Beate Flath, Eva Klein (eds.)
Advertising and Design

Cultural and Media Studies

Beate Flath, Eva Klein (eds.)

Advertising and Design

Interdisciplinary Perspectives on a Cultural Field

[transcript]

Supported by: Land Steiermark, Abteilung 8: Wissenschaft und Gesundheit (Province of Styria, Department 8: Science and Health); University of Graz; Faculty of Humanities and Arts – University of Graz; Forschungsstelle Kunstgeschichte Steiermark (Research Center for Styrian Art History); pop/musik+medien/kunst (Department of Musicology, University of Graz); Raiffeisen-Landesbank Premium Private Banking.

Bibliographic information published by the Deutsche Nationalbibliothek

The Deutsche Nationalbibliothek lists this publication in the Deutsche Nationalbibliografie; detailed bibliographic data are available in the Internet at http://dnb.d-nb.de

Cover layout: Eva Klein
Proofread by Laura McGuire, Camilla Nielsen, Nicky Imrie, Maret Schweiger
Typeset by Beate Flath, Katharina Wierichs
Druck: Majuskel Medienproduktion GmbH, Wetzlar
Print-ISBN 978-3-8376-2348-2
PDF-ISBN 978-3-8394-2348-6

Content

Your Ad Here ...

Advertising & Design: Preface

BEATE FLATH & EVA KLEIN

If you look up the word »advertising« in a popular search engine, about approximately 1,460,000,000 results appear in 0.15 seconds. If you look up the word »sex«, you get approximately 1,940,000,000 results in 0.14 seconds and for the word »sustainability« you get 82,500,000 results in 0.23 seconds. Assuming that the Internet provides a sort of mirror of human values, this is interesting. It seems that advertising in all its manifestations pervades our lives. This motivated the editors to organize a lecture series on advertising, which was held at the University of Graz in the winter term of 2012/13 and which received the teaching award »Lehre: Ausgezeichnet« (teaching excellence) in 2013. The purpose of this series was to bring together different perspectives to provide a possibly deeper understanding of this phenomenon of everyday life.

Interdisciplinary approaches[1] are more than to agree on differences when it comes to defining the »hunting grounds« of scientific disciplines and are

---

1 Interdisciplinary scientific thinking is challenging in various ways: besides the different subjects, methods and especially scientific cultures, there are different ways of arguing on the basis of scientific literature, evidence and statistical data. These ways are formalized in different types of citation. To underline the existence of these differences the editors decided to give the authors the possibility to choose between two types of citation (Footnote and Harvard citation style) so

insofar challenging as they *could* provide an opportunity to reflect and argue apart from historical grown imperatives (dos or don'ts).

In general they raise the question if it is possible to understand each other and to collaborate at all. What is a discipline's subject? Which terms occur and what do/could they mean? Which questions are asked and what kind of methods are used? Why are some questions never asked? Where is the line drawn between philosophy of science and traditions of thinking? These questions are difficult enough to answer within *one* discipline, not to mention within a collaboration *inter* many disciplines.

Employing an *interdisciplinary approach* which assumes that targets and methods of scientific disciplines do not change in interdisciplinary work (as opposed to the concept of *transdisciplinarity*)[2] this anthology is based on the image of a kaleidoscope, where more or less stable scientific disciplines resemble little coloured stones forming structures, making it possible to change perspectives/perception on/of so-called ›reality‹.

The approach of this anthology is to look for key terms that can serve as centres of gravity for different scientific disciplines. Regarding the basic definition that advertising is a specific, unilaterally form of communication used to influence three general terms are extracted: *communication*, the aim to *influence* (propaganda) and the cultural environment of (*mass-)media*. These three aspects are determining factors regarding to that cultural field mentioned in the title of this anthology.

This anthology opens with contributions focussing on *communication* in a wide sense. Communication basically means the transfer of information,

---

that they could argue within their respective structure of thinking and culture of science.

2   See Mainzer, K. (1993). Erkenntnis und wissenschaftstheoretische Grundlagen der Inter- und Transdisziplinarität. In Aber, W. (Ed.) *Inter- und Transdisziplinarität – Warum? Wie?* Bern/Stuttgart/Wien: Haupt, p. 18.; Mittelstraß, J. (1996). Transdisziplinarität. In Mittelstraß, J. (Ed), *Enzklopädie Philosophie und Wissenschaftstheorie* Band 4 (Sp – Z). Stuttgart/Weimar: J. B. Metzler, p. 329; Völker, H. (2004). Von der Interdisziplinarität zur Transdisziplinarität? In: F. Brand, F. Schaller & H. Völker (Eds.) *Transdisziplinarität. Bestandsaufnahme und Perspektiven. Beiträge zur THESIS Arbeitstagung im Oktober 2003.* Universitätsverlag Göttingen: Göttingen. p. 14.

dependent on the dispositions of the communicators. Within commercials
this process is optimized with respect to a certain target group to ensure that
the general aim of advertising is reached. From the perspective of cognitive
neurosciences, musicology, English studies and art history aspects of communication within advertisements are presented in detail: the use of sound-
design from the perspective of multisensory communication, sound-design
in the context of the Digital Mediamorphosis, the linguistic and semiotic
analysis of advertising texts and images using a constructionist approach
and the use of the very famous painting of the Mona Lisa as a cultural icon
in advertisements.

Charles Spence focuses in his article »Multisensory Advertising & Design« specifically on the contribution of the field of multisensory de-
sign/communication out of the perspective of cognitive neurosciences. A
number of illustrative examples of the intelligent use of sound in product
and packaging design, in digital applications, in advertising, and in experiential design are presented and some of the key potential benefits that the
cognitive neuroscience inspired approach brings to research in this area are
discussed.

Beate Flath's contribution »The Sound of Image« focuses on sound
communicating additional emotional values in mass media given the specificities of digital communication- and information technologies to outline a
picture of sound in mass media. Based on the premise that mass media
communicate via emotional bonding the basic theoretical mechanism of
emotional conditioning and its cause variables, especially the concept of
involvement, are discussed within the cultural framework of the digital
Mediamorphosis.

Bernhard Kettemann's contribution »Semiotics of Advertising and the
Discourse of Consumption« seeks to gain insight into the construction of
advertisements and to provide a means for a de-manipulative look at the
discursive construction of social and cultural identities through consumption. This leads us to the linguistic and semiotic analysis of advertising
texts and images based on a constructionist approach, combined with the
analytical framework of social semiotics, visual design, rhetoric, stylistics,
text linguistics, and critical discourse analysis.

Eva Klein focuses in her contribution on »Multiple Mona Lisa. Art as
tool of Advertising«, on probably the most famous art icon of the Renaissance. Mona Lisa is removed from her original »Aura« and transferred to a

new medium that offers many possibilities of contextualization. By citing recent examples of advertising, the author analyses different strategies of positioning content in the context of design.

The very controversial aspect of the *influencing power* of advertising covers a broad spectrum of scientific issues: strategies for bypassing scepticism and the disaffirmation of recipients, the question of self-determination with respect to identity, moral-driven influence of advertising and political propaganda. These aspects are the main issues of contributions from the perspective of communication sciences, sociology, cultural anthropology and history of art.

Jörg Matthes focuses on certain strategies that are able to lever out shields of advertising. His contribution »Advertising Effects Despite Scepticism: Eroticism, Humour, and Celebrities« addresses mechanisms of advertising to deal with scepticism of recipients. On the basis of empirical data, which show that people are very critical and the theoretical framework of dual-process models (Elaboration-Likelihood-Model and the Heuristic-Systematic-Model) the author presents specific techniques of advertising. He critically reflects potential and boundaries of erotic appeal, humour and celebrities and discusses research methods as well as experimental designs.

As mentioned above, one striking aspect within the discussion of the influencing power of advertising is identity construction through the media. This issue is discussed from the perspective of sociology and cultural anthropology. The article »Advertising. Creating People and Worlds« by *Manfred Prisching* focuses on the interrelation between advertising and identity in terms of how it relates to the concept of a consumer society. The change of human needs as a basis for advertising is put into a historical and sociological context before some perspectives on consumer analysis are outlined (e.g., the theory of needs, the theory of sovereignty, the theory of manipulation and the theory of leisure class) and the problem of identity and the creation of an individualistic society are addressed in greater detail. Based on the conclusion that it is ultimately through advertising that we understand how the world works and through which we construct ourselves, the text ends with the statement that in the end we will, quite possibly, no longer understand anything at all.

Johanna Rolshoven focuses in her contribution »Wine Advertising and Biography« on an analysis of print advertisement to use advertising as a source for popular culture studies. Using the example of wine labels, she discusses biographic models of men and women with respect to intentions and meanings of advertising, namely as a producer of economically and socially attractive images and an influential medium with relevance for the everyday.

When thinking about the influential power of mass media, and of course also advertising, identity construction and purchasing intention are only half of the picture: the power to influence cultural and moral ideas are relevant as well. This brings us to moral-driven advertisements and political propaganda: in two quite different cases visuals are discussed with respect to their influence on cultural values as well as political ideology.

Margit Stadlober seeks to elaborate on the varied iconological interpretation of Peter Fendi's painting »Ein Mädchen vor einem Lotterie-Gewölbe (Girl at the Lottery)« by discussing solely the sociocultural context and the pictorial elements. She directs her focus to a work of traditional art history whose subtle messages provide information about the advertising component of the lottery system and also gambling.

Using the specific example of a Nazi propaganda poster, *Barbara Aulinger* in her text »›Raise the flag and make propaganda‹ On the semiotics of National Socialist wooing« follows up the question to what extent it can actually be understood as an advertisement in the modern sense in the semiotic as well as cultural and historical context and further discusses the connotations of those political posters.

Basic principles of advertising are derived from structures and mechanisms of *(mass-)media*. So the final part of this anthology is dedicated to this topic – albeit from different perspectives: the interdependence of structures of mass-media and advertising and the critique of structures of mass-media regarding to the concepts of high and low culture respectively of art and advertising.

The contribution of *Werner Jauk* »Pop & Ads« addresses the link between the paradigms of pop(-music) and advertising. Proceeding from the assumption that emotional bonding is their common basic principle, the author discusses (socio)psychological, technological and aesthetic aspects with respect to theoretical approaches and empirical evidences.

The text by *Holger Schramm* and *Nicolas Ruth* is »›The Voice‹ of the music industry. New advertising options in music talent shows« considers advertising opportunities and their impact in German music talent shows. Based on an analysis of the final episode of Season 2 of Voice of Germany, the authors classify the different advertising options for the music industry. In a next step two studies examine differences between DSDS and Voice of Germany. These two studies indicate that different music talent shows are perceived in different ways: while Voice of Germany is rated as musically superior, DSDS is still capable of establishing strong viewer commitments to the show. However, both shows clearly impact consumer behavior, both through their unique formats and the advertising opportunities described. The authors conclude that talent shows are highly profitable for everyone involved; however, it remains to be seen whether they are enough to rescue the declining music industry.

In his text »Capitalism Propaganda. Adorno's Kulturindustrie and Freedom of Creativity«, *Friedrich Weltzien* reflects on Adorno's *Kulturindustrie* and the diverging treatment of advertising and art by switching perspectives and suggesting that the categories be modified.

The diverging treatment of the field of advertising by art history is also the subject of *Bernadette Collenberg-Plotnikov's* contribution »›... things that people don't need to have but that – for some reason – would be a good idea to give them.‹ Discussions on drawing the line between art and advertising«, which is characterized and put in a context of the history of ideas. The key question of the inequality of that which seems equal is reconstructed by the use of the example of the relationship between art and advertising.

Although this anthology adheres to the definition of interdisciplinarity and therefore the idea of contributing to a research subject from the perspective of various disciplines without changing particular methods and research concepts, we suggest improving ›transdisciplinary‹ approaches in order to bring theories and methods to the meta-level of discussion and reflexion. This would be an advantage for the research subjects as well as for philosophy of science.

For giving us the opportunity to explore these issues, we would like to express our gratitude to everyone who supported this anthology and made it possible: first of all the authors – without them it wouldn't be possible to provide such a plurality. We would like to thank our lecturers and last but not least we thank the funding sponsors, namely the *Land Steiermark* (Province of Styria), the *University of Graz*, the *Faculty of Humanities and Arts* of the University of Graz and the *Raiffeisen-Landesbank Styria Private Banking*. We would also like to thank the *Forschungsstelle Kunstgeschichte Steiermark* (Centre for Styrian Art History) and *pop/musik+medien/kunst* (Department of Musicology) for supporting our project. As this publication also built up on the previous lecture series from the winter term 2012/13, we would like to thank the *Vizerektorat für Studium und Lehre* (Department of Vice-Rector for studies and teaching) of the University of Graz.

Multisensory Advertising & Design

Charles Spence

> »…the most successful new products ap-
> peal on both rational and emotional levels
> to as many senses as possible.«
> (Neff 2000: 22)

Introduction

While vision has always tended to play a dominant role in product and service communications, the last few years have seen the growth of a much
more multisensory approach to advertising, design, and branding. This transition has, on the one hand, been fuelled by the growing number of sensory
marketers extolling the virtues of connecting with the consumer via as
many senses, or sensory touch points, as possible (e. g. Hultén 2011; Hultén, Broweus, & van Dijk 2009; Krishna 2010, 2012, 2013; Lindstrom
2005a, b). On the other hand, the rapid expansion of research on the topic
of multisensory perception within the academic field of cognitive neuroscience has thrown up many exciting, not to mention provocative, examples of
how a person's perception in one sense can be dramatically altered by
whatever happens to be occurring in the other senses at around the same
time (see Calvert, Spence & Stein 2004; Stein 2012, for reviews of the
field). So, for example, it turns out that how white your clothes look when
they come out of the wash is, in part, determined by the fragrance that you
happen to smell as you inspect them visually (e. g., Vickers & Spence
2007). Similarly, how soft a piece of fabric »feels«, or even how dry one's
skin seems to be, is affected by what a person smells or hears (Churchill,

Meyners, Griffiths & Bailey 2009; Demattè, Sanabria, Sugarman & Spence 2006; Guest, Catmur, Lloyd & Spence 2002; Jousmäki & Hari 1998; Laird 1932).

In this article, though, I wish to focus specifically on the contribution of audition to the field of multisensory design/communication. I will highlight a number of illustrative examples of the intelligent use of sound in product and packaging design, in digital applications, in advertising, and in experiential design. Along the way, I want to stress some of the key potential benefits that I see the cognitive neuroscience inspired approach bringing to research in this area.

AUDITORY BRANDING: PRODUCT AND PACKAGING SOUNDS

The majority of products make a noise when a consumer interacts with them, everything from the sound of a tissue being taken from a box through to the click on the seal as one opens or closes the packaging of the product (Byron 2012; Spence & Zampini 2006). Those product and packaging interaction sounds can play a very important role in determining what a consumer thinks about a product, no matter whether they realize it or not; and mostly the evidence suggests that the consumer does not (Spence & Zampini 2006).

In our multisensory design work here at the *Crossmodal Research Laboratory* in Oxford we always strive to achieve two things when we are commissioned to help modify the auditory design of a particular product or its packaging. On the one hand, we look for those sonic features that are most likely to convey some functional benefit to the consumer. On the other, we try to advise on the design of signature sounds (think, for example, of the sound of the Snapple pop) that help to provide a brand with a point of sensory differentiation from its competitors in the marketplace (Byron, 2012). However, rather than relying on the unconstrained results of the focus group or consumer panel, we prefer to adapt tried-and-tested psychophysical techniques. Often, such tests have been fine-tuned in the experimental psychology laboratory in order to establish the key drivers of perception and behavior, and to do so in the most robust and concise manner possible.

One of the projects that we have worked on, the results of which can now be found in the majority of the world's supermarkets, is the Lynx deodorant can (sold under the Axe brand name in many countries; see Spence & Zampini 2007). Going back a few years, the problem facing the industry was that changing regulations meant that many of the propellants that had traditionally been used in aerosols were likely going to be banned by new legislation. Hence, there was a very real danger that the product/packaging would no longer sound as forceful and powerful as the brand owners (and presumably also their consumers) had come to expect.

We were able to adapt a psychophysical paradigm in order to home in on the key attributes of the aerosol spraying sound that conveyed the feelings of forcefulness and powerfulness to consumers (Spence & Zampini 2007). Unilever was then able to go to their packaging engineers with a specific sonic profile in hand. Now, while it may not always be possible to engineer the perfect sonic design, as least the designer-engineer knows what kind of sound profile that they are aiming for. Hence, the whole product innovation cycle can be sped up by this form of virtual prototyping. The suggestion here is that this form of cognitive neuroscience-inspired product/packaging design approach will, in the long run, help to provide a company with a competitive advantage in the marketplace. Ultimately, it has to make sense for a company to understand the mind of their consumer – and who better to help with that than the commercially-minded cognitive neuroscientist?

It is, of course, possible to go too far: A couple of years ago, Frito Lay were forced to withdraw their new Sun Chip packets from the shelves in North American supermarkets when consumers complained that the packets were just too noisy (see Spence 2012a). In fact, when one picks up and gently agitates one of these packages, the sound of the packaging would come in at over 100dB! It was undoubtedly attention capturing, but ultimately not successful when it came to the sonic design. Nevertheless, despite this prominent failure, an increasing number of companies are now starting to think much more carefully about what their brand sounds like, and more importantly, what they would like it to sound like in the future.

For those working in my research group here in Oxford, the ultimate sound of success involves developing a modified product/packaging sound that both helps the brand to stand apart from the competition – that is, a signature sound, but one which also delivers a functional benefit in terms of the end user's multisensory product experience (Schifferstein & Spence, 2008). Note also that for many of our interactions with fast-moving consumer goods (FMCGs) and home and personal care (HPC) products, the end consumer experience typically represents some combination of the sound of the product and of its packaging.

ADVERTISING SOUND

Now, when it comes to advertising, there is certainly scope to enhance the product sound in order to emphasize the relevant attributes of a product in the mind of the consumer. Take, for example, another of the Unilever stable of brands, Magnum: a few years ago, consumers were complaining about the chocolate coating of the ice cream falling off when they bit into it. However, when Unilever changed the product formulation in order to eliminate this perceived problem, consumers no longer liked the ice cream as much. Why? Well it turned out that one of the subtle sensory cues that consumers actually liked was the audible crack of the chocolate coating on the Magnum (perhaps connoting freshness). Knowing this, the company was able to return to their original product formulation while, at the same time, making sure to emphasize the sound of the cracking chocolate in their television and cinema advertisements. Listen carefully, and one can hear just how many other companies are using a similar strategy in their advertising nowadays (see Spence, Shankar, & Blumenthal 2011; Spence & Zampini 2006, for some examples).

In one of our current projects, we are investigating whether it is possible to create caricatured hot and cold liquid pouring sounds. So far, the results of our laboratory tests demonstrate that people are remarkably good at discriminating the temperature of a drink on the basis of nothing more than the sound it makes when poured into a receptacle (see Velasco et al., 2013, submitted b). We are now working on the design of a range of caricatured pouring sounds that are hotter than hot and colder than cold. Once again, one could certainly foresee using such modified pouring sounds to help convey the notion of a »piping hot« or »ice cold« product offering to the consumer. (In the longer term, one might even think about developing a branded drink receptacle, or glass, that made one's product sound hotter or colder in the hope that that would actually change the consumer experience.) A similar auditory design approach has also been considered when it comes to the perception of carbonation in a beverage (Zampini & Spence 2005).

In closing, it is also worth noting how some iconic packaging sounds have actually been used as »instrumental sounds« in the jingles for the product advertisement: think here of the Heinz Ketchup bottle, or the host of jingles using the sound of a tube of Pringles that one can find on YouTube. These examples are perhaps the ultimate accolade for auditory design.

THE SOUND OF TECHNOLOGY

Those working in the automotive sector, especially those working with the premium marques, spend a lot of their time customizing exactly how their car engines should sound to the customers who have paid so much for the privilege of driving them (Ho & Spence 2013). This neuroscience-inspired approach to multisensory product/packaging design utilizes a very similar approach to sound design as that popularized in the automotive industry to perfect everything from the distinctive sound of the car engine, to the reassuring sound that the car door makes when it closes (Ho & Spence 2013; Spence & Zampini 2006).

It is, however, important to note that the neuroscience-inspired approach to multisensory design is not restricted to the sound of products and their packaging. It can also be used to help design enhanced warning sounds that more effectively capture the attention of the distracted driver (Ho & Spence 2009). Multisensory illusions involving sound have also been used to expand the dynamic range of various touch screen devices (Lee & Spence 2008). By simply changing what a user hears when interacting with one of these devices, it is possible to change what they feel. This is all the more important, given the currently limited dynamic range of many of these haptic technologies.

Auditory design can also be used to enhance a number of augmented reality applications. For example, we have recently been working with Holition technology and Condiment Junkie on a project demonstrating that people interact significantly longer with, and say that they would pay more for, clothing that they have tried on virtually if it also makes the sound of the right sort of clothing when they interact with it, rather than just providing visual feedback (Ho, Jones, King, Murray, & Spence 2013). In fact, there are innumerable potential applications for enhancing sonic design and hence improving the user experience when it comes to virtual, augmented, digital, and physical environments. Cognitive neuroscience and experimental psychology can help a sonic design company to quantify the potential benefits of a client investing in their sonic signature.

SYNAESTHETIC MARKETING

Traditionally, the music or jingle that would go with a particular product or service might have been chosen on the basis of nothing more than the whim of the sonic branding agency that had been awarded the contract. However, a new field of research is starting to emerge around the systematic matching of music to specific product/service attributes (Spence 2012c, 2013). It turns out that we all (at least all of us WEIRDo's; see Henrich, Heine, & Norenzayan 2010), match particular sensory qualities to sounds in non-random ways. These surprising cross-sensory matches are known as »crossmodal correspondences« (Spence 2011b). So, for instance, most people will match a higher pitched sound with a lighter (rather than a darker) object, with a smaller (rather than a larger) object, and with a brighter (rather than a dimmer) object. At the Crossmodal Research Laboratory here in Oxford, we have been involved in a number of innovative projects around the crossmodal matching of tastes, flavours, aromas, and textures in food and drink (not to mention perfumes; Velasco et al., submitted a) with pitch, instrument type, and a whole host of other musical parameters (see Knöferle & Spence 2012; Spence 2012b, for reviews).

SENSORY APPS

Another exciting example of auditory design that we have been working on recently relates to an interactive sensory App developed by Courvoisier (see Le Nez de Courvoisier App)[1]. Courvoisier created a kit containing each of the six key aroma notes found in their XO Imperial Cognac, including the smell of crème brûlée, ginger biscuits, candied orange, coffee, and iris flower. Next, a composer was commissioned to generate a series of short musical clips to match each of these aroma notes, based on our prior laboratory work on crossmodal correspondences (Spence 2013).

The idea here was that consumers could listen individually to each of these musical pieces, and then, once they had established (or, better still, guessed) the correct association between the various pieces of music and the aromas, they could then listen to another musical composition in which each of the individual elements had been skillfully integrated into a single, more complex, piece of music (i.e., to in some sense match the complex interplay of aromas that you might find when drinking a fine cognac). All of this multisensory, some might say »synaesthetic«, entertainment is available in an App that people can download.

While the results of our subsequent testing in the laboratory suggested that the composer had only been partially successful in composing music that people would intuitively match with the various aromas, it is important to note that composing with crossmodal correspondences is an iterative process between the creative and the psychologist/measurement scientist (see Crisinel, Jacquier, Deroy & Spence 2013). We initially provide some constraints and parameters concerning what corresponds with what to the composer or sonic branding agency. The creative team then sends us some preliminary sonic solutions. We then feed them into an experiment to see whether consumers can decode the meaning inherent in the music or soundscape. Our results may suggest that a certain musical excerpt matches the aroma, flavour, or perfume, but that the others need some tweaking. We then repeat the design process until we have a solution that all sides are happy with. (To date, researchers have tended to be much more successful when it comes to matching music to tastes, e.g., sweet, sour, bitter, and salty, see Knöferle & Spence 2012, than to aromas.)

We have also worked on a project with Starbucks to design a piece of music to complement the coffee-drinking experience. It turns out that people consistently match sweet tastes with high-pitched notes on the piano, whereas bitter tasting foods (such as coffee and dark chocolate) are more

---

1   http://courvoisier.com/uk/le-nez-de-cour voisier-app/ [29th July, 2013].

commonly matched with lower pitched notes played on brass and wood-wind instruments. These insights were used to help guide the composition of a musical score that would match the taste of coffee. Starbucks aficionados could download the music from the Web to listen to with their Starbucks Via drink-at-home coffee (Spence 2011a). I believe that in the coming years, there will be many more such opportunities to improve the customer's multisensory product experience by enhancing the auditory and other sensory aspects of the environments in which they select and use or consume those products (Spence et al. 2011).

WHAT'S THE SOUND OF YOUR BRAND:
SOUND SYMBOLISM

It is important to note that the sounds that match specific product attributes need not be restricted to the music or soundscape that is used in an advertisement. Even the speech sounds contained in a brand name can convey meaning for the consumer. The better the sound symbolism of the brand name matches the stated values of the brand, the more likely the product is to be a success in the marketplace (Spence 2012b; see also Begley 2002). So, for example, it turns out that voiced consonants such as »b«, »d«, »g«, »f«, and »z« are associated with slowness and heaviness, whereas voiceless consonants such as »p«, »f«, »k«, »s« and »t« are associated with speed and lightness. Is it any wonder, then, that the latter consonants are significantly overrepresented in the brand names of anti-cancer medications, the argument here being that this is implicitly what patients want in their heavy-duty chemotherapy medications (Abel & Glinert 2008).

NEUROMARKETING VS.
NEUROSCIENCE-INSPIRED DESIGN

It is important to note that despite the recent hype (Lindstrom 2008), the use of neuroscience methods to assess the effectiveness of advertising (not to mention packaging design) has been going on since the mid- to late-1970s (see Ambler, Ioannides, & Rose 2000, for a review). Now while some of the brain-scanning technologies have undoubtedly become much more powerful over the intervening years, not to mention much more colourful, I remain to be convinced that neuromarketing is ever going to live up to the hype that has built-up around it over the last decade or so (see also Ariely & Berns 2010; Plassmann, Ramsøy, & Milosavljevic 2012). Instead, I would argue that we are going to see the increased use of neuroscience-inspired behavioural techniques, rather than necessarily the increased use of brain scanning techniques per se. Furthermore, the crowdsourcing of data collection using experiments that can be run on Amazon Mechanical Turk, or on the increasingly ubiquitous smart-phone (Miller 2011), holds great potential for the widespread introduction of scaleable neuroscience-inspired marketing and advertising solutions (Woods, Spence, Butcher & Deroy, in press). Indeed, many neuromarketing companies are increasingly starting to lure their clients in with the promise that they will look into their consumer's brains before rapidly switching the dialog and offering up a neuroscience-inspired behavioural test instead (inspired, one hopes, by the latest that cognitive neuroscience has to offer).

CONCLUSIONS

In this review, I hope that I have managed to convince you that the field of sonic design/audio branding is coming to play an increasingly important role in the design of many of our multisensory consumer experiences. Furthermore, it is my firm belief that in order to really stimulate the senses most effectively, one increasingly needs to know something about how the senses work together in the mind of the consumer. Be it in the world of product/packaging innovation, advertising, branding, or experience design, my prediction for the coming years is that those companies who adopt a neuroscience-inspired approach are going to gain a competitive advantage in the marketplace. Finally, it is important not to underestimate the potential benefit associated with the cognitive neuroscientist's ability to help measure and quantify the effectiveness of sonic design in the marketplace for the sonic branding company.

REFERENCES

Abel, G. A. & Glinert, L. H. (2008). Chemotherapy as language: Sound symbolism in cancer medication names. *Social Science & Medicine*, 66, 1863–1869.

Ambler, T., Ioannides, A. & Rose, S. (2000). Brands on the brain: Neuro-images of advertising. *Business Strategy Review*, 11, 17–30.

Ariely, D. & Berns, G. S. (2010). Neuromarketing: The hope and hype of neuroimaging in business. *Nature Reviews Neuroscience*, 11, 284–292.

Begley, S. (2002). StrawBerry is no BlackBerry: Building brands using sound. *Wall Street Journal*, August 26, B1.

Calvert, G., Spence, C. & Stein, B. E. (Eds.). (2004). *The Handbook of Multisensory Processing*. Cambridge, MA: MIT Press.

Churchill, A., Meyners, M., Griffiths, L. & Bailey, P. (2009). The cross-modal effect of fragrance in shampoo: Modifying the perceived feel of both product and hair during and after washing. *Food Quality and Preference*, 20, 320–328.

Crisinel, A.-S., Jacquier, C., Deroy, O. & Spence, C. (2013). Composing with cross-modal correspondences: Music and smells in concert. *Chemosensory Perception*, 6, 45–52.

Demattè, M. L., Sanabria, D., Sugarman, R. & Spence, C. (2006). Cross-modal interactions between olfaction and touch. *Chemical Senses*, 31, 291–300.

Guest, S., Catmur, C., Lloyd, D. & Spence, C. (2002). Audiotactile interactions in roughness perception. *Experimental Brain Research*, 146, 161–171.

Henrich, J., Heine, S. J. & Norenzayan, A. (2010). The weirdest people in the world? *Behavioral and Brain Sciences*, 33, 61–135.

Ho, C., Jones, R., King, S., Murray, L. & Spence, C. (2013). Multisensory augmented reality in the context of a retail clothing application. In K. Bronner, R. Hirt & C. Ringe (Eds.), *(((ABA))) Audio Branding Academy Yearbook 2012/2013* (pp. 167–174). Baden-Baden: Nomos.

Ho, C. & Spence, C. (2009). Using peripersonal warning signals to orient a driver's gaze. *Human Factors*, 51, 539–556.

Ho, C. & Spence, C. (2013). Affective multisensory driver interface design. *International Journal of Vehicle Noise and Vibration* (Special Issue on

Human Emotional Responses to Sound and Vibration in Automobiles), 9, 61–74.

Hultén, B. (2011). Sensory marketing: The multi-sensory brand-experience concept. *European Business Review*, 23, 256–273.

Hultén, B., Broweus, N. & van Dijk, M. (2009). *Sensory Marketing*. Basingstoke, UK: Palgrave Macmillan.

Jousmäki, V., & Hari, R. (1998). Parchment-skin illusion: Sound-biased touch. *Current Biology*, 8, 869–872.

Knöferle, K. M. & Spence, C. (2012). Crossmodal correspondences between sounds and tastes. *Psychonomic Bulletin & Review*, 19, 992–1006.

Krishna, A. (Ed.). (2010). *Sensory Marketing: Research on the Sensuality of Products*. London: Routledge.

Krishna, A. (2012). An integrative review of sensory marketing: Engaging the senses to affect perception, judgment and behavior. *Journal of Consumer Psychology*, 22, 332–351.

Krishna, A. (2013). *Customer Sense: How the 5 Senses Influence Buying Behaviour*. New York: Palgrave Macmillan.

Laird, D. A. (1932). How the consumer estimates quality by subconscious sensory impressions: With special reference to the role of smell. *Journal of Applied Psychology*, 16, 241–246.

Lee, J.-H. & Spence, C. (2008). Feeling what you hear: Task-irrelevant sounds modulates tactile perception delivered via a touch screen. *Journal of Multisensory User Interfaces*, 2, 145–156.

Lindstrom, M. (2005a). *Brand Sense: How to Build Brands Through Touch, Taste, Smell, Sight and Sound*. London: Kogan Page.

Lindstrom, M. (2005b). Broad sensory branding. *Journal of Product and Brand Management*, 14, 2/3, 84–87.

Lindstrom, M. (2008). *Buy-ology: How Everything We Believe About Why We Buy is Wrong*. London: Random House Business Books.

Miller, G. (2012). The smartphone psychology manifesto. *Perspectives on Psychological Science*, 7, 221–237.

Plassmann, H., Ramsøy, T. Z. & Milosavljevic, M. (2012). Branding the brain: A critical review and outlook. *Journal of Consumer Psychology*, 22, 18–36.

Schifferstein, H. N. J. & Spence, C. (2008). Multisensory product experience. In H. N. J. Schifferstein & P. Hekkert (Eds.), *Product Experience* (pp. 133–161). London: Elsevier.

Spence, C. (2011a). Sound design: How understanding the brain of the consumer can enhance auditory and multisensory product/brand development. In K. Bronner, R. Hirt, & C. Ringe (Eds.), *Audio Branding Congress Proceedings 2010* (pp. 35–49). Baden-Baden: Nomos.

Spence, C. (2011b). Crossmodal correspondences: A tutorial review. *Attention, Perception, & Psychophysics*, 73, 971–995.

Spence, C. (2012a). Auditory contributions to flavour perception and feeding behaviour. *Physiology & Behaviour*, 107, 505–515.

Spence, C. (2012b). Managing sensory expectations concerning products and brands: Capitalizing on the potential of sound and shape symbolism. *Journal of Consumer Psychology*, 22, 37–54.

Spence, C. (2012c). Synaesthetic marketing: Cross sensory selling that exploits unusual neural cues is finally coming of age. *The Wired World in 2013*, November, 104–107.

Spence, C. (2013). On crossmodal correspondences and the future of synaesthetic marketing: Matching music and soundscapes to tastes, flavours, and fragrance. In K. Bronner, R. Hirt & C. Ringe (Eds.), *(((ABA))) Audio Branding Academy Yearbook 2012/2013* (pp. 39–52). Baden-Baden: Nomos.

Spence, C., Shankar, M. U. & Blumenthal, H. (2011). »Sound bites«: Auditory contributions to the perception and consumption of food and drink. In F. Bacci & D. Melcher (Eds.), *Art and the Senses* (pp. 207–238). Oxford: Oxford University Press.

Spence, C., & Zampini, M. (2006). Auditory contributions to multisensory product perception. *Acta Acustica united with Acustica*, 92, 1009–1025.

Spence, C., & Zampini, M. (2007). Affective design: Modulating the pleasantness and forcefulness of aerosol sprays by manipulating aerosol spraying sounds. *CoDesign*, 3 (Supplement 1), 109–123.

Stein, B. E. (Ed.). (2012). *The New Handbook of Multisensory Processing*. Cambridge, MA: MIT Press.

Velasco, C., Jones, R., King, S., Dove, R., Kellie, J. & Spence, C. (submitted a). Smelling a sweet tune? Assessing the influence of soundscapes on the perception of fragrance. *Chemosensory Perception*.

Velasco, C., Jones, R., King, S. & Spence, C. (2013). »Hot or cold?« On the informative value of auditory cues in the perception of the temperature of a beverage. In K. Bronner, R. Hirt & C. Ringe (Eds.), *(((ABA)))* *Audio Branding Academy Yearbook 2012/2013* (pp. 177–187). Baden-Baden: Nomos.

Velasco, C., Jones, R., King, S. & Spence, C. (submitted b). The sound of temperature: What information do pouring sounds convey concerning the temperature of a beverage. *Food Quality & Preference.*

Vickers, G., & Spence, C. (2007). Get set for the sensory side of the century. *Contact: Royal Mail's Magazine for Marketers*, November, 11–14.

Woods, A. T., Spence, C., Butcher, N. & Deroy, O. (in press). Testing the semantic hypothesis of crossmodal correspondences using an internet-based testing methodology. *i-Perception.*

Zampini, M. & Spence, C. (2005). Modifying the multisensory perception of a carbonated beverage using auditory cues. *Food Quality and Preference*, 16, 632–641.

Internet sources

Byron, E. (2012). The search for sweet sounds that sell: Household products' clicks and hums are no accident; Light piano music when the dishwasher is done? *Wall Street Journal*, October 23, downloaded from http://online.wsj.com/article/SB10001424052970203406404578074671 598804116.html?mod=googlenews_wsj#articleTabs%3Darticle [29th July, 2013].

LeCourvoisier, http://courvoisier.com/uk/le-nez-de-cour voisier-app/ [29th July, 2013].

Neff, J. (2000). Product scents hide absence of true innovation. *Advertising Age*, February 21, 22. Available at http://adage.com/article/news/ product-scents-hide-absence-true-innovation/59353/ 28/11/2012. [29th July, 2013].

The Sound of Image

Aspects of Sound Design within

the Digital Mediamorphosis

BEATE FLATH

ALL YOU NEED IS IMAGE?![1]

Since we live in a society that is itself constituted by digital information and communication technology, media are indeed omnipresent. As Marshall McLuhan writes, media shape meaning, society, perception and communication (Mersch 2006: 112).

This article is based on the premise that within Western societies one basic principle of mass media is emotional bonding in order to »sell« ideas, images of persons, products etc. within the sociological context of a so-called *Erlebnisgesellschaft* (Schulze 1992). Following this empirically based description of society »innenorientierter Konsum« (Schulze 1992: 422), which means consumption on the basis of an additional emotional benefit of a product becomes more important than the »objective« physical characteristics of a product. The hedonic aspect of a product itself as well as the communicated additional benefit is central.

If we assume that products or services are bought with their emotional additional value[2] in mind, then one has to take a closer look at media, since

---

[1] See the anthology with the same name edited by Beate Flath, Andreas Pirchner, Elisabeth Pölzl and Susanne Sackl published in 2010.

advertising is one major source of income for the media.[3] The media thus employ a target-group-driven design in order to an optimal product placement. Sound or/and music is/are part/s of this design.

The purpose of this article is to focus on sound that communicates additional emotional values – in the following text termed *image* – in the mass media and its basic principle emotional bonding under the condition of specificities of digital communication- and information technologies to outline a picture of the *Sound of Image*.

DEFINITIONS

Sound in the mass media is primarily functional sound. Especially within musicological discussions a mutually exclusive distinction is drawn between aesthetics and function, whereas functional music or sound are denied having an aesthetical impact or an aesthetical additional value. In this context, value can be read and understood in the double sense of the word – in nearly every case the aesthetic value *is* the value that determines something becoming a musicological scientific subject.

In this article, aesthetics is defined in terms of the concept *Aisthesis*, which sees aesthetics as being based on perception processes. Aesthetics is therefore not grounded on attitudes of some less (»Ästhetik von oben«, Fechner 1876) but on individual perceptions of specific characteristics of stimuli (»Ästhetik von unten«, Fechner 1876; »New Experimental Aesthetics« Berlyne 1974). Based on this approach, the differentiation between aesthetic *or* function is excluded and sound is discussed in terms of its functional aesthetics. Following this approach, sound is defined as a perception-based quality of acoustic stimuli; with regard to empirical studies it is operationalized in terms of acoustical parameters.

As mentioned above, the cultural context of discussing sound in the mass media is the sociological concept of an »Erlebnisgesellschaft«. Addi-

---

2   Within an image-driven society the social value of a brand becomes an economic value (see *Interbrand*, http://www.interbrand.com/de/best-global-brands /2012/Best-Global-Brands-2012.aspx [30th July, 2013].

3   For a more detailed argumentation of the connection of advertising, media and sound see the contribution of Werner Jauk within this anthology.

tional emotional values can be seen from the specific perspective of the concept ›image‹. *Image* is defined and operationalized with respect to various perspectives; in this article we will adhere to a definition taken from economics:

»The image is generally the image that a person creates of any subject of opinion. It is based on objective and subjective, perhaps also false and strongly emotional ideas, ideas, feelings, experiences, knowledge regarding a subject of opinion.« (Zentes/ Swoboda 2001: 209, translated by Camilla Nielsen)[4]

The following article considers a concept of a perception-based functional aesthetics of sound, which is put into a context of an image driven society.

THEORETICAL PERSPECTIVES AND EMPIRICAL EVIDENCE

When putting sound into the context of communicating images via mass media, we have to take into account the theory of *emotional conditioning*. As a learning process it is based on the transfer of the emotional quality of one stimulus (unconditioned) to another, the neutral stimulus (conditioned) when they are presented simultaneously and repeatedly (Kroeber-Riel 1982: 199). The unconditioned, emotional stimulus could be the emotional quality of music, sound, pictures, smells or textures of surfaces, which are transferred to the conditioned stimulus, e.g., products, persons, ideas, etc.

Empirical evidence shows that this effect is limited by certain constraints: the number of the conditioned stimuli, the experiences with the unconditioned and the conditioned stimuli and the fitting (Stout/Leckenby 1988; Roth 2005) of the unconditioned and the conditioned stimulus (Moser 2002: 138). Following this, experience with the unconditioned and/or the conditioned stimulus, which means experience with the emotionally laden content and/or the product, the idea, the person, etc. are linked to

---

4   The concept of image has to be distinguished from the concept of *attitude* – in the following, we define attitude as being more denotative, image as being more connotative (Hofer 1991: 14 quoted from Mayerhofer 1995: 52). Following this, an image is defined as a connotative impression of an object, a person, etc.

the concept of *Involvement* (Sherif/Cantril 1947) – one of the core concepts regarding the effects of advertising. *Involvement* is a multidimensional concept (Trommsdorff 2003: 56) and refers to the individual importance of a certain product, service, idea, media content, etc. It can also be defined as the level of activity or the level of motivation to seek for information, to uptake information, to process information and to storage information (Trommsdorff 2003: 56).[5]

Empirical evidence has shown that a high product or music-related involvement goes hand in hand with a small effect of emotional conditioning (Kellaris/Cox 1989; Park/Young 1986; Gorn 1982).[6]

So which theoretical approach to sound are we referring to with this line of argumentation? We suggest that music be seen as a *phenomenon of mediatization* (Jauk 2009) which means that music is seen as cultural transformation of the emotional expression in sound (Knepler 1977) and body movement (Blacking 1977) – from a phylogenetic and ontogenetic point of view the origin of music thus lies within communication.

The term mediatization underlines the process of cultural transformation from »un-mediated« communication in sound and body movement

---

5   A distinction is made between stimulus depending, situation- dependent or subject-dependent involvement (Kroeber-Riel 1990: 377). Following this, involvement can be operationalized as a personality trait, as an individual intern state, as stimulus-salience and as a stimulus property (Schenk 2007: 274).
    Additional involvement can be described in terms of its intensity, direction and duration (Andrews/Durvasula/Akhter 1990).

6   Involvement also influences information processing. This connection is formulated within the dual-process model Elaboration Likelihood Modell (ELM) (Petty/Cacioppo/Schumann 1983). This model distinguishes between two different routes of human information processing, two routes – the peripheral and the central route. They are related to a low respectively a high involvement, with a high involvement not having to be an objective analysis with a certain object, since it is an intensive analysis and can also be biased. Following this line of argumentation, a low-involvement condition encourages information processing via the peripheral route. In addition to this music, pictures, smells or textures of surfaces are more likely to be perceived via the peripheral route, facilitating persuasive communication.

to mediated (e.g., fixation through signs/notes) forms of music. This approach is based on anthropological theories (Illie & Thompson 2006, McDermot & Hauser 2005, Brown 2000, Stockmann 1982, Wallin 1984) and provides a framework for effects of sound or music: complementing to musicological or linguistic approaches, the possibility of »im-mediate« (Langer 1953, Nöth 1990: 112, Jauk 2013b) communication through sound is taken into account.[7]

Accordingly, the concept of Aisthesis sound and its design in mass media is based on the relation of acoustical parameters in frequency and time domain and human perception: amplitude, frequency, the number of partials and their relation and attack-time are main parameters of a) physical associations (e.g., Köhler 1947; Ohala 1994; Jauk 2007), b) specific sensations of sound-qualities like sharpness (e.g., Bismarck 1974; Ueda & Akagi 1990; Jauk 2007), softness (e.g., Stevens, Guiaro & Slawson 1965), compactness, concentration, hardness, brightness (e.g., Bismarck 1974; Zwicker & Fastl 1999: 240f) and c) emotional connotations within a categorical as well as within a dimensional concept of emotion (e.g., Zenter & Scherer 1998; Sundberg 1987; Balkwill & Thompson 1999; Bruhn & Oerter 2002; Illie &Thompson 2006; Rösing 2002; Flath 2011, 2012).

Based on this theoretical framework, we argue in favour of a communicative quality of sound in the mass media.

The theoretical socio-aesthetic framework of this argumentation is the model of *Mediamorphosis* (Weber 1921; Blaukopf 1989; Smudits 2002). It formulates the relation of technological transformation and implications for cultural/musical work. The *digital Mediamorphosis* focuses on the influence(s) of digital information and communication technologies on cultur-

---

7   This converges with the empirical evidence of Zhu and Meyers-Levy who did
     an experimental study on the design of radio commercials with respect to *embo-*
     died meaning (»which is purely hedonic, context-independent and based on the
     degree of stimulation, the musical sound affords« Zhu/Meyers-Levy 2005: 333)
     and *referential meaning* (»which is context-dependent and reflects networks of
     semantic-laden, external world concepts« Zhu/Meyers-Levy 2005: 333). The au-
     thors find that »background music can confer either referential or embodied me-
     anings« – with the level of meaning used depending on the intensity of percepti-
     on and on the requirements of the cognitive processes.

al/musical work and aesthetical, social and also economic values. Sound ideas and values in mass media depend on technological developments and their implications for culture, respectively for mass media and economic processes – as mentioned in the introduction. Following Marshall McLuhan, media can be seen as constituting meaning, society, perception and communication (Mersch 2006: 112).

To sum up these different theoretical approaches originating in different scientific fields, we were able to note that based on the assumption that *one* main target of mass media is emotional bonding (theoretically formulated in the process of emotional conditioning); the concept of involvement and the perception of sound are main parameters. The functional aesthetics of sound and its communicative quality is addressed with respect to anthropological theories and empirical evidence of the connection of acoustical parameters and physical associations, sensual associations and emotional connotations based on the theoretical framework of music being a phenomenon of mediatisation. These approaches are embedded within the model of the Digital Mediamorphosis.

Proceeding from this, we will proceed to outline some aspects of *The Sound of Image*.

THE SOUND OF IMAGE

It has been suggested that the *Sound of Image* has its origins at the intersection of mass media, economy and everyday life. It is created to sell ideas, products and images of persons, etc., which gratify the needs of individuals. Looking at this multidimensional network sound in mass media gives us a »big public screen« of those needs and their conceptual structures. Marshall McLuhan's statement »The Medium Is The Message« formulates this aspect very precisely. Technological changes have influenced the usage of media as well as media contents and their design. We thus then presented the striking technological changes of the last decades with respect to their implications for sound within the process of emotional bonding. These technological changes are categorised in terms of a) the omnipresence of media and music and b) structural changes of time and (cultural) space, namely acceleration and globalisation.

We should start by focussing on *time*, which must be seen as giving structure to cultural manifestations, which occur in time, like music or sound (see the concept »Dynamisation« following Jauk 2009). Following Paul Virillo (1992) and his term »L'Inertie polaire« (The Racing Standstill), which is based on the observation of the acceleration through technology, we have argued that structures of mass media and their design have changed. We have observed that there is less time available for long spots or intros; jingles disappear, the number of audio logos rises. Sounds in mass media become more precise, more professionalised and are more empirically based. Time is money. Communicating through sounds or music has to work in increasingly shorter periods.

Beside Virillo's observation regarding to the concept of time and velocity in Western cultures, the intersections of mass media, everyday life and economic structures and mechanisms have changed; they have become omnipresent. Regarding this, we have suggested adopting the results of empirical studies on the extra musical motifs to listen to music. *Adaptivity* (which means that music has to fit to various moods), *connectivity* (it has to be possible to be connected with other people) and *availability* (music has to be available everywhere and at any time) are main motifs of the selection process of music, which are not related to stylistical parameters (Borgstedt 2011: 234). These motifs put characteristics of music and media reception within Digital Mediamorphosis into concrete terms. Sound design within mass media could be derived from these aspects. This link lies within the interrelation of the aesthetic values of sound in mass media and sound ideas of a culture, which are influenced by the integration of music/sound in every day life. The motifs mentioned above – adaptivity, connectivity and availability – thus influence sound specific aesthetic values within a culture.

To elaborate on this in more detail, we should cite the concept of involvement, especially stimulus-related involvement, and its role in emotional bonding (see above). Analogous to the sociological theory of creating plural and fluid identities, plurality within listening to music in every day life should be stated, plurality not (necessarily) implying plurality in musical taste; it tends to be accompanied by a broader familiarity with a lot of musical styles. Following the premise that the consumption of music is indicative of aesthetic taste because it is nearly unlimited available, the results of Peterson and Kern suggest an empirically based differentiation between two types of recipients of music, namely ›Univores‹ (people who prefer a small number of musical styles) and ›Omnivores‹ (people who prefer a huge number of musical styles) with respect to the cause variables income, profession, age and cultural capital (Peterson & Kern 1996). What the authors found in the U.S.A. in the 1990s should be applied (with respect to the digital Mediamorphosis) to the expansion of music and the access to a huge diversity of music. We do not wish to argue that sound design has become more plural but that influencing variables of emotional conditioning, especially involvement, have changed as a result of the broader familiarity with different musical styles.[8] The often discussed results of Peterson et al. could be claimed to be closely related to processes of informalisation and the rise of popular music – which is defined in this article as music that developed with electronic mass media since the 1950s (Jauk 2009: 54). This goes hand in hand with empirical results that suggest that more than half of young people agree with the statement, that they have no concrete musical taste and listen to ›everything‹ (Borgstedt: 2011: 234).

To come back to the main subject of this article, we could first state that assuming the ubiquity of music/sound (also the ubiquitous possibility to be surrounded by music or sound) – the motifs above could be summed up with respect to this – basic factors and constraints of the effect of emotional bonding through sound in the mass media have changed. So if these basic factors have changed how can we describe the terms implications for sound design in the mass media? *One* possible suggestion is that sounds have become more abstract in the sense of communicating less denotatively and communicating more connotatively.[9] This could be seen according to Philip Tagg who states the decline of the figure and the rise of the ground (Tagg 1994) to describe a shift to sound-dominated forms of popular music. This

---

8   Following this, involvement has to be seen differentiated and put into a perhaps postmodern context. Possibly the definition of involvement and therefore the cutting-scores of high and low or emotional and cognitive involvement have to be reflected on a meta-level of philosophy of science too.

9   It should only be alluded to that within music therapy the extra musical meaning as a kind of involvement is eliminated by using unknown musical instruments and sound.

aspect has led to the interrelation of popular sound concepts or sound ideas and mass media. Sound or even music in the mass media are popular – not only jingles or intros are whistled or are in someone's mind. Also in a very holistic and abstract way sound spheres or sound ideas are part of popular sound-culture(s). Sound-Logos of Pro7, Sat 1, MTV or famous brands like Intel, BMW of T-Mobile are part of popular sound aesthetics. This popularity is linked to a shift in the concepts of cultural *spaces*. Possibilities, especially the interconnectedness of digital information and communication technology, have created more fluid cultural spaces in the sense of globalisation. Following Thomas Hecken who states that popular culture is what is noted by many (Hecken 2006: 85) and Peter Gross who suggests that popular is what is successful (Gross 2003: 33), global sounds in mass media have become part of a popular aesthetic of every day life within a culture dominated by the West.

To sum up our main arguments, it should be stated that the core cause-variable of emotional bonding, involvement, – as a core mechanism of mass media – has changed with respect to media-driven changes. Those changes could be termed as omnipresence of media and music and as structural changes resulting from acceleration and globalisation. With respect to music related involvement – which has to be low regarding to the effect of emotional conditioning – it is suggested that sound design – regarding to a certain cultural environment – should be more connotative than denotative to minimise music-related involvement. This means that using denotative qualities of music or sound within the process of emotional conditioning is more likely to trigger some kind of involvement. If involvement should be avoided, its connotative qualities of sound or music are more favourable. Of course, the particular marketing concept has to be taken into account when making a decision related to sound design!

SUMMARY AND OUTLOOK

This article is based on the premise that one basic principle of mass media is emotional bonding – sound being one part of this process. The basic theoretical approach to this is emotional conditioning, the effect of which is limited by music related involvement, among other things: the lower the involvement, the higher the effect of emotional conditioning. Putting this into the context of communicating images within the specific setting of the so-called digital Mediamorphosis, we can assume that the *Sound of Image* becomes more connotative and intuitive.

Reference is made to theoretical approaches from various disciplines. From a musicological point of view, from the perspective of the theory that stated music is a phenomenon of mediatisation, it is assumed that in an image-driven society sounds or music in mass media are more likely to communicate in an »im-mediate« and intuitive way. This seems to be a crucial point in musicological thinking, because there is still a lack of theoretical approaches that work with various levels of communication in sound and music.

REFERENCES

Andrews, J. C., Durvasula, S. & Akhter, S. H. (1990). A framework for conceptualizing and measuring the involvement construct in advertising research. *Journal of Advertising* 19, 27–40.

Balkwill, L.-L. & Thompson, W.-F. (1999). A Cross-Cultural Investigation of the Perception of Emotion in Music: Psychophysical and Cultural Cues. *Music Perception* 17,1, 43–64.

Berlyne, D. E. (1974). The New Experimental Aesthetics. In D. E. Berlyne, (Ed.), *Studies in new experimental aesthetics. Steps toward an objective psychology of aesthetic observation* (pp. 1–25). Washington: Hemisphere.

Bismarck, G. v. (1974). Sharpness as an Attribute of the Timbre of Steady Sounds. *Acoustica 30*, 159–172.

Blacking, J. (1977). Towards an Anthropology of the Body. In J. Blacking, (Ed.), *The Anthropology of the Body* (pp. 1–28). London: Academic Press.

Blaukopf, K. (1989). *Beethovens Erben in der Mediamorphose. Kultur- und Medienpolitik für die elektronische Ära*. Heiden: Niggli.

Borgstedt, S. (2011). »Hauptsache ich bin ›on‹«. Milieuspezifische Medienpräferenzen Jugendlicher und ihr lebensweltlicher Kontext. In Ch. Jost, D. Klug, & A. Schmidt et al. (Eds.): *Populäre Musik, mediale*

Musik? Transdisziplinäre Beiträge zu den Medien der populären Musik. (pp. 233–243) Baden-Baden: nomos.

Brown, S. (2000). The »Musilanguage« Model of Music Evolution. In N. Wallin, B. Merker & S. Brown (Ed.), *The Origins of Music* (pp. 271–300). Cambridge: MIT Press.

Bruhn, H. & Oerter, R. (2002). Die ersten Lebensmonate. In H. Bruhn, R. Oerter & H. Rösing (Eds.), *Musikpsychologie. Ein Handbuch* (pp. 276 283) Hamburg: rororo.

Fechner, G. T. (1876). *Vorschule der Ästhetik.* Leipzig: Breitkopf & Härtel.

Flath, B., Pirchner, A., Pölzl, E. & Sackl, S. (2010). (Eds.) *All You Need Is Image?!* Graz: Leykam.

Flath, B. (2011). Sound & Image. Sound & Image. An experimental study on the influence of acoustical parameters on the perception of a product's image in TV-commercials. In K. Bronner, R. Hirt & C. Ringe (Eds.), *Audio Branding Year Book 2010* (pp. 229–238) nomos: Baden-Baden

Flath, B. (2012). *Sound & Image. Eine experimentelle Untersuchung zum Einfluss von Klangqualitäten auf die Wahrnehmung eines Produktimages im Kontext von Fernsehwerbung* (= Osnabrücker Beiträge zur Systematischen Musikwissenschaft 23) Osnabrück: epOs.

Gleichmann, A. (2001). Sounddesign im Fernsehen am Beispiel des Senders ProSieben. In J. Neubauer, & S. Wenzl (Eds.), *Nebensache Musik. Beiträge zur Musik in Film und Fernsehen* (pp. 61–82). Hamburg: von Bockel.

Gorn, G. J. (1982). The Effects of Music in Advertising on Choice Behavior: A Classical Conditioning Approach. *Journal of Marketing* 46, 1, 94–101.

Gross, P. (2003). Pop-Soziologie? Zeitdiagnostik in der Multioptionsgesellschaft. In M. Prisching (Ed.), *Modelle der Gegenwartsgesellschaft* (= Reihe Sozialethik der Österreichischen Forschungsgesellschaft Band 7) (pp. 33–64). Wien: Passagen Verlag.

Hargreaves, D. & North, A. (1999). The Functions of Music in Everyday Life: Redefining the Social in Music Psychology. *Psychology of Music* 27, 71–83.

Hecken, T. (2006). *Populäre Kultur.* Bochum: Posth Verlag.

Hofer, M. (1991). *Imagetransfer – Die Wirkung Österreichtypischer Exportwerbung für Investitionsgüter unter besonderer Berücksichtigung apparativer Verfahren*. Dissertation, Wien.

Illie, G. & Thompson, W. (2006). A comparision of acoustic cues in music and speech for three dimensions of affect. *Music Perception 23*, pp. 319–329.

Jauk, W. (2001). Musik --> Sound: psychologisches Interface im multisensorischen Gefüge der Neuen Medien. In B. Enders & M. Gieseking (Eds.), *Digital & Multimedia Music Publishing. KlangArt-Kongress 2001* (= Osnabrücker Beiträge zur Systematischen Musikwissenschaft 11) (pp. 45–66). Osnabrück: epOs.

Jauk, W. (2007). The Visual and Auditory Representation of Space and Net-Space. *Musicological Annual XLIII/2*, 361–370.

Jauk, W. (2009). *pop/music+medien/kunst. Der musikalisierte Alltag der digital culture.* (= Osnabrücker Beiträge zur systematischen Musikwissenschaft 15) Osnabrück: epOs.

Jauk, W. (2013a) ... What You Hear is What You Are in ... Experimente aus Wissenschaft und Kunst. Zur Spezifität des Höres – Immersion. In S. Hanheide & D. Helms (Eds.), *»Ich sehe was, was du nicht hörst.« Etüden und Paraphrasen zur musikalischen Analyse* (pp. 173–186) Osnabrück: epOs.

Jauk W. (2013b). Beyond semiotics? Music – a phenomenon of mediatization: The extension of the hedonistic body and its communicative aspects. In D. Davidović & N. Bezić (Eds.) *New unknown music. Essays in Honour of Nikša Gligo* (pp. 407–421). DAF: Zagreb.

Kellaris, J. J. & Cox, A. D. (1989). The Effects of Background Music in Advertising: A Resessment. *Journal of Consumer Research* 16, June, 113–118.

Klein, Naomi (2005). *No Logo! Der Kampf der Global Players um Marktmacht. Ein Spiel mit vielen Verlierern und wenigern Gewinnern.* München: Goldmann.

Knepler, G. (1977). *Geschichte als Weg zum Musikverständnis. Zur Theorie, Methode und Geschichte der Musikgeschichtsschreibung.* Leipzig: Reclam.

Kroeber-Riel, W. & Meyer–Hentschel, G. (1982). *Werbung. Steuerung des Konsumentenverhaltens* (= Konsum und Verhalten 1) Würzburg: Physica Verlag.

Köhler, W. (1947). *Gestalt Psychology. An Introduction to New Concepts in Modern Psychology.* New York Liveright Publishing Corporation.

Langer, S. (1953). *Feeling and Form. A Theory of Art Developement from Philosphy in a New Key.* London: Routledge.

Mayerhofer, W. (1995). *Imagetransfer. Die Nutzung von Erlebniswelten für Positionierung von Ländern, Prdouktgruppen und Marken.* (= Empirische Marketingforschung 13) Wien: Service Fach Verlag.

McDermot, J. & Hauser, M. (2005). The Origins of Music. Innateness, Uniqueness, and Evolution. *Music Perception 23,1*, 29–59.

Mersch, D. (2006). *Medientheorie. Zur Einführung.* Hamburg: junius.

Moser, K. (2002). *Markt- und Werbepsychologie: Ein Lehrbuch.* Bern/ Toronto/ Seattle: Hogrefe.

Nöth, W. (1990). *Handbook of Semiotics.* Bloomington: Indiana University Press.

Ohala, J. F. (1994). The frequency code underlies the sound-symbolic use of voice pitch. In L. Hinton, J. Nichols & J. Ohala (Eds.), *Sound Symbolism* (pp. 325–365) Cambridge: Cambridge University Press.

Park, W. C. & Young, M. S. (1986). Consumer Response to Television Commercials: The Impact of Involvement and Background Music on Attitude Formation. *Journal of Marketing Research 23*, 11–24.

Peterson, R. A. & Kern, R. M. (1996). Chaning Highbrow Tast: From Snob to Omnivore. *American Sociological Review*, 61/5, 900–907.

Petty, R. E., Cacioppo, J. T. & Schumann, D. (1983). Central and Peripheral Routes to Advertising Effectiveness: The Moderating Role of Involvement. *Journal of Consumer Research 10*, 135–146.

Roth, S. (2005). *Akustische Reize als Instrument der Markenkommunikation.* Wiesbaden: Deutscher Universitäts-Verlag.

Rösing, H. (2002). Musikalische Audrucksmodelle. In H. Bruhn, R. Oerter, & H. Rösing (Eds.), *Musikpsychologie. Ein Handbuch* (pp. 579–588) Hamburg: rororo.

Schenk, M. (1987). *Medienwirkungsforschung.* Tübingen: J. C. B. Mohr.

Schulze, G. (1992). *Die Erlebnisgesellschaft. Kultursoziologie der Gegenwart.* Frankfurt a. Main: Campus.

Sherif, M. & Cantril, H. (1947). *The psychology of ego-involvements, social attitudes & identifictions.* New York/ London: J. Wiley & Sons.

Smudits, A. (2002). *Mediamorphosen des Kulturschaffens. Kunst und Kommunikationstechnologien im Wandel.* Wien: Braumüller.

Stevens, St., Guirao, M. & Slawson, W. (1965). Loudness, a product of volume times density. *Journal of Experimental Psychology* 69/3, 503–510.

Stockmann, D. (1982). Musik – Sprache – Biokommunikation und das Problem der musikalischen Universalien. *Beiträge zur Musikwissenschaft 24*, 103–111.

Stout, P. A. & Leckenby, J. D. (1988). Let the Muisc Play. Music as a Nonverbal Element in Television Commercials. In S. Hecker & D. Stewart (Eds.), *Nonverbal Communication in Advertising.* (pp. 207–223) Lexington, MA: Lexington Books.

Sundberg, J. (1987). *The Science of the Singing Voice.* DeKlab: Northern Illinois University Press.

Trehub, S. (2000). Human Processing Predispositions in infancy: an update. In N. Wallin, B. Merker & S. Brown (Eds.), *The Origins of Music* (pp. 427–448). Cambridge: MIT Press.

Trommsdorff, V. (2003). *Konsumentenverhalten.* Stuttgart: Kohlhammer.

Ueda, K. & Akagi, M. (1990). Sharpness and amplitude envelopes of broadband noise. *Journal of the Acoustical Society of America* 87,2, 814–819.

Virilio, P. (1992). *Rasender Stillstand.* München: Hanser.

Wallin, N. L. (1984). Gedanken über Musik und Sprache. Ein neurophysiologisches Entwicklungsmodell. *Jahrbuch der deutschen Gesellschaft für Musikpsychologie 1*, 73–91.

Weber, M. (1921). *Die rationalen und soziologischen Grundlagen der Musik.* München: Drei Masken Verlag.

Wicke, P. (2001). Sound-Technologien und Körper-Metamorphosen. Das Populäre in der Musik des 20. Jahrhunderts. In P. Wicke (Ed.), *Rock- und Popmusik* (pp. 13–60). Laaber: Laaber.

Zenter M. & Scherer, K. (1998). Emotionaler Ausdruck in Musik und Sprache. *Musikpsychologie. Jahrbuch der Deutschen Gesellschaft für Musikpsychologie 13*, 8–25.

Zentes, J. & Swoboda, B. (2001). *Grundbegriffe des Marketing. Marktorientiertes globales Management-Wissen.* Stuttgart: Schaeffer-Poeschel Verlag.

Zhu, R. J. & Meyers-Levy, J. (2005). Distinguishing between the meanings of music: When background music affects product perception. *Journal of Marketing Research* 42, 333–345.

Zwicker, E. & Fastl, H. (1999). *Psychoacoustics. Facts and Modells*. Heidelberg/ New York: Springer.

Internet Source

http://www.interbrand.com/de/best-global-brands/2012/Best-Global-Brands-2012-Brand-View.aspx [30th July, 2013].

Semiotics of Advertising and the Discourse of Consumption

In this article I will discuss possible approaches to the use of semiotics, semantics and pragmatics in the analysis of advertising discourses in English-language media, and the rhetoric of the image and the stylistics of consumption.

The aim here is twofold: by analysing advertising discourse, I want to gain insight into the construction of advertisements and at the same time provide a means for a de-manipulative look at the discursive construction of social and cultural identities through consumption. This leads into the linguistic and semiotic analysis of advertising texts and images using a constructionist approach, combined with the analytical framework of social semiotics, visual design, rhetoric, stylistics, text linguistics, and critical discourse analysis.

What is my point? It is that, actually, it is the consumption of meanings which is important and not the consumption of goods. Of course, you buy goods as items, but what you need is their meaning and not the items as such. You could very well be happy with other, similar goods, not necessarily the ones bought. What I am saying is that the purchase, the possession and the use of goods, i.e. the consumption of goods in a broad sense, have become prime signifiers in our lives and are thus instrumental in the discursive construction of identity.

As a social constructionist, I do not believe in essentialism, which means things do not mean anything by themselves. They may or may not exist, ontologically speaking, but they are meaningless before we assign meanings to them, mostly meanings shared within a society. So, in a sense, we make them, produce them. The word »facts« derives from the Latin »factum« which means »the produced« and this is exactly what we are dealing with: »the produced«, constructed in our own representation of reality. We, as societies, give things meaning; create facts.

We are constructing reality, in its interpretations and representations in our minds. So, everything we know is constructed. I am not denying that there is a »wall«. I notice that there is a »wall« when I walk into it. But I am not concerned with the ontological reality of the thing out there. I am concerned with the representation of this not in reality but in our minds. In this sense this »wall« is not a »wall«. It is a »wall« only because we interpret it as such. It is not solid because there is no solid matter. However, I cannot walk through it, because inside it is highly unstable; it is full of electrons, neutrons, anions, positrons and all these other particles, moving around incredibly fast. It is a »wall« because I say it is a »wall«, or because you say it is a »wall«, or because we all say it is a »wall«, and because we all agree, it is a »wall« and not because it is a »wall«. (Cf. von Foerster, von Glasersfeld 1999; von Foerster, von Glasersfeld, Watzlawick, Schmidt et al. 1997; von Glasersfeld 1997; Watzlawick 1981).

If reality is a construction, truth as a monolithic, unquestionable epistemic category does not exist. There are only different truths at different times. If we here in our society agree on something, then this is true for us here and now. If we do not agree, it is not true. There is no truth independent of our current interpretations which, in turn, depend on our culture. Martyrs and believers have died because of this; scientists and dissidents have gone to prison because of this; this is what drives innovation and change; racism, xenophobia, populists and dictators thrive on this, their own truth. It does not exist.

Consumption of goods has become a symbolic activity and thus meaningful for the social construction of identity. Now, I am not talking about the »wall« any more, now I am talking about us as people; about the construction of the meanings of ourselves, i.e. our identities; and about the social communication of interpretations of ourselves to others, which seems to be one of the most central activities in life. We are not careless in our projections of our identities, instead we try to present meanings to others that we assume they consider desirable. We are therefore constantly presenting signifiers of our sociability, our competence, our intelligence, and our beauty irrespective of whether the signifiers point to any signifieds at all. But who cares?

Consumption, i.e. the purchase, possession and use of goods and services, as previously mentioned, has become the major signifier in today's society. We consume something in order to project an identity of ourselves to others. We live in a consumer society; this is what we participate in. As we live in a consumer society, we have to consume in order to belong. And we want to belong. You sign up to the consumer society's ethos by consuming; you are the *pouvoir constituant* of the consumer society; and you give it its consumerist ethos and subject yourself to it at the same time. You produce society's consumer ethos and reify it by consuming.

And what do we consume? Well, I have given it away already: not goods, but meanings (cf. Benjamin 1982; Weber 1972).

Assume it is winter in the Northern hemisphere: you buy a coat because the weather is cold. You wear this coat because the weather is cold. However, you buy the specific coat because you want to project an image of yourself to other coat wearers and non-coat wearers around you, and not because it is a warm coat, but because it is an Yves Saint Laurent coat or a Barbour jacket. Why are you wearing Barbour? It means you are an upper-class person (e.g. an aristocratic hunter). There are additional meanings. Why do I buy Nike shoes? Because I want to project cool athleticism; because I am a second Messi or a third Beckham. Why do I drink Red Bull? Because I think Felix Baumgartner is cool. Because I like the Red Bull Air Race. Because I have heard of Hangar Five. I do not consume Red Bull; I consume Red Bull Media. There is nothing less important to Red Bull than the sugary liquid in the can. What is important, are the cliff divers; daredevil pilots; extreme runners; base jumpers; and stratospheric »I am going home guys.« I repeat, it is not the product, but the meaning of the product that we consume in order to construct ourselves.

Now, how do we consume meanings? We do this by a transfer of meaning of something in the advertisement through an objective correlative. In print advertisements, the scenario presented in the text and the image constitute an objective correlative for the quality and value of the emotional satisfaction of a need or a desire. The scenario usually represents desirable social circumstances; usually, but not necessarily, including the product to be promoted and the consumer. These circumstances emphasize social attraction and integration associated with beauty and happiness. Such an objective correlative is closely linked to the consumption of the product advertised so that eventually product, scenario and desired features of social identity merge in people's minds. In other words, the consumption of the product is supposed to transfer conceptually this quality and value to the consumer. So, we have bought a signifier after we have followed the advertisement to the point of action. We have bought a meaning, not a function. The most important social desire is to belong to a group and to be loved by others. We believe that we need to consume what we think makes us loved, because we want to be loved. This is why advertising works.

The idea of the objective correlative is taken from T.S. Eliot's essay »Hamlet and his problems« (1919), where he states that you need the objective correlative to express emotion in art. Art touches you through the objective correlative. Art does something to you; changes something in you; and makes you feel something.

The only way of expressing emotion in the form of art is by finding an »objective correlative«, i.e. a set of objects, a situation, or a chain of events which become the formula of that particular emotion. The formula is such that when the external facts, which must terminate in sensory experience, are given, the emotion is immediately evoked.

What Hamlet is for Eliot, Dove, Head & Shoulders, and Chanel No. 5 are for me. It is my claim that advertising is actually a form of art. By finding an objective correlative, which is the formula for that particular emotion, you can still bring the emotion back by remembering the advert even when the external facts cease (i.e. when you no longer take notice of the advertisement).

How and why do we consume meaning? We can sum this up with references to important social theoretical concepts:

- The regime of representation (the discursive construction of reality, cf. Foucault 1980; 1988)
- talks you into existence in order to consume a sign (the commodification of meaning, cf. Baudrillard 2005)
- with the aim of taking part in (look and be seen, cf. Benjamin 1982)
- or being part of something (through e.g. shared tastes, cf. Bourdieu 2001)
- in order to be someone (in order to have someone (in order to be someone ...)) (cf. Freud 1948)
- to create your own regime of truth in the endless construction of myths (cf. Barthes 1957).

Let me explain: the regime of representation produces the discursive construction of reality. This also means you are discursively constructing yourself, primarily by the meanings of the things you consume. This is what Jean Baudrillard (2005) calls the commodification of meaning: you buy meaning by consuming commodities endowed with meaning.

We consume a sign with the aim of taking part in something, i.e. to look at and to be seen by other people. While doing this, there is a certain voyeuristic pleasure for all of us. Why do we have reality TV? Why do we enjoy watching ordinary and extraordinary people carrying out unpleasant tasks or eating disgusting things? Why are they taking part in these modern-day *circenses*? Because we are voyeurs and exhibitionists, i.e. we want to look and to be seen. This is a major idea in Walter Benjamin's *Passagen-Werk* (1982).

The idea of fashion is the immediate result of the aim of taking part in or being part of something through shared tastes. None of us is dressed now as people dressed in 1850. Why not? Because it would be strange. People would laugh at us. This is why we do not do it. There is nothing wrong with dressing in this way, as such, though perhaps the clothes would be stiff and heavy. Today, we have to look relaxed and cool. This is nothing but an attitude that we must have in order to share with other people, in order to belong. If you are not a relaxed and cool follower of fashion, you do not belong.

We must have shared tastes in order to be someone. And why do we want to be someone? Because we want to have someone. And why do we want to have someone? Because we want to be someone. And so on and so forth, and therefore it never ends. And why do we do all of this? In order to create our own regime of truth in the endless construction of myths.

A regime of truth is constructed through discourse. We are embedded in discourse: we read newspapers; we listen to the radio; we watch TV; we talk to people; everything we take in is discourse on something. Here in Austria, at the end of 2012 for example, we have a discourse of corruption in the media which includes Grasser, Meischberger, Hochegger, Birnbacher, Martinz, Mensdorff-Pouilly, Strasser, Scheuch and twenty other names. We did not know about them before, but now, and perhaps for some time to come, they will be part of our discourse. We construct reality through discourse. For example, think of something like hysteria. This illness emerged around 1860 and it more or less disappeared around 1960. Before and afterwards there was no hysteria. It was constructed through discourse, by institutions and academics, and during that time, by people like me teaching people like you about hysteria.

We consume these meanings by way of consumption – i.e. buying, possessing, using – the product, so that the latter gradually loses its importance as a level in its own right, becoming a signifier instead. This makes it possible for us in our construction of our own selves to take part in or be part of something, in order to be someone, in order to have someone, in order to belong to an imagined community, whatever it is.

Our question now is, how do we construct a sign? How do we create meaning? How does meaning happen? What do we do in order to make meaning?
The next question is, how do we construct a myth? How do we »unmean«? First we mean something, and then we »unmean« something.

How do we create meaning? We make meaning by using linguistic signs. The most famous example of a model of the linguistic sign is Ferdinand de Saussure's (1916: 33), which was later modified by Ogden and Richards (1923: 11).

Figure 1: The linguistic sign

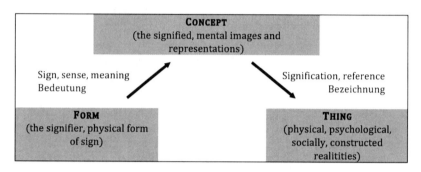

De Saussure starts with the form, which, in French, he calls *le signifiant*, and this evokes *le signifié*, the concept. The signifier is the physical form of the sign, i.e. what you hear when I, for example, utter the word »desk«. You hear »desk« and this invokes in your mind the signified, the idea, the concept of a »desk«. This connection is arbitrary. We do not know why we call something »desk« or »table«. We do not know why we name these things using these words. Once the connection between form and meaning has been established, you have to use the form to evoke the meaning. You cannot walk around and call a table »horse«. Society does not accept »horse« for a »table«. The linguistic sign is arbitrary but conventional. This means you must follow the rules of society in order to communicate.

Not all signs are arbitrary, though. According to American philosopher Charles Sanders Peirce (1982–89), we can distinguish between three types of signs based on the relationship between signifier and signified, besides other distinctions he introduced.

First, there is an icon. An icon is a sign where there is a relationship of similarity between the signifier and the signified, i.e. this relationship is motivated. This is why you have a photograph of you in your passport. It identifies you, assuming that the picture is sufficiently similar to your current appearance.

Second, there is an index. This is a sign where there is a relationship of contiguity or causality between the signifier and the signified. For example, when you see smoke, what is this an index of? Fire, because we know that fire produces smoke. Or when you see clouds, then you will say or think something like »It is going to rain«, because rain comes from clouds.

The third type is the symbol. This is a sign where there is an arbitrary relationship between the signifier and the signified. So, all of language (or most of it) is symbolic. Every word in a language is a symbol because there is an arbitrary relationship between the signifier and the signified. So language is the symbolic system in human communication.

Having discussed the sign, let us now move on to myths. This is a term coined by Roland Barthes (2001 (originally 1957): 187–188) in his book *Mythologies*. In it he claims that in myth there are two semiological systems operating on top of each other, the second system emptying the first of its meaning and changing the sign into a myth, and so to mean something else. This is where my »unmean« mentioned above comes in. The myth changes the meaning.

The first system is the normal linguistic system. You have a signifier and a signified; a word and then the concept that is evoked, and this means something. On the level of myth, this sign now enters into a second system of meaning as a new signifier. The linguistic sign becomes a signifier again and is related to a signified that creates another meaning, a second meaning, which empties the first sign of its meaning.

Here is Barthes' example of advertising.

Figure 2: Panzani Pasta ad:
Roland Barthes (1964).

Picture credit: Maryvonne Longeart,
Interprétation d'une publicité Panzani

This is an advertisement for spaghetti. Why is there a net? What does this mean? Perhaps it means daily shopping at the local market. Why is the background red? What does red mean here? Perhaps tomato sauce. We have the fresh vegetables:

onions, a tomato and a mushroom. What do they mean? What does this adver-tisement do to us? We have fresh market produce, Panzani spaghetti and sauce. This is Italian; the name and the colours of the Italian flag on the product, and there is natural freshness. But the problem is that we have all this in the shape of an industrial French product. The sauce, *pâte, sauce, parmesan, à l'italienne de luxe*, comes in a tin. It is an industrial French product and it produces in us the idea of natural fresh Italianness! This is a myth. The French meaning is gone. So, how do you turn an industrial French copy into a natural, Italian original? Here are the two steps:

Myth: first level of signification:

- Signifier: Panzani (plus pictorial elements)
- Signified: French Pasta and sauce
- Sign: French pasta and sauce with an Italian name

Second level of signification:

- Signifier: French pasta and sauce with an Italian name
- Signified: Italianness
- Sign: Italian pasta and sauce (original, real, fresh, natural, good, home-made, etc.)

Look at the next example: This is an advertisement for a perfume by Christian Dior with the name *Hypnotic Poison*. We see a woman. The background is red. What does red mean here? Perhaps passion and love. She wears a string of red pearls. What do strings do to people? They keep people in place. There is an el-ement of danger; action; dynamism; temptation. There is something dangerous about the woman. Her eyes look like cat's eyes. What about her finger nails? What is she going to do with those finger nails? Perhaps scratch your back in ec-stasy. The name of the product is *Hypnotic poison*: she is going to kill you, and you will love every minute of it. What about the bottle? It is roundish and blood-coloured. Perhaps something inside you? Perhaps a womb, for example. She is going to hold on to you, after she has scratched you. And all this is going to hap-pen because of Christian Dior.

Figure 3: Christian Dior Hypnotic Poison

Another myth: This is an advertisement for a man's fragrance, a »real« man's fragrance.

Figure 4: Extreme Sport Polo Ralph Lauren

The »real« man is doing something dangerous. He is sky boarding, an extreme sport connoting freedom, power, pleasure, coolness, courage. What about the colours? Black, silver, grey, red and blue. Compared to the Dior advertisement above with its hot colours, these are cool. And coolness is what men need. Remember: women are passionate; men are cool. What about the shape of the bottle? Probably a phallic symbol. And you can unscrew the top. Just *Extreme Polo Sport* by Ralph Lauren.

Let us have a look at some other perfume advertisement:

Figure 5: Paco Rabanne Ultraviolet Man

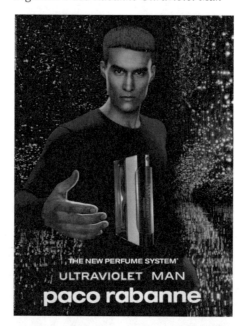

This is Paco Rabanne *Ultraviolet Man*. The product suggests that for a modern man it cannot just be a perfume, it has to be a *new perfume system*. How can there be such a perfume system? It is inconceivable. It is simply a perfume. But this perfume is a system because men are systematic, logical, rational, clear, cool, and not emotional. Men do not cry. What about the colour? What about the background? What about the picture? What about his hair? What about the man? What does he look like? He appears to have come from outer space. He has a demanding look. Perhaps he has been borrowed from *Star Trek* or *The Matrix*. He is in outer space. This is cool because of the cool colour, blue which is connected to space. You have the Milky Way behind him, and he is floating in space. We know that he is floating rather than standing on the earth because the perfume bottle is not connected to any surface.

Is it now possible to predict the advertisement for the woman's fragrance? Let us look at Paco Rabanne *Ultraviolet Woman*. It will not say *system* because that does not do anything for women. Remember, they are unsystematic. What is our prediction about the colour? Pinkish or reddish, probably. That is the colour. There will be the Milky Way again, and so on, quite similar probably. And the dress? The hair? What kind of hair will she have? Alright, straight or short hair, basically. What about the dress? Probably quite tight fitting; nothing loose or airy. What is our prediction for the shape of the perfume bottle? Not phallic and blue, but round and red. Here is the advertisement. Please compare the predictions.

Figure 6: Paco Rabanne Ultraviolet Man

Let us now look at the structure of an advertisement. I analyse advertisements on three different levels: the pragmatic level; the semantic level; and the semiotic[13] level.

---

13 I use the term *semiotics* here for what actually is limited to visual analysis, i.e. the analysis of the semiotic potentials of still images.

On the pragmatic level, what you have is an appeal to buy the product, and normally this appeal to buy is put into words and expressions such as »enjoy«, »try«, »use«, »new«, »better«, »now«, »just for you«, and so on. And remember, when an advertisement says »you«, it does not mean you personally. The advertisement has no idea about you.

The semantic level is the level of meaning production. We have a proposition that consists of an argument and a predicate. The argument is about product identity, the product itself, whatever it is. The predicate refers to some quality ascribed to the product. In a car advertisement, this is *Vorsprung durch Technik* or *Freude am Fahren* etc. In an advertisement for perfume or shower gel it is »If you smell like this product, you will have hundreds of men or women running after you« (e.g. Lynx). The product is good for you. Advertisers use metaphors, connotation, and myth – as we have seen – and what this suggests are qualities such as happiness, love, beauty, peace, power, eternal youth, a perfect life and so on.

Figure 7: Breguet Classique
7787 model chronometer

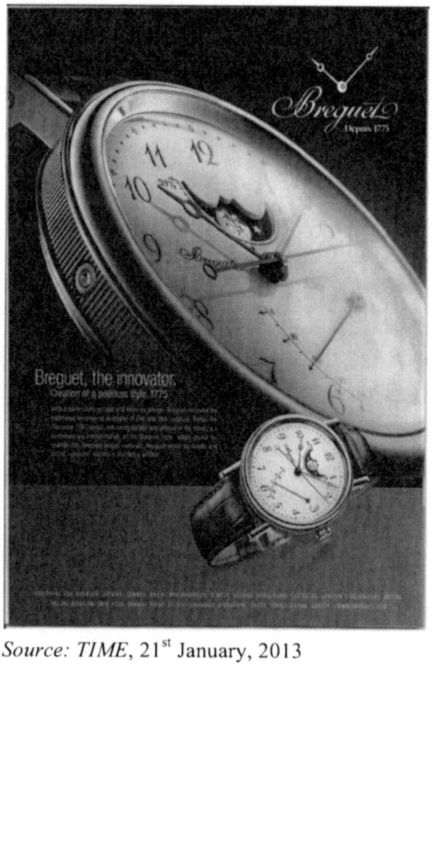

Source: TIME, 21st January, 2013

Here we have a watch, a Breguet Classique 7787 model chronometer. This will be interpreted as beautiful as a result of the aesthetically pleasing visual composition of shapes and colours in the advertisement. It represents a fantasy. It combines beauty, function and professionalism with the mystery of the moon. So this is not just beautiful, this is iconically beautiful. It is the sort of perfect instrument that puts a man in control of day and night. Thus, we also have the beauty of professionalism in time management.

Figure 8: Calvin Klein Eternity

Here is an example of a relationship of contiguity to beauty. This is a fragrance again. Which bottle is for men and which is for women? By now you should be able to answer this question. The larger bottle is for men. Do you realize that you are exposed to these concepts through discourse for around 16 hours every single day? The larger bottle is for men. This is natural. The man in the advertisement is handsome. The woman is beautiful. The little boy is beautiful. This man has a beautiful wife and this couple have a beautiful son. We have a product combined with beauty and family happiness. This is what will happen to you if you use this product.

Then you go shopping in a beautiful place in order to look and be seen; in order to fulfil your voyeuristic and exhibitionist dreams. We all have these to variable degrees. So, you go shopping in a beautiful mall, like the Galleria Vittorio Emanuele in Milan. This is a city famous for its style, fashion and opera. The mall was built in 1867 and named after the first king of the united Italy. You go there in order to buy things because you can afford to; because you are a consumer; and you want to be seen consuming because you want to belong to this new Italian society. We consume because we want to be happy. This is not an interpretation, but is actually expressed in the following advertisement.

Figure 9: Media Markt Graz, »Kauf dich glücklich«

Source: Scan from print advertisement in a flyer by
Bernhard Kettemann 2012

Kauf dich glücklich! (Buy yourself happy!) There is no longer fulfilment in personal relationships; in jobs; or in meeting moral and ethical standards. It is not idealism or social work that make you happy, it is consumption. Buy and consume in order to be happy! Buy, buy, buy!

ILLUSTRATIONS

Figure 1: The lingustic sign

Figure 2: Panzani, http://johnnyholland.org/wp-content/uploads/panzani2.jpg [15th January, 2013].

Figure 3: Dior, Hypnotic Poison, http://www.polyvore.com/dior_hypnotic_poison _ad/thing?id=18843432 [15th January 2013].

Figure 4: Ralph Lauren, Extreme Sport, http://www.advertisingarchives.co.uk /assets/thumbnails/82/3/eee228fcdaf9c85b8b3c2afec56a5da8.jpg [15th January 2013].

Figure 5: Pacco Rabbane, Ultraviolet Man, http://lambre.by/gallery/pics/paco _rabanne_ultraviolet_man_1.jpg [15th January 2013].

Figure 6: Paco Rabanne Ultraviolet Woman, http://2.bp.blogspot.com/_7yqWRH Raihk/SqON7dg3TeI/AAAAAAAADWw/q8EtZ77EWmU/s400/paco_rabanne_ ultraviolet_advertising_fragrance.jpeg [15th January 2013].

Figure 7: Breguet Classique 7787 model chronometer, TIME, 21st January 2013.

Figure 8: Calvin Klein Eternity, http://www.missparfum.be/PubDoubles/Klein Calvin/index.html [10th May 2013].

Figure 9: Media Markt Graz, »Kauf dich glücklich«, Scan from print advertise-ment in a flyer by Bernhard Kettemann 2012.

REFERENCES

Barthes, R. (1957/2001). *Mythologies*. Paris: Editions du Seuil.

Barthes, R. (1964). Rhétorique de l'image. *Communication 4*, 41–42.

Baudrillard, J. (2005). *The System of Objects*. London: Verso.

Benjamin, W. (1982). *Das Passagen-Werk*. (2 vols., Ed. Rolf Tiedemann) Frankfurt: Suhrkamp.

Bourdieu, P. (1991/2001). *Langage et pouvoir symbolique*. Paris: Editions du Seuil.

de Saussure, F. (1916). *Cours de linguistique générale*. Lausanne, Paris: Payot.

Eliot, T.S. (1919/1971). *Hamlet and His Problems*. In H. Adams (Ed.) Critical Theory Since Plato (pp. 788–790). New York: Harcourt Brace Jovanovich.

Flath, B. & Klein E. (Eds.) (2013). *Advertising and Design. Interdisciplinary Perspectives on a Cultural Field*. Bielefeld: transcript.

Foucault, M. (1980). *Power/Knowledge: Selected Interviews and Other Writings 1972-7*. Hemel Hempstead: Harvester.

Foucault, M. (1988). »Technologies of the self« In L. H. Martin, H. Gutman & P. Hutton (Eds.), *Technologies of the Self: A Seminar with Michel Foucault*, (pp. 16–49). Amherst, MA: University of Massachusetts Press.

Freud, S. (1948ff.). *Gesammelte Werke* (18 vols.). Frankfurt: S. Fischer.

Kettemann, B. (2008). »Lifestyle als soziale Semiotik. Identitätsstiftender Anglizismengebrauch im Deutschen.« In S. M. Moraldo (Ed.), *Sprachkontakt und Mehrsprachigkeit. Zur Anglizismendiskussion in Deutschland, Österreich, der Schweiz und Italien* (pp. 167-175). Heidelberg: Winter.

Ogden, C. & Richards, I. (1923). *The Meaning of Meaning*. New York: Harcourt.

Peirce, C. S. (1982–89). *Writings of Charles S. Peirce* (4 vols.). Bloomington, IN: Indiana University Press.

von Foerster, H. & von Glasersfeld, E. (1999). *Wie wir uns erfinden. Eine Autobiographie des radikalen Konstruktivismus*. Heidelberg: Carl Auer.

von Foerster, H., von Glasersfeld, E., Watzlawick, P., Schmidt, S. J. et al. (1997). *Einführung in den Konstruktivismus*. München: Piper.

von Glasersfeld, E. (1997). *Radikaler Konstruktivismus. Ideen, Ergebnisse, Probleme*. Frankfurt a. M.: Suhrkamp.

Watzlawick, P. (Ed.) (1981). *Die erfundene Wirklichkeit. Wie wissen wir, was wir zu wissen glauben? Beiträge zum Konstruktivismus*. München: Piper.

Weber, M. (1972). *Wirtschaft und Gesellschaft: Grundriss der verstehenden Soziologie*. Tübingen: Mohr Siebeck.

Multiple Mona Lisa

Art as a tool of advertising

EVA KLEIN

> »...the desire of contemporary masses to bring things ›closer‹ spatially and humanly, which is just as ardent as their bent to overcoming the uniqueness of every reality by accepting its reproduction.«[1]
>
> WALTER BENJAMIN

Leonardo Da Vinci's »Mona Lisa« is certainly the best-known work in art history, but it is also the one that is most shrouded in riddles. The portrait gives a perfect rendition of a person at ease with herself and in almost perfect harmony who unites all the potential so that always a bit of uncertainty remains.[2] She is endowed with a universal aura that is free of pretensions, styling or decoration.[3] The mystical smile of the woman portrayed here as

---

1   Walter Benjamin, The Work of Art in the Age of Mechanical Reproduction, in: *Illuminations*, London 1973, 216f. *(German: Das Kunstwerk im Zeitalter seiner technischen Reproduzierbarkeit*. Drei Studien zur Kunstsoziologie. Frankfurt a. M. 1977, 15.) (First published in French in 1936).

2   Cf. Jutte Held, Norbert Schneider, *Sozialgeschichte der Malerei: Vom Spätmittelalter bis ins 20. Jahrhundert*, Cologne 2006, 197–200.

3   Cf. Gernot Böhm, *Aisthetik. Vorlesungen über Ästhetik als allgemeine Wahrnehmungslehre*, Munich 2001.

well as her mysterious aura and the unknown background of the painting have certainly given rise to innumerable interpretations and speculations.

Traditionally, this woman was identified as being Lisa del Giocondo, the third wife of the Florentine merchant Francesco di Bartolomeo di Zanobi del Giocando. This assumption was corroborated by the discovery of a hand-written entry of the Florentine chancellery official Agostino Vespucci dated October 1503, which refers to a portrait of Lisa del Giocondo which was supposedly painted by Leonardo da Vinci. Yet even after this discovery by the university library in Heidelberg in 2008, this was called into question, since the entry could not be clearly ascribed to this painting. A further theory cites Giuliano II de' Medici and his illegitimate son Ippolito de Medici and his lover Pacifica Brandani. After Brandani, the mother of the little son, died in childbirth, the painting was supposed to have consoled the bereft. The name given to the painting at the time –»La Giocanda« – the consoling woman – would bear out this assumption. A further, less widespread theory is based on Leonardo da Vinci's allegedly homosexual orientation. He is said to have lived together with Gian Giacomo de Caprotti alias Andrea Salaino Florentine and to have called him, alluding to his distinct character, »mon Salai« – spawn of Satan – which would, in turn, be reflected in the combination of letters in the title »Mona Lisa«. Other theories, by contrast, identify the woman as being Caterina Sforza or Isabella d'Este. In spite of many attempts to nail down her, she ultimately remained the great unknown woman, which not only gave her a certain appeal but also, more importantly, gave rise to further speculation.[4]

Employing the *sfumato* painting technique he himself had refined, Leonardo Da Vinci created an artwork that not only continues to raise questions and to be the subject of innumerable studies. It is also still exerts a fascination on masses of viewers, luring hordes of tourists and culture vultures to the Louvre daily.

The veritable hype surrounding the Mona Lisa has been taken up by the mass media and reinforced. The high-brow culture icon of the Mona Lisa is

---

4   Cf. Frank Zöllner, *Leonardo da Vinci. Mona Lisa. Das Porträt der Lisa del Giocondo, Legende und Geschichte*, Frankfurt am Main 1994; Cf. Maike Vogt-Luerssen, *Wer ist Mona Lisa?*, Norderstedt 2003; Cf. Giussepe Pallanti, Marianne Schneider, *Wer war Mona Lisa? Die wahre Identität von Leonardos Modell*, Munich 2007.

a popular motif that is used in a number of different ways. In the following we will show the strategies visual communication employs and how the art icon is deliberately staged to make a specific statement. We will also trace the cultural and historical developments that paved the way for today's deployment of art in advertisement.

DEMYSTIFICATION AND TRANSGRESSION OF BOUNDARIES: A BREAK WITH TRADITION

The artwork Mona Lisa has enraptured onlookers for centuries and also served as a model for Raphael and Titian. In the 20th century the *La Jaconde* became a media icon, with numerous artists creating different versions so that the art icon became detached from its original context, now appearing in a new guise.

In 1887 Eugéne Bataille created a Mona Lisa smoking a pipe and gave it the name *La Jaconde fumant la pipe* in Le Rire.[5] In 1914, Kasimir Malevich presented his cubist composition *Partial Eclipse with Mona Lisa*. Marchel Duchamp's L.H.O.O.Q from 1919 finally marked a break with the traditional, seemingly sacred veneration of the artwork. The readymade consists of a Mona Lisa reproduction in the form of an ordinary postcard, which Marcel Duchamp changed by simply painting a mustache and adding the title L.H.O.O.Q. The title, when spoken in French, sounded like *Elle a chaud au cul*, which translates as *She has a hot ass*.[6]

Mona Lisa was also featured in works such as Ferdinand Léger's *La Jaconde aux clefs* from 1930, Philippe Halsman's *Dali as Mona Lisa* from 1954, Fernando Botero's *Mona Lisa Age Twelve* but also in Andy Warhol's *Thirty Are Better Than One* from 1963. In the latter, a postcard depicting Mona Lisa was reproduced thirty times on a canvas, with the title alluding to a central theme of pop art – that of the consumer world and concomitant mass production. Mona Lisa as a motif was torn out of its medial context and subject to a process of mass production so that the motif was once again, and here all the more patently, robbed of its exclusive status.

---

5   Illustration of *Le rire* ed 1887, author Coquelin Cadet, by Sapeck.

6   Cf. Jerrold Seigel, *The Private Worlds of Marcel Duchamp. Desire, Liberation, and the Self in Modern Culture*, Berkeley/Los Angeles/London 1995, 119.

Even if the roster of prominent artists who draw on the Renaissance motif in their works could be extended, it already becomes clear that the seemingly sacrosanct quality of traditional art was undermined by modernism. Or to paraphrase it with the words of Walter Benjamin: the artwork was robbed of its original aura. Thus the transgression of boundaries was set in motion, a process that resulted in the original barriers between highbrowculture and everyday culture, good and bad taste, art and non-art becoming blurred. The previously seemingly insurmountable barriers gradually crumbled.

ART INFLUENCES ADVERTISING: THE BEGINNINGS OF A DISCIPLINE

The overlap between advertising and art is, however, no invention of the 20th century. This goes back even further all the way to the beginning of modern advertising and thus marks the advent of the newly established discipline known as graphic design or visual communication.

The services of artists were enlisted to help modernize advertising in response to growing competition. The printing procedures, now more affordable, allowed elaborately designed images to be produced – one significant prerequisite. The first modern poster advertisement is generally seen as being one of the few still surviving English posters from this period – Fred Walker's *Women in White* from the year 1871. The artistic advertisements designed by the English were then also followed by many great French poster artists such as Jules Cherét or Toulouse Lautrec. Significant impulses for modern advertising came from Germany and Austria, most notably from the Secessionists and their conception of a *Gesamtkunstwerk* (a total work of art).[7] In the first edition of the art journal *Ver Sacrum* we can read:

---

7 Cf. Eva Klein, *Das Plakat in der Moderne. Der Beginn des Grafikdesigns in der Steiermark im Kontext internationaler soziokultureller Entwicklungen*, Unpublished doctoral diss., University of Graz, Graz 2011 *(German: The Poster in the Modern Age. The Beginnings of Graphic Design in Styria in the Context of International Socio-Cultural Developments)*.

»We know no distinction between high art and low art, between art for the rich and art for the poor, art is a good to be shared by all.«[8]

As a result of this approach and further socio-cultural developments as well as the rapid growth of advertising that led to a veritable poster boom, ever more artists were turning to the field of visual communication. The artist thus brings the style of his time and his own personal style to advertising. Gradually this field blossomed into a discipline in its own right – culminating in today's graphic design and visual communication.[9]

In advertising, the discipline of graphic design or visual communication was thus able to draw from the pictorial and theoretical knowledge of art history and to make use of society' pictorial repertory built up over centuries.

RENAISSANCE ICON IN A NEW GUISE

In his piece *Thirty Are Better Than One* from 1963, Andy Warhol addresses what advertising claims today: Mona Lisa as an icon of the mass media and commercial advertising.

KnowOne.de, Germany's first online dating service 2007 features the all-too-familiar single woman in its advertisement. (Fig.1) As opposed to advertisements that place the art icon in the background or use it as an illustrative element, Mona Lisa appears here as the messenger so that a story is subsequently created. The advertising agency Schwarzspringer from Stuttgart then swiftly adds a young boy at her side who affectionately puts his arm around her. Together, the enamored couple seem to have been a model for Leonardo Da Vinci who captures their happiness for posterity.

Poster advertising confronts the viewer with an interplay of visual and verbal messages which, in semiotic terms, are based on a code.[10] The image is recognized and the code deciphered. Mona Lisa is related to acquired knowledge, opening up a horizon of associations. Here, however, the famil-

---

8   *Ver Sacrum. Mittheilungen der Vereinigung Bildender Künstler Österreichs*, Heft 1, Wien 1898, 6.

9   Claudia Friedrich, Eva Klein, *Große Schau der Reklame. Reklame in Graz zwischen Umbruch und Kontinuität*, Graz 2009.

10 Cf. Umberto Eco, *A Theory of Semiotics*, München 1972.

iar motif appears in a new, strange context, which can trigger irritation and heightened curiosity. The advertisement ends with an amusing text that elucidates the mysterious appearance, promising: *Never again Single!*

Depending on which aspects of the art icon are underscored in the advertisement, the artwork can be reinterpreted in the new context. The original message of the artwork remains secondary in the process.[11]

The Renaissance icon has a special kind of beauty, offering a number of links to the beauty industry. In 2007, the hair-care brand Pantene used Mona Lisa in Australia to advertise for a hair-care spray (Fig. 2), which was supposed to let damaged hair appear radiant and full again, alluding to the subtly brittle structure of the old oil painting. The agency Grey in Melbourne used image processing to help give Mona Lisa a flowing mane. The natural beauty now emanates an irresistible charm, now used to advertise a product: Pantene Time Renewal. Restores age-damaged hair. In addition to the hair, the chapped lips are then »restored« one year later by the Isreali agency Shalmor Avnon Amichay Y&R Interactive Tel Aviv with the help of the lip care balsam Blistex. The use of a well-known artwork suggests an aesthetic quality in advertising, which, ideally, affects the perception and then assessment of the product.

High-ranking artworks such as that by Leonardo DaVinci appeal to a sense of beauty. Put in general terms, the masterwork is seen as being »beautiful«, with its timeless creative spirit resonating throughout. Art is part of our cultural heritage but it also signals prosperity. This applies above all to the status of oil paintings. The value of an artwork is thus both ideally and materially controversial in society.[12] Moreover, advertising also addresses the way the potential customer perceives beauty, since Renaissance artworks are largely perceived as »beautiful« and »aesthetically appealing«.[13]

---

11 Cf. Georg Felser, *Werbe- und Konsumpsychologie*, Stuttgart 2001, 377–410.

12 Cf. Jürgen Harten, Michael Schirner, *Art meets Ads. Kunst trifft Werbung in der Ausstellung Avantgarde & Kampagne*, Kunsthalle Düsseldorf, 18.-27. September 1992.

13 Cf. Ingo Huyer, *Bildende Kunst in der Produktwerbung am Beispiel Anzeige und Plakat*, Salzburg 1992.

Fig. 1: Online Dating Service KnowOne.de, agency: Schwarzspringer, Stuttgart, Germany, 2007.

Fig. 2: Pantene hair-care product, agency: Grey, Melbourne, Australia, 2007.

Fig. 3: Travel agency Hana Tour, agency: JWT Adventure, Seoul, Korea, 2011.

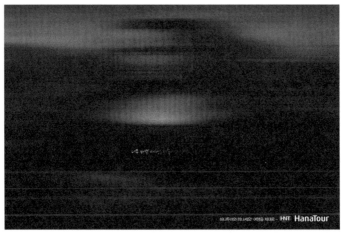

H/L : If you're tired of hectic schedule...
B/C : Enjoy proper tour! Hana Tour

*Fig. 4: Nageldesign Le Nail,
agency: OGILVY & Mather, Gurgaon,
India, 2011.*

In 2011, the Korean agency *JWT Adventures Advertising Agency* fo-cused on the pleasure associated with viewing this unique piece of art. (Fig. 3) It was advertising for the travel agency *Hana Tour*, which lures the po-tential customer with the following words: *If you're tired of a hectic sched-ule...* The statement is first left open – here, too, the advertising agency works with visual irritation, since in order to solve the riddle and to recog-nize the meaning of the statement it is necessary to read the text placed next to the *Hana Tour* logo: *Enjoy a proper tour!* What is being constructed here is the situation of the museum visitor who because of time pressure is only able to race by the Mona Lisa and is thus unable to fully take in the art-work. The picture of Mona Lisa thus appears distorted and blurred in the background of the poster. In order to avoid this perception and to be able to enjoy art to the full, as the advertisement insinuates, one must go a trip with *Hana Tour*.

The Indian advertising agency *Ogilvy & Mather* has also adopted the strategy of visual irritation as can be seen immediately in a Mona Lisa of 2011 (Fig. 4) a fat fly has been placed over the beauty's face so that her en-chanting smile is concealed by the hairy, repellent looking fly. A clear break with aesthetics in this case results in a visual irritation that only dis-appears once the viewer discovers the company the picture is advertising for. In this case it is *Le Nails* promoting nail design. It is not an overly large-sized fly but – in keeping with nail design - an artwork shrunk to the smallest possible dimensions. This advertisement, like the one cited above, shows that the Mona Lisa can be distorted and concealed to the point of non-recognition and still be perceived as such.

This is also true in the advertisement produced by the Mexican Playboy in 2011. (Fig. 5) Here the agency MADE censors the image of Mona Lisa, commenting it as follows: *It's a crime to censure Beauty.*

The viewer is not just expected to know the artwork, he/she should also be familiar with certain values of art and the actual artistic content, mean-ing that the advertisers deliberately draw on the cultural value system and the overall social mechanisms.[14] In the famous artwork not just the aesthet-

---

14 Cf. Hermann Ehmer, Zur Metasprache der Werbung. Analyse einer DOORNKAAT-Reklame, in: Hermann Ehmer (Ed.), *Visuelle Kommunikation. Beiträge zur Kritik der Bewusstseinsindustrie*, Cologne 1971, 162–178.

ic and ideal values resonate but there is also always a material quality which, for instance, the Israeli agency *Shalmor Avnon Amichay Y&R Interactive Tel Aviv* deployed in 2011 - in a further rendition of the Mona Lisa used to promote *Magimix* mixer with the slogan *Only the exceptional last*. (Fig. 6) The illusion to the singularity of Mona Lisa can be easily understood. It should, ideally, affect the product being promoted. The mixer is so exceptional that it even – as the advertisement promises us – chops vegetables so small with the result producing a reconstruction of Mona Lisa. As opposed to the previous advertisements that were a processing of the original, what we have here is a copy that renders the artwork in a new abstract way.

In 2010, the agency *Twiga Advertising Ukraine*, subverted the sacrosanct beauty of the motif for *Consilum Medicum*, a journal for medical professionals. (Fig. 7) Drawing on one of the many theories relating to Mona Lisa's smile, the advertising agency tapped this mythic image, revealing the underpinnings. Mona Lisa's unique smile can thus, be traced to a facial paralysis known as *paralisis nervae facialis*. The advertisement addresses this and marks the copy of the painting at certain spots with medical details. In addition to the paralysis, attention is also drawn to the Xanthelasma around the eyes and the Lipoma on the right hand. Here the claim to perfection that seems to define the painting and the rendition is deliberately subverted with the slogan: *What you see is what you know*.

Even the fast-food chain McDonalds had a response to the riddle related to the enchanting smile. In 2011, the corporation ran a commercial in Belgium that was designed by the TBWA agency in Brussels. In this commercial the viewers found themselves in Leonardo Da Vinci's studio. The great artist is standing in front of his easel and is in the process of eternalizing his model but the perfect smile is slow to appear on her face. The inspiration: A furtive bite from a *Big Mac*, which alone is able to give the Mona Lisa its unmistakable smile and posterity the perfect artwork. The commercial ends with the slogan: *Big Mac. Part of the legend*.

Fig. 5: *Playboy Mexiko, agency: MADE, Mexico City, Mexico, 2011.*

Fig. 6: Toshiba Magimix, agency: Shalmor Avnon Amichay Y&R Interactive, Tel Aviv, Israel, 2011.

Only the exceptional last
magimix

Fig. 7: *Professional journal Consilium Medicum, agency: TWIGA Advertising, Kiev, Ukraine, 2010.*

In 2013, Mona Lisa is even brought to life by the agency *Publicis Con-sell* for the mobile phone company *Orange* in France. The commercial is based on the principle of a hidden camera, which captures the reactions of the visitors to the Louvre here confronted with an unexpected situation. In this case the advertisers exchanged the original painting with an animated version of Mona Lisa so that when one looks at the artwork, Mona Lisa suddenly blinks or twitches her lips. The reactions of the surprised viewers were captured in the You Tube video that was deliberately so that it would be widely diffused through postings in the realm of social media. The heading was: *The most mysterious painting in the world just got even more so*, alluding in an amusing way to the surprises awaiting a mobile phone user abroad. With this video and the accompanying web and print advertisements, Publicis Consell has thus created a strong campaign with a great viral potential.

Only through the break with tradition and the demystification of the artwork and its aura is it possible to cultivate such a light and humorous approach to the myth-shrouded Renaissance icon, which is able to elicit a smile on the viewer's face. Apart from visual irritation, humor is used as a central element in advertising, creating new stories relating to the mythic icon.

While the list of current advertisements and commercials relating to the icon of Mona Lisa could be extended, this selection already shows how the icon can be used in a diverse and inter-cultural way the icon quotes are deployed. The icon seems very amenable to transformation, since it can be used for almost any product – from Big Mac to a medical journal and from Playboy to a mixer. A product targeting the masses instead of the original seems to be the call of the day.

Yet even if the advertising industry is able to bring the Mona Lisa – as in the recent initiative of *Orange* – back to life and to do all sorts of things with her, advertising remains a reproduction of the original, which represents the artwork thematically but never replaces it. Moreover, advertising is a relatively short-lived medium.[15] It thus remains to be seen how many times the original can be reproduced or how many reproductions the original will be able to survive.

---

15 Cf. Marshall McLuhan, Understanding Media. The Extensions of Man, New York 1964.

ILLUSTRATIONS

Fig. 1: Online Dating Service KnowOne.de, agency: Schwarzspringer, Stuttgart, Germany, 2007. Source: http://de.coloribus.com/werbearchiv /printwerbung/online-dating-service-mona-lisa-10893955 [17th August, 2013].

Fig. 2: Pantene hair-care product, agency: Grey, Melbourne, Australia, 2007. Source: http://theinspirationroom.com/daily/2007/pantene-restor es-mona-lisa-with-time-renewal [11th August, 2013].

Fig. 3: Travel agency Hana Tour, agency: JWT Adventure, Seoul, Korea, 2011. Source: http://www.coloribus.com/adsarchive/prints/travel-agen cy-mona-lisa-16640555 [17th August, 2013].

Fig. 4: Nageldesign Le Nail, agency: OGILVY & Mather, Gurgaon, India, 2011. Source: http://www.advertolog.com/le-nails/print-outdoor/mona-lisa-143145 [3rd June, 2013].

Fig. 5: Playboy Mexiko, agency: MADE, Mexico City, Mexico, 2011. Source: http://www.coloribus.com/adsarchive/prints/playboy-magazine-mona-lisa-15874055 [17th August, 2013].

Fig. 6: Toshiba Magimix, agency: Shalmor Avnon Amichay Y&R Interactive, Tel Aviv, Israel, 2011. Source: http://www.coloribus. com/adsarchive/prints/magimix-mona-lisa-14407255 [11th August, 2013].

Fig. 7: Professional journal Consilium Medicum, agency: TWIGA Advertising, Kiev, Ukraine, 2010. Source: http://adsoftheworld.com/media/ print/consilium_medicum_mona_lisa [17th August, 2013].

REFERENCES

Benjamin, Walter, The Work of Art in the Age of Mechanical Reproduction, in: *Illuminations*, London 1973. *(German: Das Kunstwerk im Zeitalter seiner technischen Reproduzierbarkeit. Drei Studien zur Kunstsoziologie. Frankfurt a. M. 1977.)* (First published in French in 1936).

Böhme, Gernot, *Aisthetik. Vorlesungen über Ästhetik als allgemeine Wahrnehmungslehre*, München 2001.

Eco, Umberto, *Einführung in die Semiotik*, München 1972.

Ehmer, Hermann, Zur Metasprache der Werbung. Analyse einer DOORN-KAAT-Reklame, in: Hermann Ehmer (Ed.), *Visuelle Kommunikation. Beiträge zur Kritik der Bewusstseinsindustrie*, Köln 1971, pp. 162–178.

Felser, Georg, *Werbe- und Konsumpsychologie*, Stuttgart 2001.

Friedrich, Claudia & Klein, Eva, *Große Schau der Reklame. Reklame in Graz zwischen Umbruch und Kontinuität*, Graz 2009.

Harten, Jürgen; Schirner, Michael, *Art meets Ads. Kunst trifft Werbung in der Ausstellung Avantgarde & Kampagne, Kunsthalle Düsseldorf*, 18.-27. September 1992.

Held, Jutta; Schneider, Norbert, *Sozialgeschichte der Malerei: Vom Spätmittelalter bis ins 20. Jahrhundert*, Köln 2006.

Huyer, Ingo, *Bildende Kunst in der Produktwerbung am Beispiel Anzeige und Plakat*, Salzburg 1992.

Klein, Eva, *Das Plakat in der Moderne. Der Beginn des Grafikdesigns in der Steiermark im Kontext internationaler soziokultureller Entwicklungen*, Unpublished doctoral diss., University of Graz, Graz 2011.

McLuhan, Marshall, *Understanding Media. The Extensions of Man*, New York 1964.

Pallanti, Giuseppe, Schneider, Marianne, *Wer war Mona Lisa? Die wahre Identität von Leonardos Modell*, München 2007.

Seigel, Jerrold, *The Private Worlds of Marcel Duchamp. Desire, Liberation, and the Self in Modern Culture*, Berkeley/Los Angeles/London 1995.

Ver Sacrum. *Mittheilungen der Vereinigung Bildender Künstler Österreichs*, Heft 1, Wien 1898.

Vogt-Luerssen, Maike, *Wer ist Mona Lisa?* Norderstedt 2003.

Zöllner, Frank, *Leonardo da Vinci. Mona Lisa. Das Portrait der Lisa del Giocondo, Legende und Geschichte*, Frankfurt am Main 1994.

Advertising Effects Despite Scepticism: Eroticism, Humour, and Celebrities[1]

JÖRG MATTHES

ADVERTISING AND THE SCEPTICAL CONSUMER

Advertising is, without doubt, an integral component of modern media society. Every day we are confronted with an estimated average of 500 advertising messages (Bovee & Arens 1995; Elliot & Speck 1998). We encounter
advertising on TV, the internet, and the radio, as well as on the street, in
bars, on public transportation, at bus stops, and, sometimes, even on pizza
boxes or toilet paper. In recent decades, there has been a noticeable increase
in advertising in various media. As data from the USA shows, up to half of
some magazines and newspapers are filled with advertising and the share of
advertising on prime time TV accounts for up to one quarter of air time (Elliot & Speck 1998).

The results of this flood of advertising are threefold. First, recipients
give less and less attention to advertising. That is, advertising messages are
increasingly processed in passing and as a result, recipients do not invest
much cognitive energy when they are confronted with advertisements. Second, citizens actively try to avoid being confronted with advertising, for
instance by changing the TV channel or by refraining from buying a newspaper containing too much advertising. Third, advertising can anger and

---

1   This paper is a revised and shortened version of a chapter in the Czech language
    published in the book »Úvod do teorie a výzkumu spotřební kultury«. I thank
    the Czech publisher Academia and the editor Pavel Zahrádka for permission.

bother recipients. In turn, this can impact the advertised brand so that instead of a positive advertising effect, a negative one follows.

Against this background, it comes as no surprise that research has repeatedly found that people are not always willing to change their viewpoints and opinions during or after the reception of advertising (Dickenberger, Gniech & Grabitz 2001; Matthes, Schemer & Wirth 2007). In fact, surveys point to widespread and ongoing scepticism toward advertising (Obermiller, Spangenberg & MacLachlan 2005). As a result of their socialization, consumers nowadays are rather sceptical of advertising and this makes it difficult for marketers to achieve strong and lasting advertising success. In a survey of US households, Pollay and Mittal (1993), for instance, identified several types of recipients:

- The first group, the *contended consumers,* has a positive attitude toward advertising. These people appreciate the information that is communicated by advertisements and they acknowledge the economic necessity of advertising. Furthermore, this group experiences advertising as entertaining. They account for 38% of all consumers.
- The second group is referred to by the authors as the *deceptiveness wary.* This group accounts for 7% of the surveyed individuals. These people recognize the necessity of advertising and they regard the information value of advertising as moderate. However, for the most part, this group considers advertising as wrong and misleading.
- The third group accounts for 16% of the surveyed individuals and is referred to as the *degeneracy wary.* While this group also sees a moderate information value in advertising, it also refers to advertising as wrong and misleading. Moreover, these people deem advertising to be damaging for social values and they criticize the materialism underlying most advertisements or the advertising industry more generally.
- The last group, the *critical cynics,* is the most sceptical. In the study by Pollay and Mittal, they account for 39% of all surveyed individuals. This group has no appreciation whatsoever for advertising and rejects advertising completely.

The study by Pollay and Mittal (1993) reveals that the majority of consumers are critical of advertising. In view of these findings, some authors even speak of a crisis in advertising: »The emergent picture is really one of ›advertising in crisis«« (Mittal 1994: 35). Yet, there are a number of demo-graphic differences (see Obermiller et al. 2005; Shavitt, Lowrey & Haefner 1998): men have a more positive attitude toward advertising than women, feel less bombarded by it, and feel that state advertising regulations are less reasonable; older people are usually more critical than younger people and feel more misled and bombarded. Ultimately, advertising appeals more to less-well educated people than to those with a higher level of education.

Those who are sceptical of advertising also have a more negative attitude toward advertising and for this reason are less won over by advertising. This also affects the reception process: if the level of scepticism toward advertising is high, advertising is given less attention, advertising messages are avoided, and other sources are used to acquire product information (Obermiller et al. 2005). Taken together, this shows that consumers have gathered plenty of experience of advertising attempts during their socialization and, as a result, have developed strategies to deal – and cope – with advertising messages.

In light of these aspects, scholars, marketers, and practitioners increasingly ask the question of how advertising can still reach its target audience and achieve measurable effects. The goal of this short introductory chapter is to answer this question briefly by pointing to three select modern techniques used by advertisers to reach increasingly sceptical consumers. To re-iterate, if the majority of recipients believe advertising to be wrong and misleading and if they try to avoid advertising, then advertising may hardly attain significant effects. The fact that this is not the case is evident by merely glancing at the immense advertising expenses incurred by companies around the world. The question arises, therefore, of how we can address this paradox. There is a range of answers to this question. Below we will focus on three current trends which are gaining in importance, and which are clearly capable of breaking down the protective shield around consumers. All three techniques make advertising more pleasant, interesting, and enjoyable for at least a large proportion of consumers. Furthermore, the techniques discussed below are – to some extent – built on the assumption of low consumer involvement.

THE PROCESSING OF ADVERTISING MESSAGES

Involvement plays a key role when predicting advertising effects. The high relevance of involvement can be best explained by the dual-process models used in social psychology: the elaboration likelihood model (ELM, Petty & Wegener 1999), and the heuristic-systematic model (HSM, Chen & Chaiken 1999). In both models, the assumption is that information processing can follow either a systematic/central or a heuristic/peripheral route. In systematic information processing, people think carefully about the information presented, and based on that, they draw their own conclusions and create their own opinions. On this route, persuasion is determined by the strength of the arguments that are presented. Although systematic processing does not imply that recipients process the information in an unbiased manner, this route does, however, equate to the idea of a rational decision-maker. The systematic route of information processing is especially likely when the advertised products are important to us, meaning, that our involvement is high.

Yet, recipients do not always have the motivation or ability to deal intensively with advertising messages. This notion corresponds to the second route, heuristic information processing. In heuristic information processing, the persuasiveness of the argument plays a minor role. Crucial are the so-called peripheral characteristics of the message or the communicator, such as the number of arguments in advertising, the attractiveness of advertising models, music, the general appeal of the advertisement, or reference to the names of experts in advertising. That is, when following the heuristic route, people do not think intensively about the message, but, instead, use rules of thumbs to reach a decision.

Dual-process models assume that heuristic processing requires less effort and less cognitive capacity than systematic processing. The heuristic route is chosen if the motivation and ability to process information are low, and if corresponding heuristics are available and can be applied to the given situation (Chen & Chaiken 1999). When it comes to the reception of advertising, this is often the case: if we are not very interested in the advertising messages, we only process them in passing. It follows that advertising arguments are less relevant than heuristic cues. Moreover, dual-process models theorize that attitudes acquired through systematic information processing are more stable over time and have a higher predictive value on behaviour than viewpoints formed using heuristic cues.

Alba and Marmorstein (1987) illustrate the role of peripheral and central routes in the reception of print advertising. The authors showed participants information about two comparable camera brands. Twelve characteristics shared by both cameras were described. Camera A had three characteristics that were superior to Camera B, but these were the most important characteristics for a camera (i.e. strong arguments). Camera B had eight characteristics that were superior to Camera A, but these were of secondary importance. The ability to process advertisement arguments was manipulated by restricting processing time: one group had only two seconds for each characteristic; another group had five seconds; and a third group could take as much time as it wanted. The findings show that the group which only had two seconds per characteristic preferred Camera B. The group which had five seconds to consider still favoured Camera B, albeit to a lesser extent. Only the group which took enough time to compare the cameras preferred Camera A. The explanation is that people with little time applied the peripheral route and relied solely on the number of positive characteristics without taking a closer look at them. The group with plenty of time, however, applied the central route. The decisive factor when following the central route was the persuasiveness or strength of the arguments.

The findings of Alba and Marmorstein (1987) in particular, as well as dual-process models more generally, are of great relevance to advertising research: often advertising messages are only processed incidentally, meaning that recipients are not motivated or able to process the advertisement arguments thoroughly. As a result, peripheral characteristics of an advertising message can be more important than convincing arguments, particularly in the case of products we have little interest in or we do not think much about. In addition to such involvement, however, viewpoints toward advertising also play an important role: if people generally reject advertising or judge it negatively, persuasive effects can hardly be expected to materialize, neither on the central nor on the peripheral route (Obermiller et al., 2005).

SOME PROMINENT TECHNIQUES
USED IN ADVERTISING

Given that people generally want to avoid advertising or find it unpleasant, the advertising industry has reacted with techniques and stylistic devices to make advertising interesting, exciting and pleasant. In other words, advertising is designed in such a way that recipients want to expose themselves to it, which is an important prerequisite for advertising effects. There is a long list of stylistic devices and the following section will look at just three of these: eroticism, humour and celebrities. As this short review will demonstrate, these techniques can yield significant effects on brand memory, brand rating, and consumer behaviour despite consumers' widespread scepticism toward advertising.

Erotic Appeal

Eroticism in advertising is regarded as a key stimulus, which recipients can hardly ignore. If eroticism is used in advertising, recipients instinctively react with increased attention as per human evolution. Eroticism in advertising is not just nudity but also erotic movements, insinuations, or signals of sexual interest (e.g., eye contact or body language; see Reichert 2002). Content analyses show that the proportion of eroticism has increased over the last 30 years, especially in Western societies (Reichert & Carpenter 2004). Also, the proportion of female models is greater than that of male models, and eroticism in advertising is primarily used for certain products such as fashion, jewellery, accessories, perfume, or cars (Reichert & Carpenter 2004). Research on eroticism in advertising reveals that eroticism can both hinder and promote advertising effects (Reichert 2002). According to the so called *recall enhancement* thesis, a recollection of brand names is more likely when eroticism is used in advertising. According to the *distraction* thesis, however, recollection of a brand worsens when erotic advertisements are used. Overall, available empirical findings tend to point in favour of the distraction thesis (Reichert 2002). While it is clear that eroticism draws increased attention for an advertising message, it can, however, interfere with the processing and storing of the brand name, especially when the degree of eroticism is too strong. In short, recipients may still recall the erotic stimuli, but not the advertised product. However, eroticism is more effective if it is connected with the message or the brand name. If eroticism leads to increased attention for an advertisement, then the recollection of information in connection with eroticism should also increase. In contrast, if eroticism is used without creating a link to the product or brand, it will hinder the recall of product information and tend to prevent a persuasive effect.

Severin, Belch and Belch (1990) show that eroticism in advertising can make recipients rate a brand better and make them more likely to buy. The reason is that eroticism distracts recipients from critically reflecting on an advertising message. Erotic stimuli bind the cognitive resources of recipients which they would otherwise need to question the arguments or appeals that are transported by advertising messages. At the same time, while critical elaboration is dampened, consumers may perceive exposure to erotic stimuli as pleasant. This pleasant feeling in response to erotic advertisements is then transferred to the product and, as a consequence, the desire to buy the product increases.

In terms of dual-process theories (Petty & Wegener 1999), erotic stimuli used in advertising serve as heuristic cues that individuals may rely on when they are not motivated to process a message thoroughly. One could phrase such an underlying heuristic as follows: »If I like the advertising, then I should also like the product«. However, it is important to note that recipients may also find the presentation of attractive and sexually provocative models as irksome and obscene, which can prevent any positive effect of erotic advertising being achieved (Reichert 2002). Current research suggests that the link between gratuitous use of sex in advertising and the depicted interpersonal commitment can be decisive for persuasive effects. Dahl, Sengupta and Vohs (2009), for instance, found that women's spontaneous dislike of sexual advertisements was softened when the advertisement included cues for relationship commitment offered by men to women. However, men's positive attitudes toward sexual advertisements were not influenced by these cues.

Humour in Advertising

Humour is one of the most important stylistic devices in advertising. According to studies, humour is used in ten to 42% of all advertising messages (Kellaris & Cline 2007). As with eroticism, humour is primarily used for expressive, low-involvement products which we do not give much thought to, such as alcohol or snacks (Weinberger & Gulas 1992). A response elicited by humour can be defined as a »person's subjective cognitive reaction to a stimulus configuration or, more accurately, the person's perception of this reaction (specifically, ›amusement‹) rather than in terms of an observed response to the stimulus« (Wyer & Collins 1992). However, there are different ways in which advertisements can elicit humorous responses. Catanescu and Tom (2001) distinguish between personification, exaggeration, pun, sarcasm, silliness, surprise, and comparison.

The effect of humour in advertising is quite similar to that of eroticism. Humour can, on the one hand, promote advertising effects, but, on the other, can also dampen the measureable outcomes of advertising (Eisend 2009). Studies show that humour can improve or worsen the recollection of advertised brands depending on how closely the humour is related to the product (i.e., how closely humour relates to the characteristics of a product or brand; see Weinberger & Gulas 1992). If there is a strong connection between humour and the product, the attention, which is created by humour, is also automatically directed to the product or the characteristics of the product (Cline & Kellaris 2007). In contrast, if there is no connection between humour and the product, humour generates attention for the advertisement, but recollection of the product or the brand name will be impaired or prevented. Like eroticism, humour can also support persuasive effects of advertisements. There are at least four reasons for this (Eisend 2009; Lyttle 2001; Matthes 2013; Meyer 2000; Weinberger & Gulas 1992; Young 2008).

- First, humour can increase the credibility of the communicator because humour signals shared values. If advertising makes us laugh, in a sense we laugh together with the communicator or the creator of the advertisement. This builds a connection between the recipient and the communicator, and as a result, the credibility of the communicator can be strengthened.
- Second, humour puts us in a good mood. This means that negative information becomes less accessible in human memory. In other words, if we are in a good mood, positive product attributes are easier to retrieve from our memory stores than negative product attributes. The underlying process is what is known as *affective priming* (Forgas, Bower &

Krantz 1984; Kühne et al. 2012). This means that recipients are more likely to access and retrieve information from their memory, which is congruent to their current mood. A very impressive illustration of this process is provided by the seminal study by Forgas et al. (1984): some of the test participants were put in a positive mood and others in a negative mood. They were then asked to watch videos showing themselves one day prior to the study. Participants who were in a positive mood saw much more positive and astute behaviour in their own videos than those in a negative mood. Translated to advertising messages, humorous ads may put people in a positive mood. As a result, people are more likely to see positive product or brand information compared to negative information.

- Third, as with eroticism, humour reduces the motivation and the ability of the recipients to analyse advertising arguments thoroughly and critically (Young 2008). Furthermore, understanding humour itself requires some amount of cognitive energy. This is quite obvious if we think of jokes. In order to understand a joke or the punch line, you have to concentrate on the content of the joke. This requires precious cognitive resources, which are taken away from processing the humorous advertisement critically. Thus, the ability to analyse arguments critically is reduced. The same is true for motivation. Humour puts us in a good mood. This automatically activates the motivation to maintain this mood. Elaborating critically on advertisement arguments could dampen our good mood, and therefore, humour decreases our motivation to reflect on advertisement arguments.

- Fourth, humour ensures that the recipients like the advertising. That is, humorous advertisements are generally more liked than non-humorous advertisements. However, as no cognitive resources are available to reflect on the content of an advertisement critically, people may use their liking for an advertisement as a simple cue to evaluate the brand or advertised product. This is in line with the logic of the dual-process models (see Petty & Wegener 1999). For instance a simple heuristic, similar to that described above for eroticism, may be used: »if I like the advertising, then the product or the brand must be good.«

Celebrities in Advertising

Another technique, which can circumvent recipients' protective shield, is the use of famous personalities or celebrities in advertising. A celebrity endorser is »any individual who enjoys public recognition and who uses this recognition on behalf of a consumer good by appearing with it in an advertisement« (McCracken 1989: 310). The key idea behind celebrities in advertising can be described as follows: if people do not like to see advertisements, then advertising has to incorporate people who recipients do like to see. There are several reasons for why celebrities in advertising work (Erdogan 1999). First, celebrities increase the attention for advertising. Second, celebrities appear to ›prove‹ the benefit of an advertised product, and they testify that with their names and their credibility. In the context of dual-process models discussed above, this can serve as a cue for consumers to like a product. The underlying heuristic could be that, »if celebrity XY likes it, then it must be a good product or brand«. Third, celebrities serve as role models for the wider public. Based on their success, their looks and their social status, they give recipients someone to identify with.

Research unanimously shows that using famous people increases the recall of advertising messages (Erdogan 1999). In addition, it has been shown that the positive image or evaluation of the famous person can be transferred to the brand or product. The mechanism responsible for this effect is called *evaluative conditioning*. In evaluative conditioning, an unconditioned (i.e., neutral) stimulus (the brand) is repeatedly presented with a conditioned (i.e., positive or negative) stimulus (the celebrity) (Till, Stanley & Priluck 2008). Translated to celebrities in advertising, this means that the positive endorsement of the conditioned stimulus transfers to the unconditioned stimulus, i.e., the product or brand (Allen & Janiszewski 1989). However, there is one important condition required for this process to work: the celebrity's image and the product statement must match, that is, they must be congruent to each other (Till et al. 2008). If the celebrity does not have a product-congruent image, then the celebrity does not fit the characteristics of the product or brand. As a result, a celebrity is not regarded as an authority for that product. Moreover, it becomes apparent that the celebrities' statements are artificial and lack authenticity. For instance, advertisers advise attractive celebrities to promote beauty products. Likewise, athletes are commonly used to endorse fitness or health products. However, it is important to stress that conditioning effects can also be negative (Schemer et al. 2008). For instance, when celebrities are involved in scandals or when they show negative behaviour, this can influence brand and product attitudes. More specifically, once there is conditioning between the celebrity and the product, the image or evaluation of the product can follow the deterioration of the star's image (Till & Shimp 1998).

SUMMARY AND OUTLOOK

In this short chapter, we have learned that advertising is rated negatively by a large proportion of the public. As a result, advertising messages are given little attention and the statements made in advertising are often questioned critically. In light of this trend, the advertising industry has reacted with creative techniques to circumvent such advertising fatigue. This has been carried out by using stylistic tools such as eroticism, humour, and celebrity endorsement, all of which make advertising more interesting and pleasant for recipients. Additionally, there is an abundance of evidence to show that these techniques can have substantial influence on brand recall, product and brand attitudes, and purchase intentions. It is important to stress that this chapter has introduced just a few of these stylistic techniques. Other techniques such as emotions, music, guerrilla advertising, personalized advertising, or viral advertising are at least equally important, omnipresent and can also exert a considerable influence on consumers.

Yet, we have also seen that each creative technique is subject to boundary conditions that determine whether advertising appeal is effective or not. As in all media effects research, these boundary conditions include characteristics of the recipients, the products, the situation in which a message is processed, and the connection between product and advertising. The complexity of these boundary conditions is not yet fully understood in current advertising effects research. In addition, the underlying mechanisms behind these effects are not always explicitly modelled in empirical studies. Moreover, advertising effects research still faces some serious methodological challenges. Most studies rely on experiments that are often flawed by simplified advertising stimuli, exposing subjects to isolated extracts of advertisements in controlled and often unrealistic settings. As a result, the effects of eroticism, humour, or celebrity endorsement might be overrated, at least to some extent. Related to this, there is little knowledge on the stability, that is longevity, of advertising effects, especially with respect to low involvement persuasion processes. This is especially true when it comes to dynamics, that is, effects that unfold and change over time. Despite using one-shot, student-based experimental studies, research should strive to examine the dynamics of various brand exposures in multi-wave experimental settings with quota-based samples that vary in important demographic characteristics. That is, rather than exposing participants to advertisements at one point in time, we need to learn how consumers react to multiple, additive exposure in a complex and, therefore, realistic media environment. Only by working with such experiment designs, we will be better equipped to draw substantial conclusions about the ultimate power of advertising effects in a modern media environment.

REFERENCES

Alba, J. W. & Marmorstein, H. (1987). The effects of frequency knowledge on consumer decision making. *Journal of Consumer Research, 14*, 14–25.

Allen, C. T. & Janiszewski, C. A. (1989). Assessing the role of contingency awareness in attitudinal conditioning with implications for advertising research. *Journal of Marketing Research, 26*, 30–43.

Bovée, C. L. & Arens, W. F. (1995) *Contemporary advertising*. Homewood, IL: Irwin.

Catanescu, C. & Tom, G. (2001). Types of Humor in Television and Magazine Advertising. *Review of Business*, Summer, 92–95.

Chen, S. & Chaiken, S. (1999). The heuristic-systematic model in its broader context. In S. Chaiken & Y. Trope (Eds.), *Dual-process theories in social psychology* (pp. 73–96). New York: Guilford.

Cline, T.W. & Kellaris, J.J. (2007). The influence of humor strength and humor-message relatedness on Ad memorability. *Journal of Advertising, 36*, 55–67.

Dahl, D. W., Sengupta, J. & Vohs, K. D. (2009). Sex in advertising: Gender differences and the role of relationship commitment. *Journal of Consumer Research, 36*, 215–231.

Dickenberger, D., Gniech, G. & Grabitz, H.-J. (2001). Die Theorie der psychologischen Reaktanz. In D. Frey & M. Irle (Eds.), *Theorien der Sozialpsychologie.* Bd. I: Kognitive Theorien (pp. 243–273). Bern: Huber.

Eisend, M. (2009). A meta-analysis of humor in advertising. *Journal of the Academy of Marketing Science, 37,* 191–203.

Elliott, M. T. & Speck, P. S. (1998). Consumer perceptions of advertising clutter and its impact across various media. *Journal of Advertising Research, 38,* 29–41.

Erdogan, B.Z. (1999). Celebrity endorsement: a literature review. *Journal of Marketing Management, 15,* 291–324.

Forgas, J. P., Bower, G. H. & Krantz, S. (1984). The influence of mood on perceptions of social interactions. *Journal of Experimental Social Psychology, 20,* 497–513.

Grossman, R. P. & Till, B. D. (1998). The persistence of classically conditioned brand attitudes. *Journal of Advertising, 27,* 23–31.

Kellaris, J. J. & Cline, T. W. (2007). Humor and ad memorability: On the contributions of humor expectancy, relevancy, and need for humor. *Psychology & Marketing, 24,* 497–509.

Kühne, R., Schemer, C., Matthes, J., Wirth, W. (2011). Affective priming in political campaigns. How campaign-induced emotions prime political opinions. *International Journal of Public Opinion Research, 23,* 485–507.

Lyttle, J. (2001). The effectiveness of humor in persuasion: The case of business ethics training. *Journal of General Psychology, 128,* 206–216.

Matthes, J. (2013). Elaboration or Distraction? Knowledge acquisition from thematically related and unrelated humor in political speeches. *International Journal of Public Opinion Research, 25 (3),* 291–302.

Matthes, J., Schemer, C. & Wirth, W. (2007). More Than Meets the Eye: Investigating the Hidden Impact of Brand Placements in Television Magazines. *International Journal of Advertising, 26,* 477–503.

Meyer, J. C. (2000). Humor as a double-edged sword: Four functions of humor in communication. *Communication Theory, 10,* 310–331.

McCracken, G. (1989). Who is the celebrity endorser? Cultural foundations of the endorsement process. *Journal of Consumer Research, 16,* 310–321.

Mittal, B. (1994). Public assessment of TV advertising: Faint praise and harsh criticism. *Journal of Advertising Research, 31,* 35–53.

Obermiller, C., Spangenberg, E. & MacLachlan, D. L. (2005). Ad skepticism: The consequences of disbelief. *Journal of Advertising, 34*(3), 7–17.

Petty, R. E. & Wegener, C. (1999). The elaboration-likelihood model: Current status and controversies. In S. Chaiken & Y. Trop (Eds.), *Dual-process theories in social psychology* (pp. 41–72). New York, London: Guilford.

Pollay, R. W. & Mittal, B. (1993). Here's the beef: Factors, determinants, and segments in consumer criticism of advertising. *Journal of Marketing, 57*, 98–114.

Reichert, T. (2002). Sex in advertising research: A review of content, effects, and functions of sexual information in consumer advertising. *Annual Review of Sex Research, 13*, 241–273.

Reichert, T. & Carpenter, C. (2004). An update on sex in magazine advertising: 1983-2003. *Journalism & Mass Communication Quarterly, 81*, 823–837.

Schemer, C., Matthes, J., Wirth, W. & Textor, S. (2008). Does »Passing the Courvoisier« Always Pay Off? Positive and Negative Evaluative Conditioning Effects of Brand Placements. *Psychology & Marketing, 25*, 923–943.

Severn, J., Belch, G. E. & Belch, M. (1990). The Effects of Sexual and Nonsexual Advertising Appeals and Information Level on Cognitive Processing and Communication Effectiveness. *Journal of Advertising, 19*, 14–22.

Shavitt, S., Lowrey, P. & Haefner, J. (1998). Public Attitudes Toward Advertising: More Favorable Than You Might Think. *Journal of Advertising Research, 38*, 7–22.

Till, B. D. & Shimp, T.A. (1998). Endorsers in advertising: The case of negative celebrity information. *Journal of Advertising, 27*, 67–82.

Till, B. D., Stanley, S. M., & Priluck, R. (2008). Classical conditioning and celebrity endorsers: An examination of belongingness and resistance to extinction. *Psychology & Marketing, 25*, 179–196.

Weinberger, M. G. & Gulas, C. S. (1992). The impact of humor in advertising: A review. *Journal of Advertising, 21*, 35–59.

Wyer, R. S. & Collins, J. E. (1992). A theory of humor elicitation. *Psychological Review, 99*(4), 663–688.

Young, D. G. (2004). Late-Night comedy in election 2000: Its influence on candidate trait ratings and the moderating effects of political knowledge and partisanship. *Journal of Broadcasting & Electronic Media, 48*, 1–22.

Advertising

Creating People and Worlds

MANFRED PRISCHING

Advertising exists only in consumer society, in a society which lives far beyond the breadline, where resources are readily accessible and effectively exist in abundance. They can therefore be applied, distributed or consumed in diverse ways. The term »consumer society« suggests more, however.[1] It

---

1   On the homepage of the *McGregor Consulting Group* the following features of a consumer society (among others) are described: »build identities largely out of things; the key issues of enjoying life are consumption of good and services; to consume is the surest perceived route to personal happiness, social status and national success; activities that previously belonged in the domestic sector are being integrated into the market sector; [...] in a consumer society, consumption must be organized so production can continue; [...] glorification of greed and material accumulation; [...] to keep the economic machine moving, people have to be dissatisfied with what they HAVE; hence, who they ARE; everybody is a walking advertisement; [...]« (http://www.consultmcgregor.com/documents/reso urces/features_of_consumer_society.pdf) [22nd July, 2013].
The *Oxford Dictionary* defines consumer society as »a society in which the buying and selling of goods and services is the most important social and economic activity.« (http://oxforddictionaries.com/definition/english/consumer-soc iety?q=consumer+society) [22nd July, 2013].
In *The Blackwell Encyclopedia of Sociology* there is the follwing description: »The notion of ›consumer society‹ emerged after World War II and was made famous by authors such as Marcuse, Galbraith, Packard, and Baudrillard [...]. It

does not simply mean that we have a society with even greater consumption ahead of us, with an increased aggregate output and with greater wealth, but rather societies whose raison d'être and purpose in life are largely consumption; whose structural concepts lie in buying and selling; whose functional condition is economic growth; whose idea of contentedness is primarily contingent upon the sale of goods and services.[2] It is advertising which must create this mentality.

Such conceptual definitions make clear that they are connected to the wealthy industrialized and post-industrial societies of the present. It was their earlier productive success which facilitated, generated and demanded the consumer society. Consumer society first emerged between 1880 and 1930, but its real development began from the 1960s with the establishment of luxury societies.[3] It was manifest that the incredible productivity of the

---

was used to suggest that the society in which we live is a late variant of capitalism characterized by the primacy of consumption over production. At that time, the label ›consumer society‹ constituted an attack on so-called ›consumerism‹: a continuous and unremitting search for new, fashionable, superfluous things, which were branded as causing personal discontent and public disengagement.« (http://www.sociologyencyclopedia.com/public/tocnode?query=consumer+socie ty&widen=1&result_number=1&from=search&fuzzy=0&type=std&id=g97814 05124331_yr2012_chunk_g978140512433319_ss1-209&slop=1)   [22nd   July, 2013].

The *Adbusters* focus on critical aspects of advertising: »Ours is a consumer society that profits from disposability under the logic that the sooner things break the sooner they can be replaced. Production is artificially inflated through intentionally shoddy products while consumption is stimulated through commercial bombardment.« (http://subrealism.blogspot.co.at/2010/01/consumer-soc iety-is-made-to-break.html) [22nd July, 2013].

2   I often use both genders for corresponding formulations, but at times, for linguistic-aesthetic reasons, only the conventional form. In some sections I refer to both of my books Prisching (2009a) and Prisching (2009b). See also Prisching (2010b) and Prisching (2011).

3   There are theoreticians who would insist that the roots of consumer society can be found in 18th century, perhaps even in the 16th century, in the transformation of space and time, family and state, individual and society beginning at that time (McCracken 1990).

capitalist machinery at the turn of the 20th century was to be admired, that further increases in productivity were anticipated and therefore one wondered, who would buy all of the items produced. The fear of overproduction and saturation was in no way unjustified. An economic system which increased productivity year on year had to come into conflict with the virtues of the 19th century and its orientation towards moderation, frugality, humbleness, renunciation and contentedness. The virtuousness of earlier periods certainly should not be overplayed; there have always been greedy people, but a modification of the image of humanity (how people see themselves and what, in their opinion, an acceptable life is) appeared expedient, in order to rescue the market economy from its own efficiency. Advertising (in a broad sense) was the vehicle for the transformation of consciousness.[4] If

---

4   The entry for »Advertising« in the *Blackwell Encyclopedia of Sociology* reads: »Advertising is the attempt to bring attention to a product or service using paid announcements in mass media that encourage people to purchase those goods or services. The average person is exposed to innumerable advertisements. In addition to all the normal advertisements selling pharmaceuticals, cars, soft drinks, beer, and fast food, among many others, in an election year there will be many more ads ,selling' candidates. Supporters argue that ads help consumers make informed decisions about all sorts of things, and indeed, advertising can provide people with a common basis for common goals, values, and a variety of gratifications. Opponents claim advertising leads to social fragmentation, alienation, hyperconsumption, and the resulting wanton destruction of the environment. All agree that ads are everywhere.« (http://www.sociologyencyclopedia.com/public /tocnode?query=Advertising&widen=1&result_number=1&from=search&id=g9 781405124331_yr2012_chunk_g97814051243317_ss1-14&type=std&fuzzy=0 &slop=1) [22nd July, 2013].

In the *Historisches Lexikon der Schweiz* (the *Historical Encyclopedia of Switzerland*) it reads: Advertising signifies paid communication that is supposed to inform, convince and influence the clientele. According to its purpose one can differentiate between political advertising (Propaganda) and economic advertising (publicity). Advertising tactics are part of the economic as well as political marketing. The most significant advertising materials are, among others: newspaper advertisements, placards, mailshots (leaflets, catalogues or letters), film, sound recordings, as well as exhibitions and giveaways. Potential advertising media are newspapers and magazines (press), billposters, the internet, cinema,

economic growth advances into infinity, needs must also become limitless (Prisching 2009c). If a structural crisis is to be avoided, a balance between output and consumption, between supply and demand must be established. Thus, luxury must become necessity. There should never again be a moment where people are content with what they have; when they would say: »Ah, linger on, thou art so fair!«

GOODS AND THEIR IMPLICATIONS

The history of man's problems has been generally those of scarcity. More recently, however, economic crises have occurred because of superfluity, which initially is a perplexing phenomenon in people's experience. Abundance appears to be at least as dangerous as paucity. In only a few decades the significance of goods has been modified. Goods are no longer understood as necessities for life but as objects of desire. Many, in no way systematically planned, sanctions have served this reassessment. Goods are packaged as ready-prepared products, ready to access and ready to go. Packaging allows the creation of brands. Goods are displayed and stores arrange them in an attractive, and disciplined, way. Canvassing and advertising are attention-grabbing, appealing, and auspicious. Advertising pushes into the public realm. Experts and celebrities alike are now used in testimonials. The idea of fashion had to be spread further and, along with it, a corresponding mentality had to be created. Buying has grown into a public matter; city centres have been redesigned to represent sales outlets. Credit resources have been expanded, and, gradually, debt has been destigmatized.

An enormous boost to the »ideology of consumerism« came during the economic boom of the *Wirtschaftswunder*, from the 1960s onwards in particular, when people had left disaster and totalitarianism, fear and guilt behind and life had begun to enter merchandise heaven. Furthermore, the economic system assured the unexpected rise in productivity, booming turnover and rapid acceleration.

TV, radio, and realia (e.g. enamel signs). From an economic point of view, advertising can be understood as an attempt to overcome the distance, created by mass production and mass sales, to the client.« (http://www.hls-dhs-dss.ch/index.php) [22nd July, 2013].

Many elements have coincided in recent decades in the »radicalization« of advertising and consumerism. Global mass media especially have served as a stage on which to offer goods and lifestyle. As a result, the connections between information, entertainment and product promotion have become indistinct, and have turned into the most important intermediaries of consumerist ideology. Well over 90% of the images we see in the visual world are »advertisements«: the television news is in truth advertising for the respective channel; every crime film presents a plethora of goods; every appearance of a politician inevitably becomes an advertisement – for the person, the party or policies. What globalised imagery suggests is that a satisfying – even happy – life is irrevocably linked to the availability of goods and services; without a car there is only squalor; without a mobile phone, one falls from the world; the new blockbuster, tipped for the Oscars, is important, important, important!

Advertising has been professionalized. Every advertisement promotes a specific product, but what is much more significant is the meta-message, i.e. that it is important to devote oneself to the features of new goods. Every car advert not only tries to convince the observer that Mercedes, Opel, or any other brand, is the greatest possible, but also that it is necessary to devote oneself to all the refinements they have to offer, and even that purchasing one of these brands grants admission to a new life. In the contemplation of life, structures of relevance are changing: one must scrutinize design trends in Milan; one must be aware of the new spring colour in fashion; one must do so many things. Shopping malls are the synthesis of the arts where everything relevant in the world converges. What modern advertising boils down to is that shopping is not just the procurement of goods, but a symbolic sensation. Advertising knows that a chair is never just a chair. A chair is not only a Starck chair or a Breuer chair, it is an aesthetic statement, an act of presentation, a confession. Buying is an act of creativity whereby a new person, a new world or a new identity is created. One defines oneself anew via Illy, Boss or Porsche. Bobos (*Bobos in Paradise*, Brooks 2000) define themselves via cappuccinos, and a few other frivolities.

Men and Buying

We will now outline in summary some perspectives on consumer analysis and then address the problem of identity, which we will consider in more detail. The first and most simple explanation of buying is the »theory of needs«. People have needs they try to gratify with the act of purchasing. These needs can be conceptualized and arranged in diverse ways, as did Abraham Maslow, for instance. He placed tangible biological and social needs at the bottom of his model, while the desire for self-actualization and aesthetics can be found at the top (Maslow 1954). Food comes first; H&M can wait. Naturally, representatives of this simple model have difficulties explaining why so many billions are spent on advertising, which is – in the strict sense – futile, because it must merely reflect the distinct needs of each individual. The theory of needs simply declares that everything people do is the result of need, and so gives free rein to the possibility of upward development. The CEO simply has a need for an enormous yacht; a great number of managers have an »inner desire« to play golf.

A second theory is the »theory of sovereignty«. It deems people as sensible beings who are able to make decisions. The economic theory of action takes this idea a step further. In the act of buying the preferences of the individual are expressed; if an item is not prioritized, the individual would not buy it at all.[5] With »confident« consumers of this kind, debating the act of purchase is futile. There is no »good« or »bad« television programme; quota is the pertinent thing. The quota expresses what viewers desire which in some ways makes it a direct democratic decision. Markets yield the right thing. Here, individuals are the decision makers. Nobody has to buy. If one

---

5   What is overlooked in both these simple models are the decisions about those circumstances which are presumed to be »given«. Initially the type of situation must be assessed, and individuals necessarily use simplified models of reality. What is it about? Is it about a quality purchase or a bargain? Then, the individual's own preferences are not clear. *De gustibus non est disputandum* does not solve the problem, not even for the individual himself and least of all not in terms of the genesis of wishes, »needs« or »preferences«. Closely connected with this is the decision about the individual's own identity. Who am I? How do I want to live? What suits me? How do I present myself? One cannot simply allege that all of these questions are incidental to the »confident consumer«.

buys, one demonstrates free will, autonomy and sovereignty. Who but the buyer himself knows his desires best? It is after all his money, he can spend it with a variety of intentions and nobody should have the audacity to stipulate what would be sensible or good for him. The real thing is the rational thing. A purchase can never go wrong; at most an error can occur.

The objection we are addressing with the third theory, the »theory of manipulation«, is apparent. Vance Packard's classic bestseller *The Hidden Persuaders* portrays advertising strategists as manipulators, working with every psychological method to win over consumers (Packard 1960). With this, the billions directed into advertising are more easily explained. According to this view of the market system, it in no way provides freedom and consists only of adulteration and pretence. The high financial input reveals itself in the hegemony of controlling interests: the providers determine people's profound desires (not going for any product in detail, for this demand is crucial, but more in the sense of a comprehensive definition of life). In his study the *One Dimensional Man*, Herbert Marcuse addressed the problem of the true and the false consciousness, and that every critique of consumption is based on the premise that critics claim to know better than the buyer as to what would be of most use to them (Marcuse 1967). This is by no means a very liberal assumption, but is at times quite realistic.

Quite often it is feelings of pride and distinctness from others which define a purchase. These socially comparative elements are addressed in the »theory of reputation and distinction«. Thorstein Veblen in his *Theory of the Leisure Class* (Verblen 1958) devised the following demonstrative model: my car is bigger; my garden more colourful; my mobile phone is smarter; and that sweater is from Abercrombie & Fitch. Pierre Bourdieu analysed aspects of lifestyle where rivalries are fought using various sorts of tangible and intangible capital. These accompany a social habitus for which varieties of taste and competence in consumption are of importance (Bourdieu 1987). In recent years, *Sinus milieus* have been most influential. Social researchers have used them to define diverse lifestyles according to two attributes: one following the conventional model of upper class, middle class and lower class; the other following particular orientations based on values, from traditional-conservative via hedonistic to experimental values. Preferences can be allocated socially: some people have filled their homes with period furniture and pay a subscription to the symphony orchestra; whereas others put their money into a pre-owned BMW which they soup up with every possible accessory to create a sleek, supercharged set of wheels; some people are into garden gnomes; others like abstract paintings; some are connoisseurs of Chateauneuf du Pape; others need a bottle of vodka every Saturday night.

Here, we are approaching our last theory, the »theory of identity« for modern consumers. The aforementioned points may play a part, but in the late modern world, purchasing has primarily become a matter of identity formation and an aspect of the wider issue of individualisation and self-development (Berger 1996). It is a matter of the composition of the self and one's own life; about the distinctiveness and singularity of the person; about liberation from the prevailing mediocrity. One is not orientated so much towards those one wishes to impress, but towards oneself. The creation of one's own imagined personality merits closer investigation.

THE STYLISATION OF IDENTITY

Second modernity created an *individualistic* society. This means that people are obliged to develop an original identity. Children are taught not only to imitate others or fulfil expectations, but to acquire roles. They are allowed and obliged to craft their own self. They must become authentic, find themselves and pursue the self. This is the era of individualistic consciousness (Gerhardt 2000; Abels 2006; Eickelpasch und Rademacher 2004; Keupp 1999) which has incidentally in no way developed against the constraints of modern industrial society, but has been demanded by them.[6]

---

6   The world is disenchanted and secularised. This brings a certain relief, but also sobriety and boredom. It becomes a great apparatus, an immanent entity, in which a longing for something spiritual remains. The grand narratives, the ideologies and the concepts of history have also largely forfeited their credibility. The world has simply become »empty«. If nothing more can be found out there one must turn into oneself. There are several strategies for re-enchantment, to the extent of esoteric practices, but consumption pushed by advertising is one of the most powerful forces. In the past, people feared damnation; today, they fear meaninglessness. In the past, one had to battle hysteria and phobias; today, one battles the loss of the self and feelings of meaninglessness. Meaning cannot be postulated arbitrarily. How can anything count unconditionally if it can always

What sort of images and messages are conveyed by current society, and represented by parents, peers, teachers, the media, to young people in a community in particular? Of course, such a question confronts the issue of heterogeneity. In truth, »youth« exists only in the plural. Among the younger generation there are heavy drinkers who move themselves into a coma every now and then; those who go to betting shops regularly; there are the spoilt whiners and the high-achieving careerists; the alert and the dull; those who are focused on leisure or a job; those who die of burn-out syndrome; those who die of boredom; and many others. What counts for all of them is the idea of individuality, the quest for identity, singularity and authenticity.

Identity is defined by understanding what the person concerned deems as crucially relevant for his life.[7] One is obliged to shape one's own inner life and make it outwardly visible. For this, society provides a range of means, not least the consumption of goods, while advertising assumes the task of interpretation. The pursuit of the self takes place in the jungle of accessories. One must take sides on the presentation of one's aptitudes: play it cool, aloof, friendly and amenable, souped-up or worn out, vegetarian or hedonistic, cosmopolitan, politicized, football fan, philanderer, Malibu Beach or Wörthersee Playboy, rising star of science, sensitive girl or distant bra burner, seductive or chummy? Thus, one eavesdrops on oneself, listens to one's own gut and heart. Categorical answers do not always exist. In this way it is a permanent game of trial and error. Everyone is unique. Everyone is an individual case. Everyone stands alone. It is a complicated task. Advertising is basically solely a doctrine of interpretation. How is the abundance of products in a luxury society to be understood? What do these products clarify? What position do they take in the potential understanding

---

be something else? There are in fact too many rival meanings, but it is precisely supermarket model which in turns destroys every meaning.

7   It is about a package which includes ties and empathies, in the light of which one can take a stand. What is important and what is not? Moreover, there are also fundamental moral bearings. These are goods which define spiritual orientation, on the basis of which we measure the value of life. It is the goal of a successful definition of identity to construct a narrative account of one's own life, as a coherent story as opposed to a transient self. How have we become what we are and where are we going?

of the self? Advertising shows people quite plainly how happy they »could« be, and what sort of people they could be, if they only bought the correct thing. One single eavesdropping operation on one's own soul is not enough, if you want to know who you are. The individual ventures into a crafting task and the tinkering never stops. It becomes a permanently incomplete project (Beck-Gernsheim 2001; Hitzler 2003; Prisching 2010a). As one wishes to remain compatible with this authentic self, a self is created which is able to succeed on the market, the market of reputation, the partner market and the job market. What is more, one grab attention and be discernible. One must offer an »interesting patchwork identity«. Late modernity demands innovators, creative folks, originals, geniuses. This means more than the individual ordinarily has to offer (Bröckling 2007). For the *Me-Generation*, the credo of the euphoric individual is almost taken for granted (Twenge 2006). From the cradle onwards, children of this generation are asked what they want. Spaghetti? Ice-cream? Cake? They learn that »what counts is what I want, what is good for ME«.

The building of identity as well as the performance of the personality are managed by means of consumerism. Therefore, one needs money; the post-materialism of our time is based on a stable material foundation. After all, the self must be made visible via signals. Advertising is a constant lesson in the performance of the self. One must not underestimate the high level of consumer competence required to carry this out. One must be acquainted with the corresponding symbolic worlds that are hidden behind the objects themselves, because every commodity has become symbolic: sports shoes represent an easy-going attitude; Armani signifies something different from Hilfiger; a recycling bag something other than Louis Vuitton; a lip piercing signifies something different from a pearl necklace; Fairtrade coffee makes us more compassionate; with green hair we are a little freakish. There is no advertisement, no commodity, no act of purchase which is not *symbolic*. Objects are not what we use them for: a Hilfiger sweater or a Chanel suit could only signify a warming piece of cloth to a consumer philistine.

The creation of identity implies stress. One inevitably lags behind the expected self-perception and remains bound to the creation of the self. There are still few predefined rules of this game; the only axiom is to sculpt oneself into an incomparable, authentic person. This rarely is achieved and thus depression looms (Ehrenberg 2004). He who lives well, feels well, but nobody feels well. Therefore, everyone is obliged, in the hope of eluding fatigue and boredom, to labour permanently on the creation of the self through acts of purchasing. The economy has long since understood that consumers, relieved of their existential afflictions, are floating in the intangible, in the realm of simulations and illusions, dreams and reflection, but nevertheless, and precisely for that reason, need tangible things. They are not desirous of money. They simply need an abundance of goods to have the feeling of becoming a »personality« and to bring meaning to their lives. The transcendence of the afterlife has wasted away in Europe in many cases, yet the shopping mall has become a cathedral where transcendence may still be experienced. In the chaos of a world where nothing now counts, order has to come from somewhere.

Conformist individualism

Reality is apparently far less creative and original than claimed by a »strong« theory of individuality. When one walks the streets or flicks through lifestyle magazines, one does not encounter individual, authentic people. Outward appearances – the fashions, the jeans and the tattoos – are similar. Opinions are, largely, not ground-breakingly inventive either. To all intents and purposes, guidelines to draw upon are needed. Paradoxically, these make the prototypes for one's own individuality. Simultaneously, a longing for unity and the wish to belong emerge, and for that we need similarity. Moreover, one does not wish to be cast out from society entirely. True otherness is regarded as unpredictable, dubious and unfeasible. The more complex and interconnected the machinery of society becomes, the more the single individuals need to be kept on track, as illustrated by Norbert Elias (Elias 1978/79).

Individualisation must therefore not be too individualized. A conformist individualism is more desirable; a distinctive self that puts itself on display but at the same time assures its compliant purpose. Individuality has long since become a requirement of the person specification in job applications, but only if that individuality is still fit for purpose. These requirements must be met by advertising. Above all, advertising must relay the message that the all-embracing event of purchasing is the most appropriate way of translating the contradictory, i.e. individuality and conformity, into images and to make it manageable for life. How this functions can be seen in stereotypical magazine images (Reichert 2000).

TEMPORARY COMMUNIZATION

Only among other selves can one be a self (Taylor 1996:69). People are born out of interaction and this is why some communality is needed to become human, and to acquire an identity. This is understood. One cannot create an identity in isolation (Mead 1968). But communities (families, neighbourhoods, villages, associations) have, however, become more flexible, less committal, and more easy-going. A process of »disembedding« is underway. The »old« communities were, as Ferdinand Tönnies described them, permanent social surroundings, hierarchic, spreading over generations, bound to status and face-to-face (Tönnies 1991). Modern society is familiar with formal, anonymous, rationalised, flexible and fleeting interactions. Thereby feelings of deficiency are created. One cannot live in this non-binding environment; the remains intact. There is a longing for intimacy, for common experiences, and for familiarity. A solution to the problem of making the incompatible compatible, the need for freedom and singularity on the one hand, and the wish for commitment and embedding on the other, constitute temporary communitization. This can be found in adopted communities, experience milieus, lifestyle groups and the youth scene (Albrecht 2008; Hitzler 2008; Prisching 2008). Collective consumption, thereby combined identification with products. Congregation with others at pop concerts, on the football pitch, or at a vintage-car events. The event is wittnessed just as the others do (Gebhardt et al. 2000), people cheer together, and for a short period of time, one is rid of the accursed individuality. After an allotted time everything is over. One has no further obligations and is free to go home and to be spontaneous. *Brand Communities* (Lury 2004) are instruments of communitization: we both own a Harley-Davidson; you own the same scarf as me; you support Real Madrid just like I do, and this is why we take to each other at once; you think Justin Bieber is out of this world too; both of us want to see the Formula One race; »Nike, yes, but Adidas? Heavens no!« or »Adidas. Puma? No way!«; the tribe of the i-Phone fans versus the Samsung devotees.

Still a residual uneasiness remains. Unlike communities of the past, temporary communitization does not provide feelings of safety or of support. In the end, one is left all alone. This is *fast-food communitization*, the communitization of owning Fossil handbags. This does not create reliability. When you need someone, no-one is there.

THE DRIVE FOR LIMITLESSNESS

Advertising does not depict a finite world, but an unlimited one. The diversity of the world of commodities is boundless. Second modernity is a multi-option society. There are not only many more options, more opportunities, higher income, and more experiences expected, the expansion of options and their intensification are considered the substance of life. What is the meaning of life? To experience things. To experience more. To experience everything (Gross 1994; Schulze 1999). As advertising tells you: anything is possible.

You are free to choose products and services, identities and realities, ideologies and religions, biographies and residences, makes of cars, domestic partners, sexual practices, pets; and all the time, experience teaches you that there could be more, that everything could be different, that everything could be intensified, more comfortable, more thrilling. Traditions are impediments, as are values and religion. They constrain the freedom of choice. Any constraint must be avoided, which is why every commitment must be questioned. If one strives to maximize options, not anything must be valid. Detraditionalization means release, but also reduction of meaning; it represents spontaneity but also a loosening of ties and release from responsibilities (Dahrendorf 1979). Maximizing options requires a value vacuum.

The richness of options has another burdensome aspect: the necessity to choose. If one *can* always choose autonomously, one cannot elude the demand to be *obliged* to decide. However, the individual is overloaded by continuous decisions, and the result is always his own fault. Responsibility lies with the individual. If he does not achieve everything he should – which, with an »unlimited« range of options, is basically never achieved – he has made the wrong choice. Fate has been abolished. This generates a series of depressing mishaps.

The uptake of possible opportunities cannot keep pace with the increase in opportunities. One can endeavour to do this, but the promises can never be captured. Nonetheless, advertising must promise it. But there can always be more opportunities, better opportunities, opportunities for all, multi-coloured opportunities. We are too slow or too stupid or we do not have enough vigour for the limitlessness of the promised spheres. However, there is a pivotal paradox: if the meaning of life lies within the exhaustion of all potential, the matter becomes more complicated the more affluent societies are. This is because in a finite life with limited time and energy, one can try to experience everything, but affluent societies offer such a variety of options, that one can only experience an ever-smaller proportion of them. One could spend an evening in hundred different ways, yet one must select just one or two options. A constant experience of renunciation exists: more options means more sacrifice. However, advertising constantly promises more options. Advertising therefore plunges us into disappointment. Affluent societies are machineries of disappointment.

THE WORLD AS A SENSATION

In his book, *Joyless Economy*, Tibor Scitovsky took the view that boredom and stress are both burdensome, and thus people aim for an intermediate level of tension in their lives (Scitovsky 1989). However, the fear of stress seems to have been reduced, inspite of everyone still suffering from it. Advertising and consumerism build up an awareness that everything could be more beautiful, larger, newer, more gratifying; that »truly good living« has not yet been achieved but lies just ahead. One only has to seize it, that is to say buy it, to achieve that short instant of contentedness, which one must leave behind just a moment later because consumption must continue to stabilize sales and avoid crises.

Advertisements want to sell their respective products. In a society where communication has been oversaturated, there is stiff competition for *attention* (Franck 1998; Nolte 2005). Advertising must drown out all other impulses. In a world where so many (alleged) sensations exist, advertising must make use of the sensational itself. A high level of excitement, harsh stimuli and the omnipresent media all become part of the mechanism of deadening and saturation. What at first has been a sensation, becomes mundane or boring just a few years later. This is why the dosage must be increased on a steady basis to maintain a permanent level of excitement. Attention Deficit Syndrome is a plausible accompanying symptom of these mechanisms.

Fictionality is trumps. Normality is out. In the »symbolic economy«, it is words, feelings, needs and their satisfaction, interpretations and wishes that are of importance, not tangible, measurable achievements. In a virtual society, fictitious, impression-making performances are the true accomplishments which include successful communication, the production of entertainment, imaginative routes and detours, stories and arguments, illustration and persuasion. Added to these is the concept of the »star«. The proportion of young people who believe they will become a model or film star, sports star or artist – at any rate fairly rich – is growing. Ultimately, they see these people on their TV screens every day. Role models are celebrities, models, stockbrokers, world-champion hairdressers, IT gurus and star architects.

As a result, life seems to be a game of chance. Everyone deceives himself because, of course, almost nobody will become a star or a millionaire. However, the message influencing young people is »you will not make something of yourself by hard work, but by chance, by knowing the right people presenting the right gags. You have to be at the right place at the right time and have some skill.« It is a game with millions to win; some kind of *Las Vegasisation* of the world. Those who are successful deserve to be. There is no valid argument against money earned, even if it is undeserved. Late modern society needs only achievers; behind their standards, real, »normal« people lag increasingly further behind. Normal life is becoming debased. Those who do not play at the top of their game are losers. This is precisely why everyone must be happy. Pessimism is no longer a permissible lifestyle, but indicates a need for medial treatment. Melancholy rouses the suspicion of psychological deviance. Those who are not beautiful have failed in their – even surgical – responsibilities towards themselves (Prisching 2012). Ultimately, there are only beautiful people in advertisements.

The world of symbols imposed by consumer culture tells stories that leave no room for the cunning of fate, for tragic heroes, for existential victims, for complicated conflicts, for complex moods or for inherited encumbrances. In this world there can be only radiant people, victors, success, happy ends, cleanliness, good moods and luck. What is suggested, is that the world is in a euphoric state. This has consequences for the assessment of the self: there must be something wrong with those who are not constantly euphoric. They are in need of therapy. Thus, we all are in need of therapy in some way. However, these are the unintended side effects of a consumer world whose imagery is characterized by advertising. Ultimately, it is through advertising that we understand how the world works, and through which we construct ourselves. In the end, we will, quite possibly, no longer understand anything at all.

REFERENCES

Abels, H. (2006). *Identität. Über die Entstehung des Gedankens, dass der Mensch ein Individuum ist, den nicht leicht zu verwirklichenden Anspruch auf Individualität und die Tatsache, dass Identität in Zeiten der Individualisierung von der Hand in den Mund lebt.* Wiesbaden: VS Verlag für Sozialwissenschaften.

Albrecht, C. (2008). Traditionale und posttraditionale Vergemeinschaftung. Oder: von der Antiquiertheit der Modernisierungs- im Lichte der Evolutionstheorie. In R. Hitzler, A. Honer & M. Pfadenhauer (Eds.), *Posttraditionale Gemeinschaften. Theoretische und ethnografische Erkundungen* (pp. 329–336). Wiesbaden: VS Verlag für Sozialwissenschaften.

Beck-Gernsheim, E. (2001). Von der Bastelbiographie zur Bastelkultur – über binationale Paare und Migranten-Familien. In A. Brosziewski, T. S. Eberle & Ch. Maeder (Eds.), *Moderne Zeiten. Reflexionen zur Multioptionsgesellschaft* (pp. 245–261). Konstanz: UVK.

Berger, P. A. (1996). *Individualisierung. Statusunsicherheit und Erfahrungsvielfalt.* Opladen: Westdeutscher Verlag.

Bourdieu, P. (1987): *Die feinen Unterschiede. Kritik der gesellschaftlichen Urteilskraft.* Frankfurt a. M.: Suhrkamp.

Bröckling, U. (2007). *Das unternehmerische Selbst. Soziologie einer Subjektivierungsform.* Frankfurt a. Main: Suhrkamp.

Brooks, D. (2000). *Bobos in Paradise. The New Upper Class and How They Got There.* New York: Simon & Schuster.

Dahrendorf, R. (1979). *Lebenschancen. Anläufe zur sozialen und politischen Theorie.* Frankfurt a. M.: Suhrkamp.

Ehrenberg, A. (2004). *Das erschöpfte Selbst. Depression und Gesellschaft in der Gegenwart.* Frankfurt a. M.: Campus.

Eickelpasch, R. & Rademacher, C. (Eds.). (2004). *Identität.* Bielefeld: transcript.

Elias, N. (1978/79). *Über den Prozeß der Zivilisation. Soziogenetische und psychogenetische Untersuchungen.* Frankfurt a. M.: Suhrkamp.

Franck, G. (1998). *Ökonomie der Aufmerksamkeit. Ein Entwurf.* München-Wien: Hanser.

Gebhardt, W., Hitzler, R. & Pfadenhauer, M. (Eds.) (2000). *Events. Soziologie des Außergewöhnlichen.* Opladen: Leske & Budrich.

Gerhardt, V. (2000). *Individualität. Das Element der Welt.* München: Beck.

Gross, P. (1994). *Die Multioptionsgesellschaft.* Frankfurt a. M.: Suhrkamp.

Hitzler, R. (2003). Die Bastelgesellschaft. In M. Prisching (Ed.), *Modelle der Gegenwartsgesellschaft* (pp. 65–80). Wien: Passagen.

Hitzler, R. (2008). Brutstätten posttraditionaler Vergemeinschaftung. Über Jugendszenen. In R. Hitzler, A. Honer & M. Pfadenhauer (Eds.), *Posttraditionale Gemeinschaften. Theoretische und ethnografische Erkundungen.* (pp. 55–72). Wiesbaden: VS Verlag für Sozialwissenschaften.

Keupp, H. et al. (1999). *Identitätskonstruktionen. Das Patchwork der Identitäten in der Spätmoderne.* Reinbek bei Hamburg: Rowohlt.

Lury, C. (2004). *Brands. The Logos of the Global Economy.* London: Routledge.

Marcuse, H. (1967). *Der eindimensionale Mensch. Studien zur Ideologie der fortgeschrittenen Industriegesellschaft.* Neuwied et al.: Luchterhand.

Maslow, A. H. (1954). *Motivation and Personality.* New York: Harper & Row.

McCracken, G. D. (1990). *Culture and Consumption. New Approaches to the Symbolic Character of Consumer Goods and Activities.* Bloomington: Indiana University Press.

Mead, G. H. (1968). *Geist, Identität und Gesellschaft. Aus der Sicht des Sozialbehaviorismus.* Frankfurt a. M.: Suhrkamp.

Nolte, K. (2005). *Der Kampf um Aufmerksamkeit. Wie Medien, Wirtschaft und Politik um eine knappe Ressource ringen.* Frankfurt a. M.: Campus.

Packard, V. O. (1960). *The Hidden Persuaders.* Harmondsworth et al.: Penguin Books.

Prisching, M. (2008). *Paradoxien der Vergemeinschaftung.* In R. Hitzler, A. Honer & M. Pfadenhauer (Eds.), *Posttraditionale Gemeinschaften. Theoretische und ethnografische Erkundungen* (pp. 35–54). Wiesbaden: VS Verlag für Sozialwissenschaften.

Prisching, M. (2009a). *Das Selbst, die Maske, der Bluff. Über die Inszenierung der eigenen Person.* Wien: Molden.

Prisching, M. (2009b). *Die zweidimensionale Gesellschaft. Ein Essay zur neokonsumistischen Geisteshaltung.* 2. Aufl. Wiesbaden: VS Verlag für Sozialwissenschaften.

Prisching, M. (2009c). Fetisch Wachstum: Die politische Ausweglosigkeit der Steigerungsprogrammatik. *Wissenschaft & Umwelt interdisziplinär,* 13, 136–149.

Prisching, M. (2010a). Beipackzettel für Bastelexistenzen. In A. Honer, M. Meuser & M. Pfadenhauer (Eds.), *Fragile Sozialität. Inszenierungen, Sinnwelten, Existenzbastler* (pp. 179–195). Wiesbaden: VS Verlag für Sozialwissenschaften.

Prisching, Manfred (2010b). »Ich kaufe, also bin ich«: Die Person des Kapitalismus. In S. Neckel (Ed.), *Kapitalistischer Realismus. Von der Kunstaktion zur Gesellschaftskritik* (pp. 232–255). Frankfurt a. M. et al.: Campus.

Prisching, M. (2011). …ich, Ich, ICH. *Vorarlberger Zeitschrift für Literatur #26.* Identitäten. Hohenems: Verlag Netzwerk, 32–37.

Prisching, M. (2012). Über die Schönheit in der Postmoderne. *Psychologische Medizin* 23 (3), 60–69.

Reichertz, J. (2000). Das Fernsehen (und die Werbung) als neue Mittel zur Fest-Stellung von Identität. In R. Hettlage & L. Vogt (Eds.), *Identitäten in der modernen Welt* (pp. 129–153). Wiesbaden: Westdeutscher Verlag,

Schulze, G. (1999). *Kulissen des Glücks. Streifzüge durch die Eventkultur.* Frankfurt a. M. et al.: Campus.

Scitovsky, T. (1989). *Psychologie des Wohlstands. Die Bedürfnisse des Menschen und der Bedarf des Verbrauchers.* Frankfurt Main et al.: Campus.

Taylor, Ch. (1996). *Quellen des Selbst. Die Entstehung der neuzeitlichen Identität.* Frankfurt a. M.: Suhrkamp.

Tönnies, F. (1991). *Gemeinschaft und Gesellschaft. Grundbegriffe der reinen Soziologie.* Darmstadt: Wissenschaftliche Buchgesellschaft.

Twenge, J. M. (2006). *Generation Me. Why Today's Young Americans are More Confident, Assertive, Entitled – and More Miserable Than Ever Before.* New York: Free Press.

Veblen, T. (1958). *Theorie der feinen Leute. Eine ökonomische Untersuchung der Institutionen.* Köln et al.: Kiepenheuer & Witsch.

Internet sources

Adbusters, www.adbusters.org [22nd July, 2013].

Consumer Society is made to break (http://subrealism.blogspot.co.at/2010 /01/consumer-society-is-made-to-break.html, 22nd of July 2013].

Historisches Lexikon der Schweiz http://www.hls-dhs-dss.ch/index.php [22nd July, 2013].

McGregor Consulting Group, http://www.consultmcgregor.com/documents /resources/features_of_consumer_society.pdf [22nd of July, 2013].

Oxford Dictionary, Article *Consumer Society*, http://oxforddictionaries. com/definition/english/consumer-society?q=consumer+society [22nd July, 2013].

The Blackwell Encyclopedia of Sociology, Article *Consumer Society,* http://www.sociologyencyclopedia.com/public/tocnode?query=consum er+society&widen=1&result_number=1&from=search&fuzzy=0&type =std&id=g9781405124331_yr2012_chunk_g97814051243319_ss1- 209&slop=1 [22nd July, 2013].

The Blackwell Encyclopedia of Sociology, Article *Advertising* http://www.sociologyencyclopedia.com/public/tocnode?query=Advertis ing&widen=1&result_number=1&from=search&id=g9781405124331_ yr2012_chunk_g97814051243317_ss1-14&type=std&fuzzy= 0&slop=1 [22nd July, 2013].

Wine Advertising and Biography

An Essay on Advertisement Analysis in

Cultural Anthropology

JOHANNA ROLSHOVEN

1. PRODUCT ADVERTISING AS A SOURCE FOR POPULAR CULTURE STUDIES

Print advertisements as a source for popular culture studies is hardly conceptualized in German cultural anthropology.[1] This is probably due to the fact that the goals of advertising are diametrically opposed to the discipline's primary intentions. Popular culture studies aimed for a long time and with a »preconstructivist« approach to survey »real things« not »appearances«. Description and interpretation of a phenomenon were taken as a marker of authenticity, not of refraction or reflections. It was matter of the manifest, not of representations.

Other cultural and social sciences have seen similar developments of their interpretative traditions, except art history, linguistics and literature: they deal by definition with images and reproductions. Deconstructivist approaches in the interpretation of the social realm emerged under the guidance of structuralism, at first at a slow pace in the 1950s, then somewhat

---

[1] This paper has been first published in german: Repräsentationen des modernen Lebenslaufes in der Werbung, in: *Schweizerisches Archiv für Volkskunde. Alltag und Medien*, Zürich 1999, 211–224.

accelerated from the end of the 1980s. Having become part of our episte-
mological culture, they are no longer novel.

If the analysis of publicity appears hesitantly in popular culture studies, this
has not only theoretical but also ideological and practical reasons. The
propagation of publicity is closely tied to the post-war economic boom and
the deployment of the new world of commodities. It is therefore a phenomenon of modernity par excellence, and it is precisely modernity which popular culture studies had difficulties in accepting for a long time. The city,
technology, changing social and gender relationships were dealt with only
marginally by researchers and teachers. Hence, their eyes were closed to
the »new anthropological situation of a ›media civilization‹.«[2] which Umberto Eco has pointed to. Theoretical tools for media analysis have been
and are still rare. Nevertheless, there are sporadic approaches to the analysis of advertisement. The still-groundbreaking conceptual design by Wolfgang Fritz Haug for a »critique of a commodities' aesthetics«[3] and linguistic or historical works[4] contribute to a potential anthropological perspective
on mediated culture. The latter has been outlined by Kathrin Bonacker,
Hermann K. Ehmer and Klaus-Dieter Rath.[5] Their studies prove that adver-

---

2   Cited in Dieter Kramer, Marktstruktur und Kulturprozeß. Überlegungen zum
    Verhältnis von Kultur und kapitalistischer Gesellschaft, in: Utz Jeggle et al.
    (Eds.), *Volkskultur in der Moderne. Probleme und Perspektiven empirischer
    Kulturforschung*, Reinbek bei Hamburg 1986, 44.

3   Wolfgang Fritz Haug, *Kritik der Warenästhetik*, Frankfurt a. M. 1971.

4   Roland Barthes, *Mythologies*, Paris 1957; Jean Baudrillard, *Pour une critique de
    l'économie politique du signe*, Paris 1972; Umberto Eco, *Einführung in die Se-
    miotik*. Munich 1972; Hansruedi Spörri, *Werbung und Topik*, Bern et al. 1993;
    Heinrich Tappe, Der Genuss, die Wirkung und ihr Bild. Wertung, Konventionen
    und Motive gesellschaftlichen Alkoholgebrauchs im Spiegel der Werbung, in:
    Peter Borscheid & Clemens Wischermann (Eds.), *Bilderwelt des Alltags. Stu-
    dien zur Geschichte des Alltags*, Stuttgart 1995, 222–241.

5   Kathrin Bonacker, *Illustrierte Anzeigenwerbung als kulturhistorisches Quellen-
    material*, Marburg 2000; Hermann K. Ehmer, Dornkaat-Werbung im Kunstun-
    terricht. Zur Metasprache der Werbung. Versuch einer Interpretation, in: Peter
    Nusser (Ed.), *Anzeigenwerbung*, Munich 1975, 206–219; Claus-Dieter Rath,

tising is in fact one of the most important sources for the study of the everyday, because commodities and their marketing are a phenomenon of the
society as a whole which actually produces »culture«.

2. BIOGRAPHIC MODELS IN WINE ADVERTISING

Economic and social background

The relevance of wine advertising shall now be outlined by means of examples which, at first glance, may seem odd or remote. These examples are
short biographies of men and women who work in the wine sector, sum-
mary-like stories which are frequently found in wine advertising. They tell
of professional re-orientation, of changing career to winegrower, as well as
wine merchants, oenologists, gastronomists or sommeliers. They are a con-
spicuous feature and an interesting phenomenon, which recent wine advertising has taken advantage of: the winegrowers sell their product together
with their personalities and the discontinuities of their biographies. Ruptures become an advertising point. The biography of the previously anonymous producer, his or her »road to wine« is sold in a package together with
the wine. These stories tell us about the search for luck and a good life.

These examples are taken from the results of a qualitative study of the cultural and empirical contexts of wine consumption in Switzerland.[6] Since the
early 1990s, wine has become a product of heightened interest in an upscale
market. The economic and social background explains the cultural and social implications, and ultimately the practice of advertising. Global wine
production, and the European markets in particular, have been subject to a
deep structural transformation which is best summarized by the expression

Alkohol in der Werbung. Einige Überlegungen, in: *Hessische Blätter für Volks-
und Kulturforschung, 20* (1986), 129–150.

6   Gabriel Bender, Johanna Rolshoven & Justin Winkler, *La culture du vin. Etude
comparative sur le contexte culturel et social de la consommation de vin en
Suisse.* (Rapport de la recherche FNRS 1214-43310.95). Bâle, Colombier 1997.
URL: http://www.uni-graz.at/johanna.rolshoven/jr_weinkultur.pdf [16th August,
2013].

»from quantity to quality«. Thanks to agronomical and technological pro-gress, the grape harvest in the economically poor or winegrowing regions or those with moderate reputation had tended towards an ever-increasing quantity. In the 1970s, this has led to overproduction and the overstocking of the wine market.

Enormous difficulties in the disposal of stocks of wine exerted pressure that eventually led to a re-orientation towards quality wines. In Europe, the con-sumption of so-called »quality« wines has increased over the last three dec-ades, whereas the consumption of middle-rated table wine has dropped considerably.[7] This gap has led to the arrival of a large number of small winegrowers and merchants who produced and offered »excellent to out-standing« wines which were »not necessarily inexpensive« but – as it is of-ten commented – »produced as a labour of love«. These newcomers (though many of them from families rooted in winegrowing) no longer call themselves »winegrowers«, but »winemakers« – both in French and Ger-man – so as to show their activity as a cosmopolitan, postmodern craft simi-lar to that of product designer, but with a decisive stress on »nature and tra-dition«.

This offer and aestheticization answer a certain type of demand. The new »preference for wine« is currently a fashion following the leitmotiv »from quantity to quality«: good life and pleasure have become worthwhile in a saturated society. The central motive of this preference for wine is a dis-course practice: wine talk, talking about wine, and its linguistic tool, wine speak, have gained importance. French anthropologist Jean-Pierre Albert remarks, not without irony, that, the less people drink altogether or at a so-cial event, the more drinking wine is the subject of discussion: »moins on en boit, plus on en parle«[8].

Against the complex background of both the economic conditions of the wine industry as well as the socio-cultural conditions of changed consumer

7   Cf. Robert Tinlot, Situation et statistiques du secteur vinicole mondial en 1991, in: Jean-Claude Villetaz (Ed.), *L'avenir des vins. Les vins de l'avenir.* Sion 1993, 9–13.
8   Jean-Pierre Albert, La nouvelle culture de vin, in: *13* (1989), 118.

behaviour, the advertising claims of the product advertisement for the beverage wine can be read as evidence of a value shift in society.

Form and content of the advertising short stories

To begin with, the interpretation of »wine stories« needs an examination of the forms of the respective advertisements. Articles in trade journals and oenophile magazines contribute more extended versions of wine biographies. Here, wines, terroirs and producers are extensively presented (indicating addresses and prices). These are forms of indirect product advertising. In certain sectors of direct wine advertising, not to be found in magazines, but in intermediaries' and retailers' prospectuses, short forms of such biographic models are found. Both indirect and direct advertising share the narrative concealment of the fact that they are about product advertisement, an issue which is not shared by sober, pragmatic supermarket advertisements, for instance. This is, of course, deliberate. The product gains by this presentation an aura of purposelessness, seemingly disconnected from economic rationales and intentions, the proximity to the producer lends the wine a personalized »appellation d'origine privée«, an intimate designation of origin. This can operate thanks to the social values of the buyers' aspirations.

The insights from first steps suggest a consideration of the advertisements as narratives. The function and style of the short biographical stories often come close to those of fairy tales. This is neither pure coincidence nor arbitrariness. On the one hand, the formal frame of fairy tales can be characterized as offering the social model of a biography. On the other hand, every individual biography is already conceived as if it were a story.[9] Thus, there is but one step between the fictitious and documentary stories involved. Literary traditions as well as media representations provide models of reality; the recipients of advertising relate to it in thought and action. These models of reality are based on shared cultural codes to which the advertising copywriter refers.

---

9   Cf. Raphael Samuel & Paul Thompson (Eds.), *The Myths We Live By*, London 1990, New York; Pierre Bourdieu, Die biographische Illusion, in: *BIOS 3* (1990), 75f.

The variation in the following examples can be interpreted according to particular topoï which respond to the target audience's socio-professional struture, consisting of, supposedly, predominantly male wine drinkers. A first, »classical« version was found in the advertisement of a winemaker from Basel, Switzerland. It featured in a Christmas customer magazine published by retailers in the centre of Basel: two people from Basle acquired a small parcel of land in nearby Fricktal.

»They cleared it and planted Riesling x Sylvaner and Blauburgunder vines. In this way, the two – residents of and professionals in Basle (where one is a chemist and the other, a metal fitter) – satisfied the desire for a vineyard they had sustained for a long time. Even in the first years they became familiar with the closeness of good and bad times in winegrowing, when the growth of the young plants was set back by frosts. Yet, the very first vintage, 1969, was a top-class wine which even today [1995] gives pleasure.«[10]

Proving oneself abroad

The morphology of fairy tales established by Russian ethnographer and literature scholar Vladimir Propp towards the end of the 1920s[11] and which inspired Claude Lévi-Strauss' structural anthropology[12] is based on the identification of structurally significant functions. These can be found in the following short story. The hero is unsatisfied and departs for the world. Here, he has to pass a number of tests, in fairy tales usually seven. Thereby, he gains experience and »grows«. Following some errors and detours he returns to the path of virtue. Now, he either remains abroad, marries the princess and inherits the estates of the father-in-law, or he returns home, where he is recognized as capable of inheriting the kingdom of his father.

The road of the modern hero leads him from the city to the countryside, back to his roots. This is mirrored exactly by real life in the 1980s and

10 Das Magazin der Pro Innerstadt, *Basler Weihnacht, 7* (1995), 57–58.
11 Vladimir Propp, *Morphologie des Märchens*. Paris 1972. [Morfologija skazki, 1928]
12 Claude Lévi-Strauss, La structure et la forme. Réflexions sur un ouvrage de Vladimir Propp, in: id. *Anthropologie structurale II*, Paris 1973, 139–173.

1990s, the era of new preferences for rural life. In the column »Baccha-
nales« in the international wine connoisseurs' magazine *Vintage*, we read:

»in 1982, Olivier Leflaive left the Parisian stage and show business (he was a guitar
player) and took over his family's domain which had been in existence in Burgundy
since 1735. Having become a winemaker, he increased his property in Puligny,
Chassagne and Meursault by 10 hectares, and has become one of the most prominent
winemakers of the Côte des Blancs.«[13]

In this variation of the story, the hero returns home after having tried his
luck in the capital. The detour is the precondition for his success: the young
neo-winegrower subsequently manages his estate differently from his father
by using urban economic and symbolic capital. This example demonstrates
how the small stories describe sociographically concrete contemporary biographical situations, and are simultaneously a means to an end. Their symbolic dimension is doubled by economic intentions: last but not least, this
story is an advertisement and helps to sell the wine of M. Leflaive.

Another variation, taken from an article on Alsace published in a major European wine-trade journal, the hero leaves his country for the world and returns to the countryside – actually the neighbouring village – where he
finds his »princess«

»indeed, this man, aged 35, a native of Kientzheim, has already traveled some way.
A butcher's apprentice, he served his army service in far-away New Caledonia,
where one eats manioc instead of sauerkraut, and resisted the temptation to emigrate
to Texas. He met a winegrower's daughter on the occasion of the village fair.«[14]

The former butcher's apprentice's »princess«, who he ultimately married,
becomes the guarantor of his personal and economic fortune. He was able
to take over the vineyards and winery of his father-in-law. The fairy-tale
model is insofar correct here in that many tales are based on matrilineal in-
heritance, in contrast to real life. The future winemaker had first followed a
traditional career, was then uprooted by army service in the Pacific, but re-

---

13 *Vintage International Magazine* (édition française), 6 (1996), 5.
14 Thomas Vaterlaus, Chasseurs de trésors perdus, in: *Vinum, 2* (1995), 21–33, 22.

turned to his roots. This is considered the premise for innovation that ultimately guides him to success. Contrary to many traditional winegrowers in
the area, he has become a »winegrower who undertakes a lot to produce
quality wines«.[15]

... women also turn to winegrowing ...

Most stories tell of male winegrowers, but women are also involved in the
production and retailing of wine.[16] It has become more common that daugh-
ters take over their parents' estate after training in a profession quite un-
connected to wine production. An impressive example is Baroness Philip-
pine de Rothschild, who trained as an actress, and then managed her late father's Grand-Cru domain in the Bordelais. More ordinary stories tell of this
development, such as a renowned wine critique in a Basle advertising
newspaper about a Tyrolean woman growing wine in Tuscany:

»she was, in fact, a kindergarten teacher about to switch to tourism. A real estate
agent offered her a farm in Tuscany. It had eleven hectares of vineyard on a total of
98 hectares. [...] Barbara was not familiar with real estate agents, least of all in Italy.«[17]

He did indeed get the better of her, but not only that:

»worse still, at the end of July, hailstones fell and destroyed a whole year's work. In
addition there were the usual annoyances with local authorities, chamber of trade,
and also with local village people. [...]«.[18]

Finally, everything went well.

»In the meantime, Barbara has been accepted, and she has learnt how to produce
wine from Vittorio Fiore, the renowned oenologist living locally.«[19]

---

15 Ibid. 22.
16 Johanna Rolshoven, Keine reine Männersache, in: *Die Grüne, 43* (1998), 14–17.
17 -sten, Barbara und der Chianti, in: *Baslerstab, 32* (1995), 28th April, 25.
18 Ibid.
19 Ibid.

Today, she produces top wines of the designation Chianti Classico.[20]

It is not easy to turn to winegrowing. For women, this is twice as difficult. To pass the exams in this male domain is – as in real life – harder than their male colleagues. Male specialists are required to guide them on the road to success and fortune. Like the fairies in fairy tales, they have the role of mediators. These kinds of stories are usually written by male journalists. Wine reports are, like sports reporters' work, dominantly men's jobs. Therefore, these wine stories have to be read as folkloristic, male representations of »real life«. Women are, as often here, the good among bad fairies, but essentially the specialists in dealing with biographical and other transitions.[21]

Gilded fortunes

Our collection of narratives would be incomplete without spectacular stories, such as the one of a bank director from Paris and the successful Belgian businesswoman. Together, they started a »new life«, married and established themselves in his native Southern France. They acquired a wine estate in the Languedoc which they enlarged on a grand scale. Thanks to their intuition and to modern technologies (the alchemical marriage of the

---

20 Ibid.

21 Cf. Katharina Steffen, Biographieverlauf und Arbeitszeit. Alltagsweltliche Organisation und lebensgeschichtlicher Entwurf von Frauen mit abweichenden Erfahrungen, in: AG Frauenforschung in der Volkskunde (Ed.), *Rund um die Uhr. Frauenalltag in Stadt und Land zwischen Erwerbsarbeit, Erwerbslosigkeit und Hausarbeit.* Marburg 1988, 57–67; Monika Wohlrab-Sahr, Frauen in der Leiharbeit. Familienbindung oder Individualisierung im weiblichen Lebenszusammenhang, in: AG Frauenforschung in der Volkskunde (Ed.), *Rund um die Uhr, Frauenalltag in Stadt und Land zwischen Erwerbsarbeit, Erwerbslosigkeit und Hausarbeit.* Marburg 1988, 69–80; Birgit Geissler & Mechtild Oechsle, Lebensplanung als Konstruktion. Biographische Dilemmata und Lebenslauf-Entwürfe junger Frauen, in: Ulrich Beck & Elisabeth Beck-Gernsheim (Eds.) *Riskante Freiheiten. Individualisierung in modernen Gesellschaften*, Frankfurt a. M. 1994, 139–167.

female and the male elements, as it were) they succeeded in producing a high quality wine in this former mass-production area.[22]

Publication in several magazines found the story of former real estate agent, who in France represents the figure of the windy parvenu. In Roussillon, in southwest France, he had acquired a large vineyard estate close to the sea.[23] His wife is described as a kind of superwoman, able to cope with everything. She has a diploma form the prestigious Johns Hopkins University in Washington; is an international diplomat; a showjumping champion; and fluent in six languages.[24] If it was not enough that they built up the wine estate together, in addition, they realized the major Centre for Cultural Agro-Tourism which hosts, they say, among other things, several museums, workshops for handcraft, restaurants, and so on. This »megalomaniac estate« which, according to their own account, has required »efforts of Pharaonic dimensions« cultivates a total of twenty-five different grape varieties.[25] The dot on the i of this magical story is, that the marriage of the couple – not the first for either – was celebrated in their castle as if following the script of an American movie director. This staging highlights the spectacle of social mobility: the real estate agent becomes king of the castle and imitates the Barons of the Bordelais with their wines. This, in turn, nobilizes his wines from regions which previously suffered from the stigma of being inexpensive so-called mass wines.

Exceptional and sometimes spectacular biographical success stories transmitted by advertisements are interesting in their reference to wine. They conclude in wine and they communicate a mythical advertising message.

The stories depict the trajectory from city to countryside, from culture to nature, and the search for one's roots; the highly charged metaphor of longing from the current canon of desires, the desire for a home elsewhere,

---

22 Winzerportrait, Domaine de Montfin, Peyriac-de-Mer. Advertisement of La cave du soleil. Basel 1995.

23 Ernst Meier, Wo die Trauben mit nackten Füssen getreten werden, in: *Die Weltwoche 10* (1995), 9th March, 70–73; 71.

24 Béatrice Ribourel-Buyck. Un paradis sur la mer, in: *Madame Figaro, 16055* (1996), 30th March, 2.

25 Meier (see note 20), 71.

a turn in the perspective of life, a fruitful personal and professional rupture with a happy ending. We read stories of success being possible, »*refaire sa vie*«. Which man does not dream of starting a new life with another woman on a seigniorial estate in southern France? As exaggerated as this sounds at first, it is exactly the implicit message which makes wine advertising economically meaningful.

Another mythical aspect of the stories is that they invariably are set in a world where the traditional relationships between the sexes are intact, and where everyone remains in his or her place. The longing for representations of a static order of the sexes seems to be the greater, the less past anchors reach real life. Again, this is more true for men than for women. In traditional, male-dominated winegrowing, as in other domains of contemporary life, women are gaining ground.

3. INTENTIONS AND MEANING OF FORMS OF ADVERTISING

Advertising as a producer of economically and socially attractive images

The examples above are all taken from the field of high-end wine advertising which is clearly separate from the »naked« advertising for bottles of wine by supermarkets. It targets »new« and aspiring wine gourmets[26]. The boom of wine preference in our society is a deeply masculine and bourgeois passion, where »there is no decent man if not an oenologist«[27]. Wine »connoisseurship« is an extremely attractive element of habitus, because, by contrast to many central attributes of distinction such as social provenance, it can be learned. The need of consumers for briefings is answered on a large scale: specialist literature on wine, wine clubs, and the growing offer

---

26 Johanna Rolshoven, Nüchternes Vergnügen. Zur ,neuen Weinkultur' in der Gesellschaft (Lecture at the Department of Cultural Anthropology/European Ethnology at the University of Münster, 1999), 6.

27 Albert (see note 8), 119.

of wine-tasting courses. The rituals of wine tasting can be seen as the outcome of this process.

The values addressed in advertisements, consisting in an aura of spontaneous and sometimes euphoric associations, are tied to the cravings of the buyers, according to their social status. It is as in the biography of the everyday, which »in terms of form and content is differentiated along the social quality of the market where it is tendered«.[28] They indicate a social register subjected to the effects of social as well as economic and structural changes. Currently, we can observe a re-appreciation of the so-called lower senses, in particular the senses of smell and of taste, which have been subjugated by the visual. The new wine culture re-centres them and overshadows the »cold« sense of sight, figurehead of modernity. Delight and savouring become, as it were, the objective of the re-valuation. The wine connoisseur appears as a bon-vivant, even if he is fundamentally guided by choice and ratio, as the impression is created by the sometimes meticulous educational features of wine drinking. The wine connoisseur is, like a freemason, rising step by step to the status of an artist. Wine as a professional basis is the advanced version of postmodern biographical plots. Per aspera ad astra, the central credo of a capitalist society, still shapes the narrative of »wine biographies«: a sense of duty rules our earthly life, but it is gradually eclipsed by a new and subversive drive, a passion which provides individual satisfaction. [29]

The »wine biographies« tell of self-determined ruptures with happy endings as opposed to imposed obligations; individual entrepreneurs vs. employees; affluence vs. precariousness. It is not a coincidence that with the increasing scarcity of paid work, the icon of the ideal professional enters the stage of advertising, and acts the engaged, motivated, smart and innovative character. On the one hand, the labour market requires flexibility and total commitment, on the other, spontaneous dismissal is imminent.[30]

---

28 Bourdieu (see note 9), 74.

29 Cf. The ethnology of everyday passions by Christian Bromberger et al., Passions ordinaires. Du match de football au concours de dictée. Paris 1998.

30 Cf. Martin Kohli, Institutionalisierung und Individualisierung der Erwerbsbiographie, in: U. Beck und E. Beck-Gernsheim (Eds.) (see note 18), 236.

Thus, advertising stories portray individual freedom and scopes of action, an easily understood dichotomy of tradition and innovation. Traditional winegrowing and modern winemaking miraculously encompass these two poles: nature and culture; craft and technology. Intuition, sensitivity, authenticity and a sure hand distinguish the new winegrower as much as his or her rational control of the cellar technology or the domestication of the »wild« fermentation processes. The perfect amalgamation of the two sides is the real innovation, and the basis of individual satisfaction and economic success.

Recent sociological findings support the interpretations of popular culture studies. »To search for one's self«, writes biography researcher Martin Kohli, »to find oneself is what shall guarantee orientation in the world«.[31] He refers to the partial dissolution of institutionalised biographical trajectories,[32] but we can even talk of patterns of career refusal. Wine making as a profession and distinction ennoble not only the butcher's apprentice or the kindergarten teacher, but also bring managers, aristocratic leather-goods producers and academics together. The narratives of many wine »conversions« chart a descent in terms of professional prestige, and yet – and this is the interesting thing about it – they are success stories. An example is Swiss manager Jacqueline Fendt. On the very day of her dismissal as director of the Swiss national exhibition 2001, »ex-Madame Expo.01«, she flew to her vineyard in Provence, which for a couple of years had already been cultivated by a former lawyer from Geneva. With her travel journalists, who titled their report for a major Swiss newspaper: »I like the vine, it suffers, it defends against the impossible. But it survives.«[33]

Neoliberal change in the economic sphere has put an end to automatic professional advancement and asks for independent, individual biography design. This fact should not be ignored in the interpretation of the media's seemingly idealistic myth building. There is no aspiration from below, as the stories might suggest. The so-called »zero career« is not only an indi-

---

31 Ibid., 233.

32 Ibid., 220.

33 Isabelle Cerboneschi, »J'aime la vigne: elle souffre, elle se bat contre l'impossible. Mais elle survit.« in *Le Temps* 11th August, 1999, 44.

vidual choice, according to Niklas Luhmann, it follows the structure.[34] Altogether, the actual function of the texts – advertising – should not be forgotten in any cultural analysis. The biography, the distinctive story of a winemaker, has the capacity to transform any vineyard or any production zone into somewhere, a terroir, a named place. Suddenly, the rural, even rustic, confinement is seasoned with an urban scent and a breeze of cosmopolitanism. Quite concretely this is about urban capital, not only symbolic, but also monetary.

Finally, the personal qualities of the winemaker merge with the wine. The professional vocabulary which serves to characterize the wines follows age-old analogies to folk medicine: the Spanish or Sicilian is more »fiery« than any Swiss wine ever can and would be allowed to be; wines made by women are more often described »elegant« than the tartly tannic ones produced by men.

Advertisements and the everyday

Advertising is an influential medium with relevance for the everyday beyond the actual intentions to stimulate the buying of commodities. It is less an issue of rousing need against our will, as the critique in the spirit of cultural pessimist used to say, seeing advertising as a device of mass manipulation by a deceiving pretty exterior.[35] »The appearance to which one falls is like a glass where craving sees itself and takes itself as objective.«[36] Advertising ties in with existing needs, so even escapist »facade needs«[37] are real needs which deserve to be taken seriously. Therefore, audience research with cultural-studies and social-science approaches delivers reveal-

---

34 Niklas Luhmann, Copierte Existenz und Karriere. Zur Herstellung von Individualität, in: U. Beck und E. Beck-Gernsheim (Eds.) (see note 18), 198.

35 Eva Heller provides a broad overview of the ideological critique of advertisement: *Theorien und Tatsachen*. Frankfurt a. M. 1984, however, neglecting the important influence of the »critique of the culture industry« in the *Dialectic of Enlightenment* on the scientific conceptions (Theodor W. Adorno, Max Horkheimer; Amsterdam 1947).

36 Haug (see note 3), 64.

37 Cf.. Karl Oldenburg, cited by Kramer (see note 2), 46.

ing sources to explore everyday requirements. Advertising messages play on myths and desires which load everyday wishing, desires for appropriation and distinction, and escapist wishes of an often dream-like or fairy-tale quality. However, consumers differentiate better between myth and reality than scholars of social sciences tend to admit, as Roland Barthes has diagnosed. They take the product for much less important that the bourgeois scholar, who is permeated by bourgeois notions of aesthetics and moral.

The average consumer usually acts consciously against better judgement when he or she prefers beautiful appearance to the less radiant or banal practicality of the everyday. Advertising meets this need as a deeply dialectical medium by playing in its messages with facts which we accept somehow despite the obvious horizon of wishful thinking. Of course, this happens behind veils; little girls have no natural need for pink muzzled Barbie puppets, than do little boys naturally crave plastic monsters. Anthropological studies have demonstrated how much more complex and sophisticated the appropriation of the cultural environment is. The deceptive appearances as a »space of temptation« and a »ruler of the universe of meaning«[38] continues to be a challenging field in cultural studies. The images of advertising are like glasses, as Haug formulates:

»empathic, watching the bottom, hauling secrets to the surface and displaying them. In these images men constantly experience unsatisfied parts of their existence. Appearance tenders one, solves one's riddles, anticipates one's wishes, sheds light on the surface of commodities. The appearance proper to commodities recognizes men; it provides them with a language which interprets them and the world.«[39]

REFERENCES

-sten, Barbara und der Chianti, in: *Baslerstab, 32* (1995), 28th April, 25.

Albert, Jean-Pierre, La nouvelle culture de vin, in: *13* (1989), 117–124.

Anonymus, Das Magazin der Pro Innerstadt, *Basler Weihnacht, 7* (1995), 57–58.

---

38 Jean Baudrillard, *Das Andere selbst*, Vienna 1987, 49f.

39 Haug (see note 3), 64.

Anonymus, *Vintage International Magazine* (édition française), 6 (1996), 5.

Barthes, Roland, *Mythologies*, Paris 1957.

Baudrillard, Jean, *Das Andere selbst*, Vienna 1987.

Baudrillard, Jean, *Pour une critique de l'économie politique du signe*, Paris 1972.

Bonacker, Kathrin, *Illustrierte Anzeigenwerbung als kulturhistorisches Quellenmaterial*, Marburg 2000.

Bourdieu, Pierre, Die biographische Illusion, in: *BIOS 3* (1990), 75–81.

Bromberger, Christian, et al., *The ethnology of everyday passions. Passions ordinaires. Du match de football au concours de dictée*, Paris 1998.

Cerboneschi, Isabelle, »J'aime la vigne: elle souffre, elle se bat contre l'impossible. Mais elle survit.« in: *Le Temps, 44* (1999) 11th August.

Eco, Umberto, *Einführung in die Semiotik*, Munich 1972.

Ehmer, Hermann K., Dornkaat-Werbung im Kunstunterricht. Zur Metasprache der Werbung. Versuch einer Interpretation, in: Peter Nusser (Ed.), *Anzeigenwerbung*, Munich 1975, 206–219.

Geissler, Birgit; Oechsle, Mechtild, Lebensplanung als Konstruktion. Biographische Dilemmata und Lebenslauf-Entwürfe junger Frauen, in: Ulrich Beck & Elisabeth Beck-Gernsheim (Eds.), *Riskante Freiheiten. Individualisierung in modernen Gesellschaften*, Frankfurt a. M. 1994, 139–167.

Haug, Wolfgang Fritz, *Kritik der Warenästhetik*, Frankfurt a. M. 1971.

Kohli, Martin, Institutionalisierung und Individualisierung der Erwerbsbiographie, in: Ulrich Beck & Elisabeth Beck-Gernsheim (Eds.), *Riskante Freiheiten. Individualisierung in modernen Gesellschaften*, Frankfurt a. M. 1994, 219–244.

Kramer, Dieter, Marktstruktur und Kulturprozeß. Überlegungen zum Verhältnis von Kultur und kapitalistischer Gesellschaft, in: ed. Utz Jeggle et al., *Volkskultur in der Moderne. Probleme und Perspektiven empirischer Kulturforschung*, Reinbek bei Hamburg 1986, 37–53.

Lévi-Strauss, Claude, La structure et la forme. Réflexions sur un ouvrage de Vladimir Propp, in: id., *Anthropologie structurale II.*, Paris 1973, 139–173.

Luhmann, Niklas, Copierte Existenz und Karriere. Zur Herstellung von Individualität, in: Ulrich Beck & Elisabeth Beck-Gernsheim (Eds.), *Riskante Freiheiten. Individualisierung in modernen Gesellschaften*, Frankfurt a. M. 1994, 191–200.

Meier, Ernst, Wo die Trauben mit nackten Füssen getreten werden, in: *Die Weltwoche 10* (1995), 9th March, 70–73.

Propp, Vladimir, *Morphologie des Märchens*. Paris 1972. [Morfologija skazki, 1928].

Rath, Claus-Dieter, Alkohol in der Werbung. Einige Überlegungen, in: *Hessische Blätter für Volks- und Kulturforschung, 20* (1986), 129–150.

Ribourel-Buyck, Béatrice, Un paradis sur la mer, in: *Madame Figaro, 16055* (1996), 30th March, 2.

Rolshoven, Johanna, Keine reine Männersache, in: *Die Grüne, 43* (1998), 14–17.

Rolshoven, Johanna, *Nüchternes Vergnügen. Zur ›neuen Weinkultur‹ in der Gesellschaft* (Lecture at the Department of Cultural Anthropology/European Ethnology at the University of Münster, 1999), 6.

Rolshoven, Johanna, Repräsentationen des modernen Lebenslaufes in der Werbung, in: *Schweizerisches Archiv für Volkskunde. Alltag und Medien*, Zürich 1999, 211–224.

Samuel, Raphael & Thompson, Paul (eds.), *The Myths We Live By*, London/ New York, 1990.

Spörri, Hansruedi, *Werbung und Topik*, Bern 1993.

Steffen, Katharina, Biographieverlauf und Arbeitszeit. Alltagsweltliche Organisation und lebensgeschichtlicher Entwurf von Frauen mit abweichenden Erfahrungen, in: AG Frauenforschung in der Volkskunde (Ed.), *Rund um die Uhr. Frauenalltag in Stadt und Land zwischen Erwerbsarbeit, Erwerbslosigkeit und Hausarbeit*. Marburg 1988, 57–67.

Tappe, Heinrich, Der Genuss, die Wirkung und ihr Bild. Wertung, Konventionen und Motive gesellschaftlichen Alkoholgebrauchs im Spiegel der Werbung, in: Peter Borscheid & Clemens Wischermann (Eds.), *Bilderwelt des Alltags. Studien zur Geschichte des Alltags*, Stuttgart 1995, 222–241.

Tinlot, Robert, Situation et statistiques du secteur vinicole mondial en 1991, in: Jean-Claude Villetaz (Ed.), *L'avenir des vins. Les vins de l'avenir*. Sion 1993, 9–13.

Vaterlaus, Thomas, Chasseurs de trésors perdus, in: *Vinum, 2* (1995), 21–33.

Wohlrab-Sahr, Monika, Frauen in der Leiharbeit. Familienbindung oder Individualisierung im weiblichen Lebenszusammenhang, in: AG Frauenforschung in der Volkskunde (Ed.), *Rund um die Uhr, Frauenalltag in*

Stadt und Land zwischen Erwerbsarbeit, Erwerbslosigkeit und Hausarbeit. Marburg 1988, 69–80.

Internet sources

Gabriel Bender, Johanna Rolshoven & Justin Winkler, *La culture du vin. Etude comparative sur le contexte culturel et social de la consommation de vin en Suisse.* (Rapport de la recherche FNRS 1214-43310.95). Bâle, Colombier 1997. http://www.uni-graz.at/johanna.rolshoven/jr_weinkul tur.pdf [16th August, 2013].

Under the spell of the lottery – warning included

MARGIT STADLOBER

Underneath the bittersweet depiction of subjects in Viennese Biedermeier paintings lie more themes deserving of exploration. This paper (Fig. 1) aims to expand on the varied iconological interpretation of Peter Fendi's painting *Ein Mädchen vor einem Lotterie-Gewölbe*[1] (*Girl at the Lottery*) by focusing solely on the sociocultural context and the pictorial elements.[2]

---

1   *Girl at the Lottery*, oil on canvas, 63 x 50 cm, 1829, inventory no.: 2.521., first edition of a painting of the same name, dated 1830, from a private collection; a pencil sketch and two watercolour studies also from a private collection. In his dissertation, Hubert Adolph mentions: a counterpart of this painting *Mädchen mit der Niete* (*Girl with the blank*) or *Mädchen nach der Ziehung der Lotterie* (*Girl after the lottery was drawn*), dated 1878, in the Belvedere Palace in Vienna. Cf. Hubert Adolph, Peter Fendi (1796–1824), Unpublished doctoral diss., vol. 1, University of Innsbruck, Innsbruck 1951, 64; and an aquarelle study, 11.5 x 10 cm, sold at auction on 10th December 1917 by S. Kende, collection of Director Robert Schlesinger. Cf. H. Adolph, Fendi, vol. 3, 242; and two pencil drawings, 18.5 x 11.9 cm and 17 x 10.5 cm 1910, the first from Prague artist Nowotny's art album from the Prague collection of Baron Lanna sold at auction in Vienna in October 1910 for 520 krone, and under the previous ownership of Count Victor Wimpfen. Cf. H. Adolph, Fendi, vol. 4, 559, 560.
    Hubert Adolph, Peter Fendis »Ein Mädchen vor einem Lotterie-Gewölbe«, in: *Mitteilungen der Österreichischen Galerie, 49* (1961), 29.
    Hans Ankwicz v. Kleehoven, Peter Fendi, in: *Kunst dem Volk, 14*, März 1943, 8.

Fig. 1: Peter Fendi, Girl at the Lottery, *painting, 1829.*

Österreichische Gallerie (Ed.), *Peter Fendi 1796–1842*, exhibition catalogue, Vienna, 1963, 39.

2   There are already 19 papers on this painting. Cf. Hubert Adolph, Mädchen, in: *Mitteilungen*, 1961, 25f.

In 1829, the painting was one of the earliest of the Biedermeier period depicting a single person. In 1830 a replica[3] was made. At the exhibition of genre art at the Imperial and Royal Court Academy of Fine Arts in Vienna in 1830 Emperor Franz Joseph I of Austria bought this painting, exhibition number 137, for 100 guilders as well as *Kaiser Karl V. als Mönch in seiner Zelle* (*Emperor Charles V as a monk in his cell*), number 155, for only 70 guilders, to include in his collection in the Upper Belvedere, where it remains today. This acquisition, as well as the exceptional feedback the painting received,[4] could explain why the artist himself made a replica of this successful painting. Its success was further documented when it was included in a children's game of copper engravings (»Das kleine Belvedere« or »Mignon-Bilder Galerie«) sold by the M. F. Müller art shop on Kohlmarkt in Vienna in 1839. The small, hand-coloured copperplate print of Fendi's painting, 36 x 28 cm in size, occupies a central position in this collection. The original print is still held in public archives today. It differs from the usual pillorying depictions of the lottery because of its decidedly subtler illustration.

A brief explanation of the history of the lottery shall serve as a prelude to the analysis of the painting. According to Günther G. Bauer, the lottery has a 565-year history, with the first records dating back to 1445 in Sluis, Flanders.[5] Five years later, a form of gambling similar to the lottery is mentioned in Florence. There, the profits went to charitable organisations. Of further importance was Genoa, where a »5 out of 120« system, the *seminario*, was first documented on 22nd September 1643. People bet on the names of two new Great Council members who would be elected. For this purpose, the first betting office in Genoa was established in 1620. A single

---

3   The L.T. Neumann Gallery acquired this replica (also 63 x 50 cm) abroad in 1960 to include in their private collection. It was exhibited in the Österreichische Galerie Belvedere, Vienna, in 1960. Cf. Peter Fendi, 1963, 39.
     Hubert Adolph describes the replica as being subtler with warmer colours. Another difference is the lighter shadow which allows the architecture to become visible.

4   H. Adolph, Mädchen, in: *Mitteilungen*, 1961, 27.

5   Cf. Günther G. Bauer, Das Österreichische Zahlenlotto. 1752–2002, in: *Dem Glück auf der Spur. 250 Jahre Österreichisches Zahlenlotto, exhibition catalogue*, Vienna 2002, 61.

match (*estrado*) and a double match (*ambe*) were possible which increased the winnings. In 1644, the quantity of numbers, which could be betted on in the *Lotto di Genoa,* was raised to five, and in 1682, the first lottery based on »5 out of 90«, in which five girls received a dowry, was held.

In the early 18th century, Pope Benedict XIII banned gambling, a ruling which was reversed a short time later by Pope Clement XII. The Pope's endorsement of the lottery made it even more popular than before. It was held in Venice's *ridotti* until the Doge (the Venetian authorities) closed these dubious establishments in the vicinity of theatres due to suspected conspiracies. Games of chance similar to the lottery, such as the *faro* and the *biribi,* were also popular. The latter was especially preferred by women.[6] The Pope's consent was also of significance in Catholic Bavaria, where the first lottery was drawn in 1735, and subsequently introduced in Austria and Bohemia.

Empress Maria Theresa granted a charter on 13th November 1751 to introduce a lottery under the official name »Lotto di Genova« which was based on 90 numbers.[7] Count Ottavio Cataldi was granted a licence to run the lottery for ten years. The first drawing of the lottery took place at 11am on 21st October 1752 at 11am at Augustinerplatz in Vienna. Reports of numerous winners were published in both the *Wiener Diarium* and the *Wienerblatt* newspapers. The latter revealed shoemaker's apprentice, Ulrich Huber, as the winner. He received 600 ducats.[8]

---

6   Cf. Martin Hirsch, Giacomo Casanova und das Lotteriespiel im 18. Jahrhundert, in: Johann Konrad Eberlein (Ed.), *SpielKunstGlück. Die Wette als Leitlinie der Entscheidung, Die Wette als Leitlinie der Entscheidung. Beispiele aus Vergangenheit und Gegenwart in Kunst, Wissenschaft, Wirtschaft,* Vienna/ Berlin 2011, 235–250.

7   Cf. Antonia Slavnitsch, *Das Glücksspielwesen in Österreich unter Berücksichtigung der neuen Rechtslage,* Unpublished Master Thesis, University of Graz, Graz 2011, 3.
Günther G. Bauer quotes 18th August 1751 as the date of Empress Maria Theresa's edict.
Cf. G. G. Bauer, Zahlenlotto, in: *Glück,* 2002, 64.

8   Cf. 150 Jahre Lotto in Österreich, in: *Innsbrucker Nachrichten,* 3rd November 1903, 1f., http://anno.onb.ac.at/cgicontent/anno?apm=0&aid=ibn&datum=1902 1103&seite=1&zoom=2 (25th March, 2013).

After 36 years, the lottery was placed under state ownership by Emperor Joseph II, on 21[9] October 1787.[9] Even before the nationalisation, five girls of marriageable age from poor families had to receive a dowry of 30 guilders from the lottery. However, the lottery's moral reputation was questionable. It was held responsible for the lower classes chasing quick money because it was perceived as encouraging gambling and profit-seeking whilst discouraging hard work and saving money.[10]

Emperor Joseph II considered a ban on the lottery. However, as the exchequer also benefitted financially from it, he aimed only to stem compulsive gambling and eliminate misconceptions surrounding the lottery.

A new decree containing rules and regulations on the state's monopoly of the lottery was issued by Emperor Francis I on 13[11] March 1813.[11] The lottery was incorporated into the Treasury which yielded high earnings of 43,641.000 guilders between 1821 and 1830. 27,352.837 guilders were attributed to administrative costs and 23,230.352 guilders were paid out in winnings.[12] Yet, opponents continued to demand a ban on the lottery during the following decades.

Fendi's genre painting of a lottery scene must be placed and analysed within this context. In the centre of the foreground, we see a girl wearing a traditional Biedermeier costume standing in the entrance hall of an imperial-royal lottery building for Vienna and Linz (in 1828 a total of 1.227 such establishments existed in the Austrian-Hungarian Empire).[13] Details of the sombre location cast in shadows are documented in a preliminary study in watercolour. There, the entire entrance of the building is visible with an open bar in the shop window. The girl is positioned to the left, in front of a big noticeboard, wearing a slightly narrower apron and an additional shawl.[14] In the painting, the girl is wearing a dress with balloon sleeves made of a shining turquoise fabric with golden yellow stripes, and a transparent shawl over her décolleté. She protects her elegant dress with an apron at the waist. This type of dark-coloured apron was worn over day

---

9   Cf. G. G. Bauer, Zahlenlotto, in: *Glück*, 2002, 70.

10 Cf. 150 Jahre Lotto, 1.

11 Cf. A. Slavnitsch, *Das Glücksspielwesen*, 4.

12 Cf. G. G. Bauer, Zahlenlotto, in: *Glück*, 2002, 73f.

13 Cf. G. G. Bauer, Zahlenlotto, in: *Glück*, 2002, 74.

14 H. Adolph, Mädchen, in: *Mitteilungen,* 1961, here 29, ill. 20.

dresses and is also depicted in Erasmus Engert's painting *Mädchen in einer Gartenlaube*[15] (Girl in a Viennese Domestic Garden) c. 1828. In addition to her clothing, her neat, pinned-up hairstyle, with locks covering her ears, her small earrings and delicate ring on her left ring finger indicate that she comes from a wealthy background.[16] She carries a basket with a lid, suggesting a shopping activity. However, the girl is not busy with household chores; instead she studies the lottery numbers with her head slightly bowed. The right hand touching her lips shows that she is thinking carefully; the visibly reddened ear indicates emotional involvement. The number fourteen on the lottery ticket in her lowered left hand matches the drawn numbers: 19, 87, 7, 60, 14. At least two numbers are visible, thus it is not clear whether it is a double match (*ambe*) or a match with three numbers (*terne*). In the latter case, one number would be covered by the girl's hand. A larger quantity of numbers make a more expensive lottery ticket as this would increase the possible winnings. Both types of lottery tickets show the girl's higher social standing. It seems as if she looks at the notice beneath the numbers which announces the end of the lottery in Linz on Wednesday. The girl considers continuing playing, and so alludes to her gambling addiction. A dark shadow coverin the left corner of the lottery announcement has a forbidding feel to it. Behind the girl's back is a bright tobacco advertisement with pipes and tobacco tins displayed in a glass cabinet. Above the cabinet is an oriental figure of a man smoking the pipe, turning his back towards her. A similar figure appears on the open bar in Christiane Grüner's copper engraving *Ein Tabakladen*[17] (*A tobacco shop*) in which a pretty Biedermeier girl sells tobacco to a small boy, a middle-aged man and an

---

15 Erasmus Engert, *Mädchen in einer Gartenlaube*, c. 1828, oil on canvas, 30.3 x 27.1 cm, private collection.

16 »Ein Mädchen, einfachen Verhältnissen entstammend [...]«. H. Adolph, Mädchen, in: *Mitteilungen*, 1961, 25.

17 Christiane Grüner, *24 Darstellungen aus dem Volksleben. Unterhaltendes Bilderbuch für die Jugend*. Verlag Jeremias Bermann, c. 1835. 24 numbered copper engravings and one engraved title page with German texts, owned by Kunsthandlung Ch. M. Nebehay; Hubert Kaut, *Kaufrufe aus Wien. Volkstypen und Straßenszenen in der Wiener Graphik von 1775 bis 1914*, Vienna, Munich 1970, 105.

elderly man; she has an innocent air about her with her reddened cheeks whilst she sells tobacco to people of all ages.

The central message of the painting is without doubt that of a warning about gambling; a depiction of daily life rendered through an emotive and moralising lens.[18] The grim darkness lends the painting a dubious atmosphere that is enhanced by the surreptitious advertising of tobacco products, which the state had a monopoly on. The girl's apron is a symbol of domestic life which strongly suggests that the lottery shop is not the right place for her. Specialist literature mentions that there is a connection between the illustration in Fendi's painting and the 18th-century *Kaufrufe* series which depict tradesmen selling their wares.[19] Fendi may have drawn inspiration from the irony of the portrayal of a single person with their product.

This paper, however, offers a clearer understanding of the painting's background. Fendi bases his warning of compulsive gambling on an illustration which uses caricaturing elements to convey moral content: Joseph Stöber's and Matthäus Loder's print *Lotto-Sucht*[20] (*Lottery addiction*) which is accompanied by a poem by Ignaz Franz Castelli in *Zerrbilder menschlicher Thorheiten und Schwächen* from 1818 (Fig. 2):

»Ein Irrwisch, den man Glück benennt, / Versammelt hier die Schönen, / Die Dame gleich dem Bettelweib begierig rennt, / Lässt sich vom Glücksspiel höhnen; / Denn noch hat dieses Keinen reich gemacht, / Doch Viele an den Bettelstab gebracht.«[21]

(A delusion called luck / brings the beautiful here. / Ladies and beggars alike eagerly rush, / to be jeered by the game of chance. / It has not yet made anyone rich, / but has brought impoverishment to many.)

Fendi adopts the depicted location dominated by the lottery numbers. From the six women portrayed, he chooses the girl who is dressed up and

---

18 H. Adolph, Mädchen, in: *Mitteilungen*, 1961, 32.

19 Cf. Gerbert Frodl & Klaus Albrecht Schröder (Eds.), *Wiener Biedermeier Malerei zwischen Wiener Kongress und Revolution*, Munich 1992. No. 107.

20 Joseph Stöber & Matthäus Loder, *Lotto-Sucht*, no. 26 from Zerrbildern menschlicher Thorheiten und Schwächen mit einem Text von Ignaz Franz Castelli, 1818, colourised etching, 26.8 x 19.1 cm, Vienna Museum, inventory no. 186.171/15

21 G. G. Bauer, *Glück*, 2002, 230.

Fig. 2: Joseph Stöber and Matthäus Loder, Lotto-Sucht, *no. 26 from* Zerrbildern menschlicher Thorheiten und Schwächen mit einem Text von Ignaz Franz Castelli, *colourised etching, 1818.*

has her back turned to us. She carries a basket with four guilders lying visibly on top of it.

Fendi's painting differs not only in its focus on a single figure, but also abandons the caricaturing features. Instead he substitutes them with an emotive study of the figure whose origins might be found in fancy pictures.[22] The stark contrast between the innocent, youthful girl with her apron symbolising domesticity, and the advertised tobacco products[23] that lend the setting negative connotations is obvious. Although the oriental man faces away from the girl and the only connection between the two figures is the matching red of his trousers and her ear, he and his vice of tobacco consumption are still present, and is an essential part of the painting's poetry.[24] He is a reminder of the girl's addiction to gambling that is hidden behind her smart appearance. Fendi's subtleness and ordinary[25] iconography allow interpretations to unfold[26] in and of themselves.

22 Cf. Sabine Grabner, *Mehr als Biedermeier. Klassizismus, Romantik und Realismus in der Österreichischen Galerie Belvedere*, exhibition catalogue, Munich 2006, 68.

23 A standing and smoking oriental figure appears e.g. in a cabinet with lottery announcements in *Vor einer Lotto-Kollektur*, colourised copper engraving, 10.6 x 8 cm, Vienna Museum, HM, inventory no.: 81.631.

24 Ulrich Nefzger, Des Glückes Los. Fortunas Spiel und Wandel mit der Bildwelt, in: *Dem Glück auf der Spur*, 28.

25 For the philosophy of happiness, see Konrad Paul Liessmann, Wir haben das Glück erfunden – Philosophische Stationen im Spiel um das Glück, in: *Dem Glück auf der Spur*, 12–27.

26 Some of these diverse thoughts appear in Walter Koschatzky, *Peter Fendi (1796–1842) Künstler, Lehrer und Leitbild*, Salzburg/ Wien 1995, 47ff.

ILLUSTRATIONS

Fig. 1: Peter Fendi, *Girl at the Lottery*, painting, 1829. Source: Belvedere, Vienna.

Fig. 2: Joseph Stöber and Matthäus Loder, *Lotto-Sucht*, no. 26 from Zerrbildern menschlicher Thorheiten und Schwächen mit einem Text von Ignaz Franz Castelli, colourised etching, 1818. Source: Wien Museum.

REFERENCES

Adolph, Hubert, *Peter Fendi 1796–1824*, Unpublished doctoral diss., University of Innsbruck, Innsbruck 1951.

Adolph, Hubert, Peter Fendis »Ein Mädchen vor einem Lotterie-Gewölbe«, in: *Mitteilungen der Österreichischen Galerie, 5* (1961), 25–34.

Bauer, Günther, Das Österreichische Zahlenlotto. 1752–2002, in: *Dem Glück auf der Spur. 250 Jahre Österreichisches Zahlenlotto, exhibition catalogue*, Vienna 2002, 60–83.

Frodl, Gerbert; Schröder, Klaus Albrecht, *Wiener Biedermeier Malerei zwischen Wiener Kongress und Revolution*, Munich 1992.

Grabner, Sabine, *Mehr als Biedermeier. Klassizismus, Romantik und Realismus in der Österreichischen Galerie Belvedere, exhibition catalogue*, Munich 2006.

Hirsch, Martin, Giacomo Casanova und das Lotteriespiel im 18. Jahrhundert, in: Johann Konrad Eberlein (Ed.), *SpielKunstGlück. Die Wette als Leitlinie der Entscheidung. Die Wette als Leitlinie der Entscheidung. Beispiele aus Vergangenheit und Gegenwart in Kunst, Wissenschaft, Wirtschaft*, Vienna/Berlin 2011, 235–250.

Kaut, Hubert, *Kaufrufe aus Wien. Volkstypen und Straßenszenen in der Wiener Graphik von 1775 bis 1914*, Vienna/Munich 1970.

Kleehoven, Hans Ankwicz, Peter Fendi, in: *Kunst dem Volk, 14, 3* (1943), 1–9.

Koschatzky, Walter, *Peter Fendi (1796–1842) Künstler, Lehrer und Leitbild*, Salzburg/ Wien 1995.

Liessmann, Konrad Paul, Wir haben das Glück erfunden – Philosophische Stationen im Spiel um das Glück, in: *Dem Glück auf der Spur. 250 Jahre Österreichisches Zahlenlotto, exhibition catalogue*, Vienna 2002, 12–27.

Nefzger, Ulrich, Des Glückes Los. Fortunas Spiel und Wandel mit der Bildwelt, in: *Dem Glück auf der Spur. 250 Jahre Österreichisches Zahlenlotto, exhibition catalogue*, Vienna 2002, 28–59.

Österreichische Gallerie (Ed.), *Peter Fendi 1796–1842*, exhibition catalogue, Vienna 1963.

Slavnitsch, Antonia, *Das Glücksspielwesen in Österreich unter Berücksichtigung der neuen Rechtslage, Diplomarbeit am Institut für Österreichisches und Internationales Unternehmens- und Wirtschafts-recht*, Graz 2011.

Internet source

150 Jahre Lotto in Österreich. In: *Innsbrucker Nachrichten*, 3rd November, 1903. http://anno.onb.ac.at/cgicontent/anno?apm=0&aid=ibn&datum=19021103&seite=1&zoom=2 [25th March, 2013]

»Raise the flag and make propaganda.«

On the semiotics of National Socialist wooing

BARBARA AULINGER

Not only companies woo their customers, but institutions and states also woo people, and broadcast their messages. It is not immediately certain whether a Hitler Youth poster should be called an advertisement. The underlying goals are the same as in the economy: to attract attention; to show oneself at one's best; to seduce; and, also, occasionally, to cause anxiety. »You are not doing well without me. I can protect you – you and your washing machine«.

During the last third of the 19th century, several decades before the invention of the mass medium radio, the image served as an effective advertising medium, by means of the technology of lithography, and as a result of the professionalization of the graphics trade on the one hand and because of the advertising demands of large companies and institutions on the other. Not least was it the economic discovery of the »brand« which necessitated drawing of attention to the singularity of one's own products by means of posters and advertisements. Radio announcements, regardless of whether these were informative, entertainment or promotional, had one disadvantage: it was and still is dependent upon the cooperation of the listener »on the other side«, and not least upon the ownership of a radio set. The »message« – to use the terminology of semiotics – required multiple technical appliances: the broadcast station at the start; the radio set at the end; and the power supply between. However, simply by turning the knob on the radio set, the message could be sent out into the ether. Regarded from a semiotic point of view, this turn of the knob, this »no«, is part of the communication process between those who make the announcements and those who do not wish to hear them.

However, posters displayed in the public sphere could not be eluded as easily as a voice on the radio: they intruded unavoidably into peoples' lives, thwarted their paths and could not be simply turned off; posters were placed in precisely those locations one could not avoid. Until the middle of the 19th century (and also due to strict pre-1848 laws), there were only placards (*Anschläge*), loosely nailed bulletins or notices, which differed from Luther's Thesis only in their greater number and the printing technique used. After 1848, a new phenomenon developed: advertisements (*Annoncen*), and among these the billboard advertisement.

The image as a sign gained in importance over the word, became the actual/real/intrinsic message, which could be understood without words. Until around World War I, economic billboard advertising aimed at seduction by making promises. This was true for product advertising (e.g. electrical items made by AEG) just as much as it was for new ideas in brand advertising (such as washing detergent or tobacco products) or the advertising of events or recreation locations (e.g. for the Semmering resort). »Buy me; visit me; and you will be happier.« The diverse seducements can be boiled down to this simple formula: everything was aimed at consumption, even the »allure« of winter sports, established at that time, or of the summer health resorts (*Sommerfrische*).

THE IMPERATIVE MESSAGE

A National Socialist poster from 1937 unites two objects of age-old symbolic significance: waving flags and the drum. Both are carried by young men. »Out with the troublemakers!« states the demand along the top of the poster; along the lower edge, »Unity of the young in the Hitler Youth!«,

Fig. 1: National Socialist Poster, »Out with the troublemakers!«, 1937.

which should be read simultaneously as the outcome of the visual representation.[1]

Between header and footer there is intense activity. Two young men representing the Hitler Youth dominate the composition. Their bodies form an echelon pressing towards the left-hand edge of the image. The Hitler Youth at the rear, reduced in scale for reasons of perspective, holds aloft a proportionally massive flag bearing a swastika. The boy in the foreground carries an equally large, colourfully adorned drum and beats it briskly. The flag, drum and even the drummer's neckerchief emphasize the movement towards the left-hand edge. Beneath their feet, the tiny troublemakers, as the title states, run from the enormous bodies of the Hitler Youths who are forging ahead. The perspective of significance is an established visual concept: important people are depicted disproportionately large, while the insignificant, or in this case worthless, are small and diminish further in size. The addressees, those who are addressed by the message, know the signs and the code, understand the subtext, just as the ancient Egyptians, mediaeval believers and citizens of the 20th century did. The flag bearer and the drummer are, as implied on the poster, presented not only to attract attention, but also as purifiers and progenitors of a new nation, as a new breed of mankind, just as National Socialist ideology had envisioned. The dynamic posture and facial expressions of the two young men do not disclose any suspicion of barbarity. The expulsion of the troublemakers is a jolly activity.

Questions arise. What is the young drummer boy in the foreground doing? Is he drumming up interest in the Hitler Youth? Present-day understanding struggles with this down-played metaphor. Apparently, we approach the content of this poster with a different method of decoding it. The Hitler Youth poster is about more than the fulfilment of consumer wishes; apparently an occurrence is to be set in motion with the assistance of the poster, with symbolic and iconic signs (word and image). The flag and the drum are not merely props but, besides the two young men, are the actual protagonists of the image. Like the perspective of significance, the flag and the drum are age-old signs for attracting the attention of eye and ear. The

---

1 Founded in 1926, the Hitler Youth became the sole German youth organisation in 1936. From 1939, it was mandatory for all young people aged 10 to 18 years to join.

primary purpose of a flag is to function as a sign. It must tower above the crowd, carried on a pole or waving at a window. A flag hidden in a coat pocket has no purpose; only by being visible does it become a sign as defined by semiotics, and a message. As a »sign of display« it serves to differentiate and identify. Its message is »here I am, here we are, this group, this organisation, this state, dynasty, brass band, Austria«, or, indeed, even »National Socialist Germany and the Hitler Youth«. The punctuation of semiotics is the same: a rejoicing crowd and a sea of flags. If a group's flag is carried forth, then the message of the jubilant »sea of flags« is read differently. Here the message reads »Follow me!« and takes the imperative form. This is communicated by the Hitler Youth poster.

MESSAGE, CODE AND SIGN

Although semiology as the science of sign systems was initially focused on writing and language – and this found its scientific structure for the first time during the 19th century – today, it investigates all forms of human communication as semiotics. The description and analysis of the Hitler Youth poster above have already addressed several significant elements in terms of semiotics. People send messages in a wide variety of ways, however always in the belief that »the other« also picks up and understands it. In this case, this means that the addressee is familiar with the flag and knows whether it represents friend or foe; that he or she is familiar with the code and the sign »flag«. The code can be tightened up still further (Eco's »endless semiosis«): he or she understand what a pole with a colourful cloth at one end means; that it is a sign, that is »something which functions as something else in a certain (particular) way« (Pierce 1931). Here, the added »in a certain way« has a particular meaning: it refers to the »connotation« of a sign which may change its meaning. By using the sign one uses the immediately perceptible in order to refer to the not immediately perceptible.[2] Revolutionaries, who burn their sovereign's (or enemy's) flag, mean

---

2   If not otherwise stated, quotations cited in this essay are taken from the follo-
    wing works of Umberto Eco: *Das offene Kunstwerk* (first published in 1962),
    Einführung in die Semiotik (first published in 1972), *Zeichen. Einführung in ei-
    nen Begriff und seine Geschichte* (first published in 1972). From *Das offene*

the enemy, not the flag and even less the piece of cloth. However, how does this agreement on the meaning of the flag emerge? Solely, states semiotics, via the customs with which a person experiences from childhood onwards. They engender the fundamental understanding of communication, which has nothing to do with »right« or »wrong«. »A code is a system of acquired (learned) expectations and customs.« Similar wordings of this definition can be found throughout semiology and also in the works of Eco. It is the most important component in semiology, aside from the sign itself. We will return to the topic of the drum later.

The term »Hitler Youth« can only be understood through the code and knowledge of Hitler himself. Addressees in around 1910 would, for instance, have had no notion of this concept, and, therefore, the message would have been meaningless. The motion of the flag, too, is a very important criterion for attracting attention. As a sign, the waving flag stands for life; the lowered flag, death. This example shows how semiology and psychology sometimes make contact, despite the distance which semiotics would like to maintain from this science. Even during the National Socialism period, the »sea of flags« was an ideological indicator. The flag with the swastika motif implied happiness. Everyone was familiar with the code. Better than with words (»symbolic signs«), this image is depicted as an iconic sign, or in certain contexts, as an »iconographic sign«.[3]

Kunstwerk onwards, Eco's anchor for the [denkmodell] of semiotics, as he understood it, was the history of art and more specifically Alois Riegl's *Die spätrömische Kunstindustrie* (1901). In this, Eco follows Mannheim, Panofsky, Benjamin and Feyerabend, to name but a few, who all referred to Riegl. Sketched roughly, it is the »circumstances« of the message and the interpretation, which later set correlate as »connotation« to »denotation«. In his definition of a sign Eco relies on Pierce (1931).

3   In the context of National Socialism, the iconic sign of the swastika motif, which has been interpreted as a sun wheel among other things, became iconography.

SEMIOTICS AND ART HISTORY

The approach of semiotics pertaining to iconic signs is prefigured in the history of art (see footnote 2). In 1901, in his work *Die spätrömische Kunstindustrie,* Austrian art historian Alois Riegl plausibly demonstrated the dependency of art on the culture and general attitude to life in an era; effectively, a particular community's codes, although he did not refer to it in those terms. In art history itself, his concept of *Kunstwollen* (»will to art« or »will to form«) remained vague. Only via the reception of his thoughts and sociological, philosophical and semiotic discourse, which continued for several decades, was the usefulness of his approach revealed. Above all, the potential difference between his contemporaries' understanding – the real addressees of the artist – and later recipients' understanding became apparent. The origin of a new, deeper understanding of the *Kunstwollen* was Erwin Panofsky's 1920 essay *Der Begriff des Kunstwollens.*[4] The code (of a particular time, society or social class) changes, is no longer or is differently understood, and with it, the meaning of the sign in broader and in narrower terms. The notion of the connotation was born, although Riegl's terminology was different. In this context, Panofsky's three-phase interpretation of the image, »pre-iconographic; iconographic; iconologic«, became famous. Here, the iconological realm essentially corresponds to the added »in a certain way«, or as Eco put it, »the circumstances« of the production and the interpretation of a sign.

Returning to the Hitler Youth poster: above, the iconic sign of the flag, which has always been understood, was discussed. This continuous understanding means that its first function, the denotation, its express meaning and purpose remained unchanged (as far as this can be claimed under the terms of »endless semiosis«). Moreover, the sign can be read in the broader context of the Hitler Youth's call for the »cleansing« of the unworthy from the country. Thus, here, the flag changes from an iconic into a iconographic sign. This is another denotation defined by the statements along the upper and lower edges of the poster and by the tiny, fleeing human figures. These denotations are only understood »correctly« when one is familiar with the circumstances underlying the illustration, i.e. the »culture« of the National

---

4 Erwin Panofsky, Der Begriff des Kunstwollens, in: *Zeitschrift für Ästhetik und Allgemeine Kunstwissenschaft,* 1920, 330–339.

Socialists, in order to express it in such a way, the ideological connotation, which would be read differently today and would generate other associations than in 1937. Umberto Eco highlights particularly the meaning of the connotations of signs. The connotation of a sign changes, because circumstances change; because they are never the same and, potentially, are even understood entirely differently, in an inextricable context, and, so, circumstances are an »open model«.[5] However, with the altered connotation comes the altered denotation of the sign. The interpreter is involved in this process. Thus, according to Eco, one cannot speak of a »semiotic system«, rather of »semiotic research«. Semiotic research not only exposes the denotation of the Hitler Youth poster; the real shock lies in its connotation, which we read differently today than did the addressees of 1937.

Parallel to and partly concealing the flag bearer, the oversized figure of a young man in the foreground beats the drum, which hangs diagonally over and around his shoulder and armpit. Due to his dominant presence in the image, he is in fact its real message. In terms of semiotics, the drum denotes »noise«, but simultaneously more than that: the rhythm declares the connotation of the drum. Joy, appeal/call, battle, escorting the dead: each has its own rhythm. The iconography of war was embedded in the young, often child, drummers early on, and thus they became the macabre herald of death.[6] This connotation of the iconographic sign »drummer boy« pushes irrefutably into our present-day consciousness and understanding of the poster. The same image, the original political advertisement, the deliberate message, which defined the Hitler Youth poster in its day, is transformed in present-day understanding. A different code is applied; it becomes a sign of intolerance, of the harassment of outsiders; it becomes an image of deadly seduction. Though ideology, like psychology and sociology, is not the subject of semiotics, it does however belong, as Eco stresses/highlights, to those extra-semiotic residues which determine semiotic occurrences. World

---

5   Umberto Eco, Introduction, 439f. and elsewhere. It forms the basis for his thoughts on his »open artwork«.

6   In the November/December 2010 edition of *Georgia Augusta,* published by the University of Göttingen, Morag Grant devotes an essay to the phenomenon of the drummer boy. (63–69) In the drummer boy, she sees an as-yet overlooked manifestation of child labour.

views, according to Eco, are always »already segmented reality«.[7] Thus, it is possible that precisely this poster, with its two age-old iconic signs, makes it clear, that, as Eco holds, »there are no specific signs, ... however, every object can be made the signifier for/of another.«[8] Elsewhere, he writes, »society uses signs to communicate, to inform, to lie, to deceive, to control, and to liberate.«[9]

So, is that an advertising poster? Undoubtedly, it was in 1937, and undoubtedly, the message was understood in that way. (Whether it was obeyed is another question entirely, and not a matter for semiotics.) However, the meaning of the poster is just as »open« – to use Eco's terminology – as an artwork. This is because, just as undoubtedly, the connotations of the two iconographic signs, the flag and the drum, have changed in the overall context of the poster and subject to the code we apply today. Today, knowledge of the future of the flag is carried with it: the National Socialist regime and the looming war, to which the drummer boy in the foreground already points. Thus, the iconic sign »drum«, which dominates the foreground of the poster, no longer conveys the original message of uprising, joy and a feeling of togetherness. Instead, decoded by the new connotation, it conveys the terrible messages of war, death and expulsion, and thereby the metaphor of the boy who »drums up interest« effectively dissipates.

ILLUSTRATION

Fig. 1: National Socialist Poster, »Out with the troublemakers!«, 1937. Source: ZUM-Wiki – Zentrale für Unterrichtsmethoden im Internet e.V. http://wikis.zum.de/rmg/Datei:Hitlerjugend_prop3.gif [26th November, 2013].

---

7   Umberto Eco, Introduction, chapter 4, 168ff. Here, Eco (inadvertent, in any case uncited) picks up Mannheim's thoughts, which Mannheim, in reference to Panofsky and Riegl, presented widely in his *Beiträge zur Theorie der Weltanschauungsinterpretation* (Wiener Jahrbuch für Kunstgeschichte 1921).

8   Eco, Zeichen, 168.

9   Eco, Zeichen, 24.

REFERENCES

Benjamin, Walter, *Das Kunstwerk im Zeitalter seiner technischen Repro-duzierbarkeit. Drei Studien zur Kunstsoziologie*, Frankfurt a. M. 1936.

Eco, Umberto, *Das offene Kunstwerk*. Frankfurt a. M. 1962.

Eco, Umberto, *Einführung in die Semiotik*, Frankfurt a. M. 1972.

Eco, Umberto, *Zeichen. Einführung in einen Begriff.* Frankfurt a. M. 1973.

Grant, Morag Josephine, Auf den Spuren der Trommlerjungen. Zeugen einer ambivalenten Verbindung zwischen Musik und Krieg, in: *Georgia Augusta. Wissenschaftsmagazin der Georg-August-Universität Göttignen, 7* (2010), 63–69.

Mannheim, Karl, Beiträge zur Theorie der Weltanschauungsinterpretation, in: *Jahrbuch für Kunstgeschichte, 1* (1921), 236–247.

Panofsky, Erwin, Der Begriff des Kunstwollens. *Zeitschrift für Ästhetik und Allgemeine Kunstwissenschaft, 14* (1920), 330–339.

Riegl, Alois, *Die spätrömische Kunstindustrie*, Wien 1901.

Pop & Ads

The Sound of Mass Media

WERNER JAUK

LINKS BETWEEN POP MUSIC AND ADVERTISING

There are a lot of relations between pop music and advertisement – some of which are quite obvious: Pop music is used in commercial, pop music related ads by itself and made the promotion-tour, the immediate contact to the fan, to an audio-visual genre. These relations are well studied and reported. This paper will focus on the function of pop and commercials: emotional bonding – (sound-)technology will be used to intensify the excitement and the effect.

My main hypothesis is the following: Pop music and advertising are part of the operating system of mass media; their function is to facilitate emotional »bonding« by excitement – technology, the adoption of technology of mass-media, is supposed to amplify this excitement and to reach the masses by disseminating different contents: products as well as political ideologies, etc.

On the surface, pop music seems to be the film score of audio(-visual) commercials. It is just the soundtrack of a commercial giving physical and emotional underscoring through music – at least it is the use of pop music fitting, or being fitted to, the image of a specific »content«.

There are two reasons for pop songs being used in particular. First pop-music, as a low-mediated[1] formalization of bodily expression of and/or interaction with sound refers dominantly to an immediate communication of emotional qualities – the connotation of activity and evaluation, just by its sound, the dominant parameter of pop music. This is the premise for the second reason: A pop song is defined by being noticed by many people. (Hecken 2006: 85) The use of pop songs in commercials is supposed to convey these basic emotional qualities as well as the popularity of a song to the image of a product – by way of learning the image and the popularity is to be transferred to the product. Because pop formalizes the pleasant excitement by means of the dynamics of sound, these bodily qualities are transferred to the image of a product by processes similar to conditioning-processes. There are different levels and different ways of doing this.

POP – A MEDIUM FOR GENERATING POPULARITY AND CONVEYING IMAGE IN COMMERCIALS

There are songs, some sort of »extended jingle«, written for commercials just to manage moods that are expected to be of the same quality as the im-

---

1   Mediatization is a process whichs transforms immediate bodily communication to mediated communication by the means of signs and codes – it makes bodily expression and its »immediate understanding« mediated.

In emotional communication gesture uses iconic qualities to »mimic« the index of expression, symbols are unique signs set by will signing specific qualities while the digital code is of basic syntactic quality being able to sign/to code any information. Music could be seen being the mediatization of emotional communication by mediating expression: from its gestural use, its iconic picturing in the neuma, its presentation in melody contour the sound and musical form make the feeling present (Langer 1953); the notational code and at least the digital code allow to break with/to discontinue these bodily communication formalized in algorithmic compositional theories – basically the »Werk« is the composition of sound despite bodily expression because of the coded representation of sound; digital musics is the composition of sound even despite any embodied experience because of the immateriality of the digital code (Jauk 2013).

age of a product. Maybe later on, because of their its use in commercials, they become well-known songs, pop-songs.

On the other hand, as some kind of »metafunction« – the use of a pop-song as a film score (Bullerjahn 2001: 65) – a well-known pop song recorded independently of a commercial is used to promote a product. It becomes common knowledge of the image of the pop song, which should make the product known with a specific emotional image. In some cases, only well-known words of a song refer to the »content« as some kind of slogan, e.g. »I am from Austria« promotes Austrian products.

A more sophisticated approach is the coupling of an image of a well-known pop star with a content; Michael Jackson's (even very short) appearance in the Pepsi Cola spot uses Jackson as testemonial because of his worldwide popularity and image as the king of pop and makes Pepsi popular as the king of Cola ...

A COMMERCIAL FOR POP

Besides this, there is a relationship, which works the other way round: a new song needs promotion. Instead of an expensive promotion tour, which brings the mediated song and its star immediately to the audience, this immediate performance comes mediated to the audience; this was the idea of the first video clip promoting a song. According to its function as a substitute, the performance video (the filmed storage of a performance) became the first clip-genre. Media technology, the close shot, made it possible to bring the star »closer« to the viewing individual. This is a possible parallel to the »especially for you« effect of the first microphone performances where the singer had the possibility to perform breathey sounds to create intimate contact with the audience.

Video-post-production technology not only facilitated bringing the star »closer«, cutting and effects are technologies, which make the picture, its syntactic elements and structure, more intensive, more exciting, more immersive – technology »amplifies« literally as well as metaphorically the content. Here the symbiosis of pop music and multi-mediacommercials as well as an »intermedial transpostion« starts becoming popular: the intuitive »emotional« communication by sound.

What started as an aesthetic experiment to make the (abstract) picture in the abstract film dynamic became a functional structure in video clips – the commercial for a pop song. It is that point in the process of development where the transfer of musical structure to visual structure was directly motivated by increasing immersion – for commercial purposes. It was first implemented by advertising experts (e.g., Julien Temple). This is why ›intermedial transposition‹ and increasing immersion first became the dominant method of structuring video-clips – today the video-clip is structured as an audio-visual work at least following the paradigm of tension/relaxation of sound stimuli. It is composed together with sound. The video clip is the avant-garde of immersive multi-sensorial structuring in order to create immersion, to control the excitement of masses ...

To summarize: The emotional image of a star is created by immersive sound and visuals – when you substitute a star just by another product, sound and visual structuring remain the same – the immersive communication of excitement associated with any kind of »product«, to masses. Following this function, the aesthetics of music as well as audio-visuals is transformed from mediating to stimulating, from being multimedia-forms to multi-stimulating – from being multisensory excitement to building up connotative images.

The pop song and its multi-sensory video clip are commercials themselves creating emotional images – regarding a »star« – in masses of listeners using electronic mass media for distribution. At the same time, the electronic mass media use the creation of images to bind the audience emotionally – in this sense the mass media need pop music to affirm its operating system. The paradigm of the activity stimulating character of sound (and its transposition to other sensory stimuli) in order to bind emotionally is transferred to other contents: pop music becomes paradigmatic for image-commercials.

Following this introduction, our main hypothesis will be presented: Pop music and multi-sensory commercials have the same function within the »logic« of the operating system of electronic mass media – they follow a functional aesthetic, the immediate bodily excitement by sound and the transposition of this paradigm to other stimuli especially visual stimuli, with the technology of the mass media amplifying this function. Basically, pop music is at the same time low-mediated – following immediately the hedonic body – and highly mediated – technologically produced and dis-tributed, transcending the mechanistic body, while intensifying the hedonic body; the same takes place with commercials. Its function made up its use in the operating system of electronic mass media – at least it is the technol-ogy of mass media, the storing, manipulating and distributing of sounds, which makes work with sound possible and »amplifies« this immediate way of emotional communication – despite the composition of sounds by representing codes. It is technologically instrumentarized structuring of sound immediately by rules of the hedonic body presenting these hedonic qualities.

The development of mass media and pop music follow the basic theory of Mediamorphosis (Weber 1921, Blaukopf 1989, Smudits 2002) – so-cio/aesthetic changes of pop music as well as commercials are motivated in technological developments reinforcing the interests of mass media: emo-tional bonding of masses.

POP BECOMING A PARADIGM FOR IMAGE-ADS – IMMERSION BY STRUCTURING EXCITING STIMULI

Because they create an emotional connotation, multi-»medial« image-commercials at least are based on an intermedial transposition, the transfer of the structure of music following tension to structuring the picture in mo-tion. The structuring of the picture in time as well as in its »colour« follows the structuring of sound in time and frequency domain – it is based on the activating perception of the dynamics of sound, the specificity of the »audi-tory logic« (Jauk 2007a) being formalized in music (Sloboda 1985) ruled by the relation of tension/relaxation (Schenker 1935) between sounds (within a musical system). As music is the formalization of auditory per-ception, the dynamic structure of music is ruled by the relation between tension and relaxation. Basically, the dynamic structure could be seen as the composition of some kind of acoustic driving effect (Harrer 1975): the stimulation of (parallel) excitement to the listener just by tempo. With the acceleration of tempo, physical arousal increases (already synchronous) under the condition of »reagibility«, the willingness to react to those stimu-li. Reagibility is given by immersion of sound together with contents, which are biologically or culturally exciting – the latter referring to cognitive pleasing surroundings.

Dynamics is physically and psychologically related to the attack-time (of the envelope) and sharpness of a sound and becomes a cognitive quality in music – the faster a series of sound is, the more the single sounds will be percussive with a short attack and a high amount of energy in the upper frequencies and even more »noise«: this natural behaviour of sound will be perceived as »impulsive« and as being »sharper« – both are exciting qualities.

The greater the energy in the (upper) frequency domain and the more amplitude sound shows in the attack-time of the envelope of a sound, the more even a single sound will excite – and the other way round. The relative distribution of energy in frequency and time is used in sound logos to raise specific activity and connotate related feelings that are all transferred to a product.

Pop music uses this distribution of energy in time and frequency to attract attention at the beginning (some kind of gimmick) and with a specific style of playing with attack-time, treble and distortion which at least are technologically reinforced by post-effects regulating the sound in density/loudness and excitement, the compressor and exciter.

While Western »serious music« may be seen as being the cultivation of the nature of sound[2] and its hearing/perception processes and mediatized sound by its «storage« in scores – that led to the development of the aesthetics of the so-called »Werk« »com-posed« by codes for sounds dominated by »relational thinking« (Riemann 1914/15) – in some kind of counter-culture[3]

---

2 Knepler (1977) sees music as being the cultivation of the sound as part of an emotion; in addition Blacking (1977) considers music to be the instrumentarization of the behaviour that is part of an emotion (becoming sound). To avoid the modern idea of cultivation as some kind of cultural progression the author considers cultivation more neutrally as a process of mediatization leading away from immediate bodily sound/behaviour to produce sound – this allows to explain pop-music as a low mediated (immediatate bodily) and at the same time high mediated (»un-bodied« technologically generated) phenomenon.

3 Being a counter-culture against social distin bourgeois high-culture pop is the avant-garde of the 20th century postulating the common despite the distinction

pop music went ›forward backwards‹ and became a sound-dominated »functional« communication system where bodily excitement is reinforced in production and reception and is amplified by technology – this way it is central in mass communication.

An increase of dynamic entails an increase of bodily excitement – this is not the rise of a special feeling but the rise of intensity on the dimension »activity« within a dimensional concept of emotion which by itself has specific correlations to feelings within the categorical concept: anger has more activity than grief, or lust has more activity than satisfaction.

Dynamic effects of sound – in itself an artefact of physical/physiological dynamic aspects of motion/emotion – will not describe feelings but connote its activity-dimension »im-mediately«. Therefore we do not speak of mediating but just of stimulating activity by dynamic aspects of sound; this effect of sound is converted/transferred to the effect of picture to intensify stimulation. (A speaking voice may be intensified by an iconic use of the melody contour, which is part of an emotion – this again follows the activity dimension of feelings).

What sound as part of motion conveys in the process of information processing, the body-environment-interaction[4], music formalizes and cultivates as a process of overcoming ›nature‹, pop music refers to this basic nature of sound. Pop intensifies this basic principle of communication – becoming ›common‹ – by extending it to other stimuli. The video-clip transposes this aesthetic concept from auditory stimuli to visual stimuli (see above). At least this is what ads aim at: it is ruled by the communicative nature of sound.

Despite the use of sound as an index of motion or emotion as underscoring in film scores, despite using imitating the sound of motion and emotion as

---

and brings »Kunst und Leben« together; it orients itself after immediately bodily arts where the work with codes – based on cultural knowledge is replaced by the work with sound, »natural« bodily interaction common to all – the upcoming of perfomative arts is in relation to this.

4   Sound as part of motion/emotion is indicative (as an index) of the risks of motion/motion in the environment to the body and activates it to engage in survival behaviour.

an icon, as semiotic signs within narrative contexts or even a symbol with specific cultural determined meaning (related to a linguistic understanding) just the excitement of syntactic elements of sound were transposed to those of pictures. Within semiotics, Morris (Nöth 1990: 112) spoke about primitive signs just triggering. »Wirkungsästhetik« and the »New Experimental Aesthetics« of Berlyne (Berlyne 1971, 1974) were to speak of the stimulating effect of syntactic elements in sound and picture.

Excitement is stimulated by at least any kind of intensity (Wundt 1874) of a stimulus or by the structure of stimuli (Berlyne 1970) and even by expectations of variations of expected structures (Konecny 1977) – that is to say, by cognitive qualities of stimuli based on learning processes within a culture. Excitement leads to curiosity behaviour and therefore to attention behaviour at medium level of excitement which is perceived as most pleasing.

Within his bourgeois aesthetic concept of enlightenment[5] Adorno, called this immediate bodily stimulation (Jauk 2009) »sozial nicht wahr« because it works outside the control of the mind and leads to mass-seduction – at least this is what pop and ads want to achieve: an emotional climate among masses of people. Whereas in aesthetics of arts and music, the linguistic turn affirmed the narrative concepts, that the structure »tells« contents in some kind of meaning, this semiotic linguistic dominance in pop is given up more and more; an upcoming understanding of sound suppresses the understanding of codes for sound in pop music: What was hard work for musicology studies was familiar to every pop musician, who did not need any emancipation from thinking in relations of codes (representing and »recording« sound). Bodily sound structuring evolves out of (gestural work with) feelings, creating a form which makes the feeling present (Langer 1953). This stimulating function of syntactic (dynamic) elements as an aesthetic concept is »closer« to the narrative concept and is even related to the evolution of advertisement from a content-mediating process to an image connoting one – the more sensory stimulation, the better it will work. Today these

---

5   ... where art was a medium of social/political distinction of bourgeois society by achieving specific forms to emancipate themselves – at least a taking over of a political behaviour of the aristocratic society and the hegemonic societies in whole.

parallel stimulating syntactic stimuli work in some kind of multisensory intermodal stimulation not following the concept of an multi-medial narrating story – this is pop, this is advertising: the specific stimulation of the body, to get an immersive situation.

The intermedial transposition is becoming more and more of an immersive »technology«. It was first developed in abstract film, the experiments of Fischinger et al. who transposed the structure of music to the (parallel) structure of abstract visuals, even leaving music aside. While this was done mechanically by painting on film, the parallel generation of sound and pictures in the audio and video-synthesizer of Nam June Paik is the continuation of the voltage controlled series of electronic music in Köln, which is the technological formalization of the »Reihe«.

»Imagine« and »Big Eye« from STEIM are MIDI programs, which convert audio signals into visuals and the other way around. Today Max/MSP and JITTER allow real-time audio and visual generation and modulation in any kind of algorithmic connection; even in interaction with bodies. What was developed in the avant-garde movements became the dominant technology of structuring interactive multi-sensorial events in techno-culture based on the »common digit«; as an immaterial code it may be transformed into any quality of perception even parallel to multimodal perception increasing immersion.

POP, ADVERTSING AND THE »LOGIC« OF THE OPERATING SYSTEM OF MASS MEDIA

1. Bodily excitement as the aesthetitcs of pop & commercials

Pop as well as commercials follows functional aesthetics: Immersion of masses – both basically use »bodily« communication, which is technologically extended/amplified. This is »the extension of man« (McLuhan 1994), the technological mediatization of immediate bodily communication.

The role of music and especially sound in multimedia commercials emerged with the change from informative ads to image-ads. Commercials, which intend to say something about a product and its advantages primarily use media, which allow the description of these informative aspects, words and narrative pictures. Commercials which want to communicate the emotional meaning of a product to (individual) life will use »media«. This allows to convey that kind of very basic and physiologically old »meaning« which occurrences in the environment will have to the body (Gibson 1982) before its cognitive evaluation (Maturana & Varela 1984) – image-ads will connote the emotional meaning just by exciting the body.

This immediate stimulation (by all forms of intensities) is the role of sound within body-environment interaction – music will be its formalization.

While music, which came up with codes as representation of sounds, which is at least adequate for perceiving by »relational understanding« (Riemann 1913/14) of the structure of codes similar to »language« may be able to say something about »contents«. Pop music is organized by the relation of tension and relaxation made »present« by sound and connotates »feelings« just by excitement.

Pop music will refer to this basic emotional communication as part of electronic/digital mass media. As a medium of bonding, the audience emotionally music is a dominant part of the operating system of mass media – pop music does this in a very immediate way and came up with or was reinforced by the electronic mass-media radio and television.

What Nietzsche (Nietzsche 1872) assumed to be »Die Geburt des Dramas aus dem Geiste der Musik« (The birth of drama out of the spirit of music) refers to this basic immediately emotional communication by sound. In a certain sense pop goes way back to these immediate states of communication to this low mediated bodily communication of excitement, which music is assumed to formalize, while the development of symbols out of (and overcoming the index of) the expressive voice and its iconic use lead to language articulated by the sound of voice (Knepler 1977) – even giving expressive values by the melody contour and dynamics of the spoken word – by »musical« means ...

Pop music ›cultivates‹ the expressive sound; it goes back to those roots where the sound of expression and the sound of motion of things which occur in the environment are differentiated in music and language. It goes back to those states of development of multimedia arts, which started with the Greek drama: the informative dialogue of the actors was interpreted by the sounds of the choir – this is the situation of mass media: sound-dominated pop music will have assumed the role of the choir within this system and have emotionally »interpreted« contents. At least this is what pop music does, and this is also what commercials do – both do it through immediate connotative sound – this paradigm is at least applied to other non-symbolic aspects of commercials: to the structuring in time of emotionally coloured pictures, as the pop video optimizes – what was once a commercial for pop music made by advertising experts is, today, a multi-sensory piece – once again: a multisensory commercial.

Music, pop music allows basic emotional communication and because of this basic human communication – which first of all does not distinct between humans – it allows mass communication. Intended distinctions will then be made by using socialized behavior, by communication based on cultural meanings of symbols constituating different cultural »groups« by signing and distinguishing them from the »other«. This is more done by cultural use of sounds within socio-aesthetic concepts of music.

Its function to build up an emotional mass-communication system establishing some kind of emotional climate makes pop music a sound-dominated bodily music. Technology does not make this music unbodied, but it extends, it amplifies its immediate effect: the bodily excitement[6]. Because of its function, its (technological) aesthetic structuring, pop music lives in symbiosis with electronic mass media. But because of its function (in the operating system of mass media) sound-dominated music like pop music is not only made possible because of technical media storing and generating sound: its hedonic bodily existence effected even technology – mass-media technology and by this the aesthetics of mass media. Playing the electric guitar as shaping feedback sound by hedonic bodily motion became a paradigm for immediate bodily modulation of »sound« being by it-

---

6 Maybe in mediatized cultures it is not that the body but the mechanic body becomes useless (Baudrillard 1981). The hedonic body becomes more important for the selection behaviour in information explosion – in this way mediatized culture brings this »natural« body back to culture and does not cultivate it considering nature being the opposite of culture.

self produced ›un-bodied‹ by highly mediated technologies. This situation is considered an intuitive interface, at least just an extension of emotional motivated body-environment interactions creating dynamic structures (collective and collectivizing) by communication (see the Latin word »communis«), while the »Werk« is the composition (see the Latin word »componere«) the »putting-together« of codes representing sounds within the logic of a (primarily visual) system which is only more or less related to the sounds that are represented (Jauk 2007).[7]

This means that sound-dominated pop music could be seen as an almost immediate formalization of sound being part of the intended body-environment-interaction where intention is the interpretation of the sound – it informs the body about motion/emotion within the environment to interact in order to survive – sound is immediate emotional informative. Pop is this immediate (low mediated) sound which is at the same time highly mediated, technologically amplified. Although it is unbodied, generated without any mechanic instrumental behaviour, it is bodily modulated – by the hedonic body following the excitement of emotional activity and its expression.

Mass media not only reinforces pop-music production but because of the same goal – emotional bonding through emotional excitement – and because of the use of the same production technology, working on intuitive manipulation of sound and its distribution, a similar aesthetics of commercials and pop occurs within the operating system of the (electronic) mass media. The symbiosis of pop music, commercials and the mass media builds up a flow of sound immediately exciting listeners and giving emotional connotation to specific contents. From underscoring[8] and thematic

---

7   There will be arguments that this logic is based on the visual representation of sounds almost unrelated to hearing, more related to the understanding of codes emerging with the theory of »conceptual metaphor« (Lakoff 1993), the intermedial transposition of experiences from seeing to hearing (e.g., the relation of tonal height). On the other hand, there are theoretical assumptions even within semiotics that the form (of sound and music) makes the feeling present (Langer 1953) but does not represent emotional feelings.

8   Physical underscoring is the reinforcement of movements and therefore reinforces the emotional meaning to the body – physical and emotional underscoring are at least closely related

work to an »endless rise of ground and decline of figure« (Tagg 1994) to immerse not only into an »Ocean of Sound« (Toop 1997) but through an ocean of sound, the sound of pop, the sound of commercials. At least the sound of (electronic) mass media attracts attention behaviour regarding contents – commercial as well as political contents ...

Pop music and commercials are considered being central parts of the logic of the operating system of mass media and were optimized by using basic human emotional communication, the exciting sound of exciting feelings, and by using the technology of the mass media to optimize the effect by technologically structured »bodily« sounds – to directly immerse masses of people.

2. Amplification of excitement as the aesthetics of pop music & commercials

Intensifying emotional bonding means at least »amplification« of two aspects of technological mass communication: First, to intensify immersion just by »amplification« of the immediate emotional communication of sound. Second, to intensify to reach masses just by distribution. This second process of intensifying has to be based on a common, a less distinctive medium but more common »trigger«, the stimulus. Here is where the first and the second aspect meet. Technology serves to intensify the immediate excitement for individuals and multiply this immediate communication to masses; the low mediated bodily communication meets highly mediated technological communication. This basic communication makes common, makes popular – here is where pop and ads meet: designing an emotional social climate.

Pop music and commercials, the aesthetics of mass media means to excite: To achieve emotional bonding means to manage moods. To manage moods, to confirm or compensate emotions just by music, especially its characteristics in frequency- and time domain are technologically extended. It is »amplified« by the technology of mass media: from the compression of sound in the early sixties to the triggering of intense perception later on, which resulted in tools, exciter and dynamic psych-processors, which not only physically compress and amplify the sound but modulate the sound in such a way that it is (cognitive) perceived as being louder and therefore more exciting. This goes together with modulations in the frequency domain, e.g., making the sound sharper and therefore more exciting, while other modulations effect the time domain, e.g., the acceleration (of modulations) in time by the ability of intuitive modulation technology: from the cutting to serial/dynamical effects, the flow of sound is accelerated and therefore increasing excitement in time is »controlled« – acoustic driving effects (Harrer 1977) will explain these technologies stimulating excitement in time.

Whereas gimmicks opening a pop song just by cutting sound pieces (which were not recorded in »real-time«) use technology based composition techniques for cognitive attraction, the compressed »high-intensity« sound associated with the loudness war in the sixties started up a process of amplification levelling the backward and forward relations to gain a constant immersive flow of sound. Compression can be said to have supported an aesthetic change, the »decline of the figure and the rise of ground« (Tagg 1994), which came up with the function of pop in mass media and its technological realization.

These techniques of sound structuring were transposed to the (non-narrative) picture in motion. Cutting follows the paradigm of structuring music in time-domain, image-effects (changes in chroma and brightness and false colour, etc. which do not change the content of a picture like keying or mixing, etc.) follow the paradigm of structuring music in the frequency domain of music – at least both, even modulation of frequency in time, follow the functional aesthetics of pop music just to increase immersion.

To make things become louder and faster may be considered part of a common rise of the amount of information and its distribution velocity, together with an overall acceleration to a »racing standstill« (Virilio 1992). Real-time technologies and intuitive interfaces are the technological basis of modulating sound according to the momentary emotional state expressing, communicating and even regulating this state immediately and bodily within a situation of excitement.

The construction of intuitive interfaces follows this »logic«. To make the sound more bodily to be perceived it is manipulated immediate bodily; making/playing music, the instrumentarization of the emotional behaviour and/or its sound, may be seen as the paradigm for these interfaces which were used in the design of (sound-based) commercials as well as the entire format of broad-casting, it being some kind of endless commercial. Amateuristic pop music used this way of making music since its use of technological sound. Intuitive expressive handling of sound, the bodily shaping of feedback playing the electric guitar (Jauk 2007b), an artefact of amplification of the guitar, up to the use of the »KΛOSS Pad«, modulating sound just by »its« touch on a screen follow expressive behaviour.

What became standard in radio production was at the same time standard in commercial and pop music organization/composition. Recording on a magnetic-tape recorder allowed samples to be cut, leaving behind time and space, multi-track-recording made it possible to mix polyphonic sound-structures. The prerecording of parts of radio broadcast goes together with the mix of different recording sessions to put it in one structure, in one commercial and pop song into a more or less homogeneous (postmodern) collage of sound based on the remix (and context variation) of sounds with similar connotative qualities. Despite the use of analogous pre-recorded structures digital radio technology/recording technology today allows such structure to be created in real-time – making the structures more »live«, more hedonic bodily: technological produced sound is now structured by bodily sensation/perception of tension and relaxation, even technologically made – technological sound becomes immediately bodily and immersive based on the technological instrumentarization of emotional qualities of expressive behaviour.

Working on sound became bodily – technology makes it possible and intensifies it at least. New compositional programs (e.g., Ableton live) leave behind the tradition of »composing« in time & frequency like setting notes in a score following »progression« in time – it works with sound-samples which are just available and can be activated whenever it is »needed« without following a time-line and it is modulated as it is needed now, becoming a »live« interaction situation – even when the program interacts with data representing the »emotional state« of the listener now.

This means: even when this interaction is done by machines it is done based on the paradigm of interacting humans »regulated« by excitement, by tension – relaxation. What was done by hand in broadcasting is now done by means of technological interfaces at least regarding certain parts: the sound of commercials and pop is adjusted »live« to the »emtional state« of the listener.

Commercials and the sound of »radio« are automatically adjusted in time- and frequency-domain of the sound with respect to changes in the excitement of the listening body and its environment. Pop uses interactive (technological) media for self-adjusting music to the currently state of the listener, ›pro-suming‹ music by mixing pre-recorded parts individually, organising sound on demand or with mobile devices with respect to mechanisms of Mood-Management (Zillmann 1988a, 1988b, 1991; Schramm 2005) without delay.

Although today technologically available but less social accepted only the future will bring bodily action into this adoption process: the gyroscope allowing sound to be manipulated by bodily motion. This will bring together sound production and sound consumption »naturally«.[9]

CONCLUSION

It is the specificity of hearing, of auditory controlled body-environment-interaction, which makes the »auditory logic« the paradigm of creating of images: hearing »informs« about the emotional quality of motion in the environment, it is an artefact of physiological motion being part of emotion – it immediately communicates the meaning of motion to the body. Sound (as an index) thus immediately communicates or just triggers (Nöth 1990: 112) excitement. What Greek drama exposed in the choir is the basis of the logic of the operating system of modern (electronic/digital) mass media and its constitutional parts: pop music and commercials. At least this is »common« because of basic human immediate communication and is »amplified« by the technology of mass media – to reach more »listeners«, to achieve more intensive immediate stimulation in association with any kind of content: products, services, (political) ideologies: this way pop and commercials are

---

9   Experiments show that anger, stress »depression« or sadness are best compensated by an individual's own bodily action, like making/playing musik (Saarikallio & Erkkilä 2007).

parts of regulating social/political (Horkheimer/Adorno 1947) as well as emotional climates (Elias 1992) and led to a hedonistic event-culture (Schulze 1992/2000).

This is the specificity of pop music, which has emerged with electronic mass media and distinguishes it slightly from popular music as being popular in the sense of well known music of most people (Hecken 2006) like folk music as music coming out of self-organizing social structure – although those aspects are and can be essential parts of pop-music as music addressing masses.

Emotional bonding makes sound the main »medium« in mass communication. Organizing sound is thus the main task in this operating system: producing functional sound in radio, in (radio) commercials and in pop, the dominant »media« of electronic massmedia with the goal of stimulating »emotion« in order to emotionalize contents. Modulating the words of Tagg (Tagg 1994) in image-commercials the content – the figure – »declines« and the image – the ground – »rises«. This is the main strategy of image creation, sound being the adequate stimulant and paradigm to be transposed in this multi-sensory gear of pop and commercials – of advertising.

Pop is advertising – advertising is pop: both want to excite bodily. They use the same technology, broadcasting technology, to »amplify« excitement, to control and intensify basic human excitement (by means of intense stimuli) and (even in this way) broaden its range – to create emotional mass bonding. This is done by »cultivating« the paradigm of immediate emotional communication through sound in pop and advertising to create a unique functional sound of mass media; its logic is at least transposed to the structure of (abstract) pictures in time as well as to its »sharpness« in time to create a more immersive, multi-sensory mass media environment »closer« to the body.

REFERENCES

Baudrillard, J. (1981). *Simulacres et simulation*. Paris: Galilée.

Berlyne, D. E. (1970). Novelity, complexity, and hedonic value. *Perception Psychophysics*, 8, 279–286.

Berlyne, D. E. (1971). *Aesthetic and psychobiology*. New York: Appleton.

Berlyne, D. E. (1974). The new experimental aesthetics. In D. E. Berlyne (Ed.), *Studies in the new experimental aesthetics* (pp. 1–26). Washington: Hemisphere.

Blacking, J. (1977). Towards an Anthropology of the Body. In J. Blacking, (Ed.), The Anthropology of the Body (pp.1–28). London: Academic Press.

Blaukopf, K. (1989). *Beethovens Erben in der Mediamorphose. Kultur- und Medienpolitik für die elektronische Ära*. Heiden: Niggli.

Bullerjahn, C. (2001). *Grundlagen der Wirkung von Filmmusik* (=Forum Muiskpädagogik 45) Wiesbaden: Wißner-Verlag.

Elias, N. (1992). Studien über die Deutschen. In: M. Schröter (Ed.), *Macht-kämpfe und Habitusentwicklung im 19. und 20. Jahrhundert*. Frankfurt a. Main: Suhrkamp.

Gibson, J. J. (1982). *Wahrnehmung und Umwelt*. München: Urban & Schwarzenberg.

Harrer, G. (1975). Das ›Musikerlebnis‹ im Griff des naturwissenschaft-lichen Experiments. In G. Harrer (Ed.), *Grundlagen der Musiktherapie und Musikpsychologie* (pp. 3–47). Stuttgart: Fischer.

Horkheimer, M. & Adorno, Th. W., *Dialektik der Aufklärung. Philoso-phische Fragmente* [1947], Frankfurt/Main 1997 (*Gesammelte Schrift-en*, ed. Rolf Tiedemann, vol. 3).

Hecken, Th. (2006). *Populäre Kultur*. Mit einem Anhang Girl and Popkul-tur. Bochum: Posth-Verlag.

Jauk, W. (2007a). The Visual and Auditory Representation of Space and the Net-Space. In *Musicological Annual XLIII/2*. 361–370.

Jauk, W. (2007b). Der Sound des hedonisch-performativen Körpers und das Spiel der Elektrogitarre, *Jazzforschung / jazz research 39* (= Festschrift Franz Kerschbaumer zum 60. Geburtstag), 273–289.

Jauk, W. (2009), *pop/music+medien/kunst. Der musikalisierte Allteg der digital culture.* (= Beiträge zur Systematischen Musikwissenschaft 15) Osnabrück: epOs.

Jauk W. (2013) Beyond semiotics? Music – a phenomenon of mediatization: The extension of the hedonistic body and its communicative aspects. In D. Davidović & N. Bezić (Eds.), *New unknown music. Essays in Honour of Nikša Gligo* (pp. 407–421). DAF: Zagreb.

Knepler, G. (1977). *Geschichte als Weg zum Musikverständnis. Zur Theorie, Methode und Geschichte der Musikgeschichtsschreibung.* Leipzig: Reclam.

Konecni, V. J. (1977). Quelques déterminants sociaux, émotionnels et cognitifs des préférences esthétiques relatives á des mélodies de complexité variable. *Bulletin der Psychologie*, 30, 688–715.

Lakoff, G. (1993). The contemporary theory of metaphor. In Ortony, A. (Ed.), *Metaphor and thought.* Second edition (pp. 202–251). Cambridge: Cambridge University Press.

Langer, S. (1953). *Feeling and Form. A Theory of Art Developement froom Philosophy in a New Key.* London: Routledge.

Maturana, H. R. & Varela, F. J. (1984). *El árbol del conocimiento. Las Bases Biológicas del Entendimiento Humano.* Viamonte: Lumen.

McLuhan, M. (1994). *Understanding media: the extension of man.* [1964]. Cambridge MA: MIT Press.

Nietzsche, F. (1872). *Die Geburt der Tragödie aus dem Geiste der Musik.* Leipzig: Fritzsch.

Nöth, W. (1990). Handbook of Semiotics. Bloomington: Indiana University Press.

Riemann, H. (1914/15). Ideen zu einer Lehre der Tonvorstellungen. *Jahrbuch der Musikbibliothek Peters,* 21/22, 1–26.

Saarikallio, S. & Erkkilä, J. (2007). The role of musi in adolescents' mood regulation. *Psychology of Music*, 35,1, 88–109.

Schenker, H. (1935). *Der freie Satz.* Wien: Universal Edition.

Schramm, H. (2005.) *Mood Management durch Musik, Die alltägliche Nutzung von Musik zur Regulierung von Stimmungen.* Köln: Halem Verlag.

Schulze, G. (2000). *Die Erlebnisgesellschaft. Kultursoziologie der Gegenwart* [1992]. Frankfurt a. Main: Campus.

Sloboda, J. A. (1985). *The Musical Mind. The Cognitive Psychology of Music.* Oxford: UK: Clarendon Press

Smudits, A. (2002). *Mediamorphosen des Kulturschaffens. Kunst- und Kommunikationstechnologien im Wandel.* Wien: Braumüller.

Tagg, P. (1994). From Refrain to Rave. The Decline of Figure and the Rise of Ground. *Popular Music*, 13/2, 209–222.

Toop, D. (1997). *Ocean of Sound. Klang, Geräusch, Stille.* St. Andrä-Wördern: Hannibal.

Virilio, P. (1992). *Rasender Stillstand.* München: Hanser.

Weber, M. (1921). *Die rationalen und soziologischen Grundlagen der Musik.* München: Drei Masken Verlag.

Wundt, W. (1874). *Grundzüge der physiologischen Psychologie.* Leipzig: Engelmann.

Zillmann, D. (1988a). Mood management through communication choices. *American Behavioral Scientist 31*, 327–340.

Zillmann, D. (1988b). Mood manamgement: Using entertainment to full advantage. In L. Donohew, H. Sypher & E. Higgins (Eds.) *Communication, social cognition, and affect* (pp. 147–171) Hillsdale: L. Erlbaum Associates .

Zillmann, D. (1991). Television Viewing and Physiological Arousal. In J. Bryant & D. Zillmann (Eds.): *Responding to the Screen. Reception and Reaction Processes* (pp. 103–133) New Jersey: L. Erlbaum Associates.

»The Voice« of the music industry

New advertising options in music talent shows

HOLGER SCHRAMM & NICOLAS RUTH

> If I can make it there, I'll make it any-
> where...
> And find I'm a number one, top of the list,
> king of the hill, a number one...
> FRANK SINATRA, THEME FROM NEW
> YORK, NEW YORK (1979)

1. INTRODUCTION

Debuting in the 1990s, music talent shows have become one of the most successful television formats in recent years. This has been especially true in relation to the high demand for reality TV shows (Pendzich 2005). In Germany, these kinds of shows are usually referred to as *castingshows*. The most popular German examples of this genre are *Popstars* (since 2000), *Deutschland sucht den Superstar* (*DSDS*; since 2002), and *The Voice of Germany* (since 2011). These shows are broadcast during prime time slots, each reaching four to six million viewers. They obtain a market share of about 40% for the 14–49 year-old target group. The main goal of these shows is entertainment: *DSDS* won the German Television Award for »Best Entertainment Show« in 2003, and *Voice of Germany* won both the German Television Award and the Golden Camera for »Best Entertainment Show« in 2012.

These shows are music competitions that provide, in addition to media exposure for participants, a label deal and the potential of a music career. Media critics complain that the most talented performers do not always win the contest, as some of the most well-known candidates tend instead to be those who behave in an embarrassing or scandalous way on the show. This is not only an artistic complaint, but a moral one, and it is often present in critical media portrayals (Hickethier 2005; Schmidt 2003; Stavenhagen 2005, for criticism of media critics see Jacke 2005). The producers of these shows tolerate and even provoke this public criticism; they encourage scandalous behavior in participants and encourage the jury to make provocative comments, because any sort of publicity helps to market the show and the show's products. Wolf (2004) found that 15.5% of a sample of 200 young adults knew of *DSDS*, even though they had not ever watched a single show. In conjunction with the comprehensive content analysis by Lünenborg et al. (2011), it is clear that this format has gained a great deal of publicity during the past decade. The broadcasting companies behind such shows, along with the music industry, use public discourse to bring their products to market using cross-media marketing (ibid.; Pendzich 2005).

While there has been considerable research on talent shows, it is not comprehensive. Most empirical studies investigate the reasons why people – especially children and young adults – watch talent shows (Götz & Gather 2012; Hackenberg & Selg 2012; Klaus & O'Connor 2010) and how they perceive the jury and the stars-to-be (Hackenberg & Hajok 2012; Hajok & Selg 2012; Müllensiefen et al. 2005). Studies on the strategic aspects of music talent shows often neglect the shows' marketing and advertising function for the music industry (von Appen 2005; Pendzich 2005; Wolf 2004). Consequently, this article provides the first descriptive overview of the diverse options available to the music industry in supporting or producing music talent shows. The present study also compares different shows, with a focus on their advertising potential.

2. BACKGROUND

The idea of music talent shows on which young people reinterpret hit songs has existed in Germany for many years. Even in early seasons of the *Rudi Carrell Show* (1988–1992) newcomer artists imitated famous singers and were rated by the studio audience (Wolther 2009). This spared the show the expense of paying for established music stars, while providing an entertaining program with hit music (Reufsteck & Niggemeyer 2005).

All of the talent shows are very similar to each other, with only small variations between different shows and seasons. During the first round, candidates usually present themselves to the jury via a short musical performance (sometimes with instruments or dancing). Only *Voice of Germany* preselects candidates; *Voice of Germany* is also the only show which conducts blind auditions during the first round. In contrast, *DSDS* and *Popstars* allow anyone to audition. As a result of these mass auditions, the jury usually only has a few seconds to approve the participants who will move on to the next round. The jury normally consists of three or four established singers, dancers, music producers, or media experts, who compare and judge the contestants. Participants compete with each other in a series of rounds; only one singer or band wins the final round. The small number of candidates who make it to the later rounds encourages viewers to bond with performers, ensuring high sales for their first record releases.

The procedure for selecting winners differs by show. On *Popstars* the jury votes on every selection except the final, which is done by viewers; on *DSDS* the jury decides during the early rounds, while viewers can vote on each of the later rounds (including the final) which are broadcast as live shows. On *Voice of Germany* the coaches and jury members determine the outcome of the first two rounds of auditions; later rounds are determined through a combination of telephone voting and jury decision; the final winner is chosen exclusively by the viewers.

Von Appen (2005) describes how this voting process transfers the selection of the next superstar, which was once the responsibility of an artist & repertoire manager, directly to the target audience. This helps to protect against the huge risk of flops that is standard in the music industry (generally one success to ten failures). Even when juries cannot directly promote or fire contestants, the influence of the jury on the viewers should not be underestimated. Many viewers rely on the perceived skilled advice of jury members, especially when viewers are uncertain of their own musical judgment, or when they have not watched the entire show as attentively as the jury. Viewers seem to turn to the jury for help when, for whatever reason, they feel they cannot distinguish the quality of different performers (see Kopiez & Platz 2009).

Deutschland sucht den Superstar was based on the original British *Pop Idol* (first broadcast 2001), *Popstars* is a version of the New Zealand show of the same name (first broadcast 1999) and *Voice of Germany* is related to *The Voice of Holland* that was first broadcast in the Netherlands in 2010. All of these original shows were so successful in their countries of origin that they were replicated and licensed worldwide. Germany provides the fourth largest music market in the world, after the US, Japan and United Kingdom (Bundesverband Musikindustrie 2013).

3. ADVERTISING ALTERNATIVES

Like the connection between *DSDS*, the TV station *RTL* (derived from *Radio Télévisioun Lëtzebuerg*) and the music major *BMG* (Bertelsmann Music Group), there is a link between *Voice of Germany*, the TV stations *SAT.1* and *ProSieben* (which both belong to the *ProSiebenSAT.1 Media AG*) and the music major *Universal* (Universal Music Group). Internet rumors claim that candidates can only sing songs provided by the *Universal* publishing department. The jury members Nena, The BossHoss, and Rea Garvey are *Universal* artists, and all of them released their latest records under the *Universal* label. Although Xavier Naidoo, another judge, is listed as a *Universal* artist for only one audio book, his own label (Naidoo Records) may be connected to *Universal*, perhaps in the form of a distribution deal. Two winners, Ivy Quainoo and Nick Howard, received record deals with *Universal* as part of their prize.

Music talent shows are among the newest marketing tools of the music industry, with hopes that they will help alleviate the crisis of plummeting sales facing record companies (Pendzich 2005). It is therefore no surprise that the largest major label, *Universal*, has created its own talent show. These shows not only create new superstars and minimize the risk of costly flops (von Appen 2005), but serve as a very important platform for advertising. Talent shows provide opportunities to promote new products and artists (Tozman 2007), and ensure plenty of airtime for licensed music; if the contestants exclusively sing songs licensed by *Universal Publishing*, this generates royalties due to copyrights.

In the following section, we analyze the final episode of Season 2 of *Voice of Germany*[1] and catalogue all of the advertising options for the music industry. We will go through the show in chronological order, noting every type of music advertisement, and then discuss these opportunities for advertising.

Voice of Germany always starts with an introduction of all four finalists and their coaches. For the episode we analyzed these were, in order of appearance: Michael Lane (Coach: Xavier Naidoo), James Borges (Coach: BossHoss), Isabell Schmidt (Coach: Nena) and Nick Howard (Coach: Rea Garvey). After a short teaser of who the guest appearances will be, Robbie Williams performs together with the finalists. All five sing the latest single by Robbie Williams, »Candy«, and the host promises that Williams will sing his upcoming single later in the show. In 2011, Williams signed a contract with *Universal*, after his former label (*EMI*) was bought, in part, by *Universal*. It is no coincidence that, one month before performing on this final show, Williams released his album »Take the Crown«. Therefore, the first advertising option found on the final show was a guest appearance by a musician signed by the sponsoring label, who had recently produced a new single and an album.

The host, Thore Schölermann, and Robbie Williams welcome the viewers, cuing the animated intro sequence with the theme music. The jury is then introduced – they are all wearing suits for the occasion, and they cheer to the studio audience. Before the host talks to the jury members about the upcoming show, the theme music is heard once again; throughout the whole show, this music is played by the studio band, and in combination with audience applause, it serves as a transition between different scenes or commercial breaks. Schölermann explains how the show works, and how fans could have already voted for their favorite candidates by downloading their songs, which were first presented during the semi-final round, one week earlier. This advertising opportunity is unique to music talent shows: the songs played are available as downloads only moments after the performance; by downloading a song, fans can also vote for their favorite contestant.

---

1 First broadcast December 14th, 2012 and retrieved online from http://www.the-voice-of-germany.de/video/ [30th April, 2013].

At this point in the show, the voting hotlines are opened and the telephone numbers for the finalists are displayed. The running voting tally for the contestants while showing pictures or films of contestants is an obvious advertisement not only for the upcoming artist (the winner of the show) but for the songs these contestants sing. As the whole show can be seen as an advertisement for the cast of singers and their songs, we tend to not identify these moments as alternative advertising opportunities.

The backstage host, Doris Golpashin, then comes on with all of the remaining contestants in a private part of the studio. She introduces the official who oversees the voting. Viewers are invited to greet and support their chosen candidates via diverse communication channels, such as Twitter, Facebook and the social TV application Sat.1-Connect. This cross-media promotion is a special form of advertising; although it is not directly linked to a product or musician, it encourages viewers to form a stronger bond with the show by boosting their interaction through social media.

Twelve minutes into the show, the first finalist, Isabell Schmidt performs her first song with her coach Nena. Schmidt and Nena then comment on a montage of Schmidt's best moments from the whole season. Her first song was »Finderlohn« by Samy Deluxe (singing under the name of Herr Sorge), who sang along with her and Nena. Herr Sorge released an album on December 14, 2012, the same date as this episode. This is another example of advertising in the form of a guest appearance.

Schölermann thanks Schmidt and Nena for their performance, and discusses the day's prizes. Then, an establishing shot of the winner of the first season, Ivy Quainoo, is presented. The shot ends with Quainoo showcasing the extra prize for this season's winner: a new Volkswagen *Golf*. This is not only obvious product placement, but also an advertisement for the former winner. Another example of product placement is seen during Michael Lane's performance of »Mrs. Lawless«. Lane plays an acoustic guitar (recognizable by its form as an Ovation guitar) with a strap promoting the guitar manufacturer *Fender*.

Schölermann then talks to some former participants in the audience: Raffa Shira, who discusses his studio sessions for his upcoming record, and Brigitte Lorenz, who tells the viewers about her recent concert tour. While neither is listed as *Universal* artist, it is likely that both are contractually bound to the producers of *Voice of Germany* in some way. James Borges and Nelly Furtado then perform Furtado's song »Waiting for the Night«;

Furtado is signed to *Universal*, and the song was released on the same day as the show.

Following a commercial break, Schölermann presents a new compilation album with songs by the semifinalists – another advertising opportunity. While the contest winners' records are not visibly labeled as a part of *Voice of Germany*, the compilation album is clearly arranged in the corporate design of the show. Thus, the compilation is a promotional tool for every artist featured on the show.

Nick Howard then takes the stage, accompanied by his coach, Rea Garvey. They sing »One Day Like This«, a song by a *Universal* artist, Elbow. The next scene takes place backstage, where Furtado discusses her 2013 concert tour. Tweets sent by fans are displayed on-screen during the interview. Isabell Schmidt then performs »Heimweh«, followed by Michael Lane and Leona Lewis's performance of Lewis's song »Trouble«. This song, released by *Sony Music*, is the first song featured in this episode which is neither published by *Universal* nor performed by a *Universal* artist.

Following a commercial break, Robbie Williams sings his upcoming single »Different«. He then announces that his album features four additional songs only available on the German release. James Borges and The BossHoss then perform a country-style reinterpretation of »It's Not Unusual«. As this song and most of its cover versions are licensed under *Universal Publishing*, this represents yet another form of advertising. The performance not only generates royalties, but is an advertisement for an old song owned by *Universal*, originally written by Les Reed and Gordon Mills, and performed by Tom Jones.

Nick Howard then performs »Unbreakable«, followed by Isabell Schmidt and Birdy's rendition of Birdy's song »People Help the People«. Notably, Birdy, who is signed to *Warner Music*, is another guest without a connection to *Universal*. Schölermann thanks Birdy and reminds viewers about a new show, *The Voice Kids*, and about upcoming audition dates. Michael Lane and Xavier Naidoo then do a version of the Motown classic »Cruisin'« by Smokey Robinson as the last contestant and coach performance. After this song, Nick Howard discusses the final eight *Voice of Germany* contestants' concert tour, which will take place shortly after the end of Season Two. James Borges then performs his song »Lonely«.

The final performance features Nick Howard and Emeli Sandé performing Sandé's song »Read All About It«. Sandé is signed by the label
EMI/Virgin Records, which is now owned by *Universal*. The following ten
minutes offer clips of performances by finalists, as fans are urged to call in
and vote for the winner. Before the final vote count, every jury member
gives a final statement summarizing the past season. While the jury members are overtly discussing the contestants, this statement also gives them
an opportunity to promote themselves, the last advertising option on the
show. The show closes with the announcement that Nick Howard is the
new »Voice of Germany« and the winner of the second season. He performs his song »Unbreakable« once again, with a giant image of his album
cover displayed in the background of the stage.

In analyzing the advertising opportunities in this episode, we were especially interested in opportunities in addition to standard advertising and
promotion. We found that *Universal* advertised its signed musicians and
products in ways that only a music talent show could enable. The five advertising options found during the analysis were:

- Guest appearance
- Voting by download
- Compilation album
- Song selection
- Jury promotion

We found that *guest appearances* on music talent shows are more personal
than on any other type of show – not only are contestants able to sing with
superstars such as Robbie Williams, but they even have the opportunity to
rehearse and chat with the like of Nelly Furtado and Leona Lewis. An important element of the success of music talent shows is the parasocial relationship established between the fans and candidates (Schramm 2010), so
producers are sure to make these meetings highlights for contestants and
viewers. Guest appearances allow for a transfer of positive effects; the
show and contestants benefit from the image of a well-established star, and
the star benefits from the media exposure and the opportunities to promote
his or her latest releases and upcoming concert tours (von Zitzewitz 2007).

The opportunity to vote for contestants is a major factor enhancing the
emotional participation of viewers (Döveling 2007), allowing them not only

to give feedback, but to influence directly the outcome of the contest. On the show in question, phone calls were worth one vote, but if a viewer downloaded a song by one of the four finalists during the previous week, it was counted as two votes, making *voting by download* the most effective advertising option, with the potential to generate huge sales. Within this one-week time frame, sales from viewers eager for their choice to win can catapult contestants' songs into the charts (Patalong 2008), improving contestants' chances for further success.

Compilation albums are another important promotional tool for the music industry, and the cross-media promotion and corporate design of a music talent show enhances the effects of a compilation. Viewers who buy the record because they like one or two songs are likely to develop an interest in the other artists and songs after listening to the whole album. The audio CD of Season 2 includes songs by all eight semifinalists, as well as their duet battle tracks. Although digital downloads are gaining favor over CDs, decreasing the synergy of a compilation album, playlists on services such as *Spotify* and *Digster* still retain the structure of the CD.

Song selection throughout the show is an important advertising tool for record companies. This gives them an opportunity of promoting not just contemporary hits, but also classic favorites. Well-known songs are rated more highly by the audience (Schramm 2009), so they are favored; for example, 62% of the songs used during the second season of *DSDS* were among the Top Ten in the German single charts (Pendzich 2005). Although we did not analyze an entire season, as did Pendzich, it seems highly likely that the majority of the selected songs were on *Universal Publishing*'s list, or were at least performed by *Universal* artists. The record company promotes its own songs and musicians heavily during the course of the show, for example: three out of six guest appearances on the analyzed episode were *Universal* artists. The royalties earned by broadcasting *Universal*'s music is a bonus source of revenue.

Finally, *jury promotion* brings jury members almost as much profit as it does the contestants. Young viewers value jury members according to perceived authenticity, appearance and expertise (Hajok & Selg 2012) and develop an even more intimate relationship with them, as they rehearse, joke and perform with the much-loved contestants. While a jury is a fixed part of every talent show, the activity of the jury on *Voice of Germany* is remarkable, as all of the coaches present small solo showcases and performances.

As three of the four coaches in the episode we analyzed are *Universal* art-
ists, it seems clear that *Universal* uses the format of the show to promote
these artists in a special way. During the first season of *Voice of Germany*,
The BossHoss released the studio album »Liberty of Action« and Xavier
Naidoo issued his greatest hits album »Danke fürs Zuhören«. During the
second season, Rea Garvey released his first solo album, »Can't Stand the
Silence – The Encore« and Nena released her album »Du bist gut«. The
BossHoss was especially successful: the album climbed to number four in
the German charts, and the single peaked at number eight in the German
charts and at number one in the Austrian charts.

4. DIFFERENCES BETWEEN *VOICE OF GERMANY* AND *DSDS*

As discussed in the introduction, there are some differences in the way
viewers and critics receive different music talent shows. Its focus on personal stories, tragedies befalling participants, and embarrassing performances generated much discussion about *DSDS*. Other shows such as the
Voice of Germany or Stefan Raab's *Stefan sucht den Super-Grand-Prix-
Star* (SSDSGPS) focused on musical performances and were received as
being more authentic. The advertising possibilities described in the preced-
ing section differ by show; this stems not only from the musical genres featured or the influence of sponsoring record companies, but also from the
way different shows are received by viewers. Helms (2005) claims that
many German consumers perceive casting by a record label very negatively, viewing the cast singers as lacking authenticity and credibility. However, despite this fact, it seems that *Voice of Germany* provides an authentic
show with a musical focus that is very well received (Stich 2011).

Two studies (conducted at the University of Würzburg under the direction of Holger Schramm) examined differences between *DSDS* and *Voice of
Germany*. The first study investigated whether or not *Voice of Germany*
was perceived as more serious and authentic by viewers. The second study
explored whether the user behavior of music talent show viewers (parasocial relationships; appreciation of musical value; appreciation of entertainment value; and viewing frequency) influenced their purchasing behavior. The first study had a sample of 221 persons (average age 24; mostly

students; 76% female) who took part in an online survey assessing the musical seriousness and authenticity of participants and jury members. The survey also asked how participants viewed the ratings system of *DSDS* as compared with that of *Voice of Germany*. Results indicated that *Voice of Germany* is perceived as more musically serious; viewers rated the contestants as more talented and the diversity of musical styles as wider than on *DSDS*. When asked about *Voice of Germany*, survey participants assessed the jury as more competent, the candidates as more experienced and the whole format as more authentic. However, the extent to which *DSDS* and *Voice of Germany* can be compared is limited; as of 2012 there had been only one season of *Voice of Germany* but nine of *DSDS*. It remains to be seen whether *Voice of Germany* can maintain its positive image in the eyes of viewers for as many seasons.

The second study also made use of an online survey, but only persons who had watched at least one episode of both *DSDS* and *Voice of Germany* were allowed to participate. A sample of 174 persons completed the questionnaire (average age 25, mostly students, 71% female). The study sought to discover whether viewing behavior influenced purchasing behavior with regard to talent- show products. The results indicated that participants who developed a parasocial relationship with a candidate of these shows, or who watched one of these shows frequently, had enhanced purchasing behavior. This study found that *Voice of Germany* contestants were rated as more musically capable, but this only had a small influence on purchasing behavior: if a contestant on either *DSDS* or *Voice of Germany* was seen as talented, purchasing behavior was enhanced. However, the entertainment factor had only a minor influence on purchasing behavior.

These two studies indicate that different music talent shows are perceived in different ways: while *Voice of Germany* is rated as musically superior, *DSDS* is still capable of establishing strong viewer commitments to the show. However, both shows clearly impact consumer behavior, both through their unique formats and the advertising opportunities described in section three above.

5. OUTLOOK

The music industry has been in crisis for at least a decade. Although music consumption is higher than ever, sales figures are at an all-time low (von Zitzewitz 2007). Music talent shows have proven to be a salvation for the music industry. Using this format, record companies do not need to spend a fortune creating and promoting new stars: they let the shows do all the work, generating revenue in the process. As these shows have evolved, unique opportunities for advertising have also been developed and applied, further boosting the utility of such programs for record labels.

Our analysis highlights how many advertisements have been incorporated into music talent shows, both subtly and overtly. Nevertheless, many questions remain. For instance, do advertisements and cross-media promotion not become an annoyance to viewers beyond a certain point? We would suggest that future studies examine why *Voice of Germany* is perceived as more authentic. Possible factors might include the visible live band, live instrumental performances by jury members, or the more diverse range of music. A content analysis as to how much music by specific publishers is actually used over the course of one season would also help shed light on the relationship between the record labels and the shows.

Although the sales figures for the winners of these shows are not as strong as they were when the first music talent show aired (Schramm 2010), this format remains very successful, and is continuing to develop. Talent shows are highly profitable for everyone involved, however it remains to be seen whether they are enough to rescue the declining music industry.

REFERENCES

Bundesverband Musikindustrie (Ed.). (2013). *Musikindustrie in Zahlen 2012*. Berlin: Bundesverband Musikindustrie.

Döveling, K. (2007). Superstar – Supershow? – „Deutschland sucht den Superstar» im Urteil der Zuschauer. In K. Döveling, L. Mikos & J. U. Nieland (Eds.), *Im Namen des Fernsehvolkes. Neue Formate für Orientierung und Bewertung* (pp. 179–210). Konstanz: UVK.

Götz, M. & Gather, J. (2012). Die Faszination ›Castingshow‹ – Warum Kinder und Jugendliche Castingshows sehen. In D. Hajok, O. Selg & A. Hackenberg (Eds.), *Auf Augenhöhe? Rezeption von Castingshows und Coachingsendungen* (pp. 87–100). Konstanz: UVK.

Hackenberg, A. & Hajok, D. (2012). Orientierung auf Augenhöhe? Der Blick junger Zuschauer auf die Castingshow-Kandidaten. In D. Hajok, O. Selg & A. Hackenberg (Eds.), *Auf Augenhöhe? Rezeption von Castingshows und Coachingsendungen* (pp. 115–130). Konstanz: UVK.

Hackenberg, A. & Selg, O. (2012). Mehr als eine Live-Bühne – Castingshow-Formate als mediale Bedeutungsangebote für junge Zuschauer. In D. Hajok, O. Selg & A. Hackenberg (Eds.), *Auf Augenhöhe? Rezeption von Castingshows und Coachingsendungen* (pp. 131–144). Konstanz: UVK.

Hajok, D. & Selg, O. (2012). Bohlens Sprüche, Klums Tipps – Der Umgang Heranwachsender mit Castingshow-Jurys. In D. Hajok, O. Selg & A. Hackenberg (Eds.), *Auf Augenhöhe? Rezeption von Castingshows und Coachingsendungen* (pp. 101–114). Konstanz: UVK.

Helms, D. (2005). Von Marsyas bis Küblböck. Eine kleine Geschichte und Theorie musikalischer Wettkämpfe. In D. Helms & T. Phleps (Eds.), *Keiner wird gewinnen* (pp. 11–39). Bielefeld: transcript.

Hickethier, K. (2005). »Bild« erklärt den Daniel oder »Wo ist Küblböcks Brille?« – Medienkritik zur Fernsehshow »Deutschland sucht den Superstar«. In R. Weiß (Ed.), *Zur Kritik der Medienkritik. Wie Zeitungen das Fernsehen beobachten* (pp. 337–394). Berlin: Vistas.

Jacke, C. (2005). Keiner darf gewinnen – Potenziale einer effektiven Medienkritik neuer TV-Castingshows. In D. Helms & T. Phleps (Eds.), *Keiner wird gewinnen* (pp. 113–135). Bielefeld: transcript.

Klaus, E. & O'Connor, B. (2010). Aushandlungsprozesse im Alltag. Jugendliche Fans von Castingshows. In J. Röser, T. Thomas & C. Peil (Eds.), *Alltag in den Medien – Medien im Alltag* (pp. 48–72). Wiesbaden: VS.

Kopiez, R. & Platz, F. (2009). The role of listening expertise, attention, and musical style in the perception of clash of keys. *Music Perception, 26* (4), 321–334.

Lünenborg, M., Martens, D., Köhler, T. & Töpper, C. (2011). *Skandalisierung im Fernsehen. Strategien, Erscheinungsformen und Rezeption von*

Reality TV Formaten (= Schriftenreihe Medienforschung der LfM, 65). Berlin: Vistas.

Müllensiefen, D., Lothwesen, K., Tiemann, L. & Matterne, B. (2005). Musikstars in der Wahrnehmung jugendlicher TV-Castingshow-Rezipienten. Eine empirische Untersuchung. In D. Helms & T. Phleps (Eds.), *Keiner wird gewinnen* (pp. 163–185). Bielefeld: transcript.

Pendzich, M. (2005). Hit-Recycling: Casting-Shows und die Wettbewerbsstrategie »Coverversion«. In D. Helms & T. Phleps (Eds.), *Keiner wird gewinnen* (pp. 137–150). Bielefeld: transcript.

Reufsteck, M. & Niggemeyer, S. (2005). *Das Fernsehlexikon.* München: Goldmann.

Schmidt, T. E. (2003). Gute Menschen, schlechte Menschen. „Deutschland sucht den Superstar» – die einen finden Gold, die anderen sich selbst: Überleben im Karrierebrüter. *Die Zeit, 11,* 44.

Schramm, H. (2009). Die Gestaltung von Mainstream-Musikprogrammen im Radio. Eine Reflektion aus Sicht der Rezeptions- und Wirkungsforschung. In S. Trepte, U. Hasebrink & H. Schramm (Eds.), *Strategische Kommunikation und Mediengestaltung – Anwendung und Erkenntnisse der Rezeptions- und Wirkungsforschung* (pp. 205–223). Baden-Baden: Nomos.

Schramm, H. (2010). Musikcastingshows. In P. Moormann (Ed.), *Musik im Fernsehen. Sendeformen und Gestaltungsprinzipien* (pp. 47–66). Wiesbaden: VS.

Stavenhagen, I. (2005). Der gute Ton, oder: Die Funktion Daniel Küblböcks im Star-System von Deutschland sucht den Superstar und im öffentlichen Diskurs. In D. Helms & T. Phleps (Eds.), *Keiner wird gewinnen* (pp. 151–162). Bielefeld: transcript.

Tozman, I. (2007). *Castingshows. Die wahren Sieger und Verlierer.* Saarbrücken: VDM.

von Appen, R. (2005). Die Wertungskriterien der Deutschland sucht den Superstar-Jury vor dem Hintergrund sozialer Milieus und kulturindustrieller Strategien. In D. Helms & T. Phleps (Eds.), *Keiner wird gewinnen* (pp. 187–208). Bielefeld: transcript.

von Zitzewitz, M. (2007). Musikvermarktung im Fernsehen. In B. Schneider & S. Weinacht (Eds.), *Musikwirtschaft und Medien. Märkte – Unternehmen – Strategien* (pp. 237–246). München: Fischer.

Wolf, S. (2004). *Deutschland sucht den Superstar: Analyse der Erfolgs-faktoren.* Hamburg: Diplomica.

Wolther, I. (2009). Musikformate im Fernsehen. In H. Schramm (Ed.), *Handbuch Musik und Medien* (pp. 177–207). Konstanz: UVK.

Internet sources

Patalong, F. (2008). Musik-Download-Zählung. Einfalltor für Chart-Manipulationen. http://www.spiegel.de/netzwelt/web/0,1518,538302,00 .html [16th March, 2009].

Stich, J. (2011). *Warum ist »The Voice of Germany« Publikumsliebling?* http://www.augsburger-allgemeine.de/panorama/Warum-ist-The-Voice-of-Germany-Publikumsliebling-id17923886.html [12th May, 2013].

Discography

Various Artists (2012). *The Best of Finals* [CD]. Berlin: Universal.

Capitalism Propaganda

Adorno's Kulturindustrie and Freedom of Creativity

Friedrich Weltzien

POLITICS OF AUTONOMY

The history of art, the history of design, and the history of advertising run in parallel tracks but are not identical. From the point of view of visual studies (or the *Bildwissenschaften*), the combination of image and text may be one important pathway that these forms of communication do share. They are ways of communication that attract the viewer's gaze. But the theory of gaze might blur a difference between art and advertisement, between pictures and commercials, and between drawing and graphic design, which are expressed emphatically in other theoretical approaches. In the following I want to scrutinize one specific formulation, that of Theodor Wiesengrund Adorno, to show that the discrimination between the autonomy of art and the dependence of applied art at a crucial point during the last century carried an eminent political meaning. I believe that this political interest today is most worthy to be kept from oblivion.

The defamation of advertisement as a form of propaganda and the defamation of all channels of mass media as means of propaganda were in themselves political statement that were at once anti-fascist, anti-capitalist and anti-communist. In times of digital monitoring, in times of personalized advertisement through social media, and in times of ever-present ad spaces on smart phones and mobile tablet computers, it might be of some relevance to again frame the question of freedom within the discussion of the relation between art and advertisement. In doing so, I do not address the freedom of the generative system, but the freedom of people: the freedom of the producers as well as the users of images.

In asking these questions, the perspective of semiotics seems to have a blind spot, and in opposition to poststructuralist theories of signs, Adorno's critical theory is more interested in intentions and affections than in effectiveness. The functional operation of communication in art and also within design processes is not a valid criterion of a successful act of creation to Adorno. In his eyes, a good design is not necessarily a functional one. A good design is one that keeps the moral integrity of the designer, as well as that of the beholder, unsmirched. Autonomy and independence are the guardians of the possibility of a freedom of choice and a free will. Propaganda is the perfect antonym to this understanding of freedom. Advertising will make a person consume things against his or her own will; advertising may affect people to the disadvantage of their own health: this would be just a form of propaganda. Following this logic, advertisements can never be art. But Adorno is giving some hints how, or at least to what extent, contract work – and that would include all kinds of design work – could be called art.

KULTURINDUSTRIE AS PROPAGANDA

Fleeing from fascist Germany to England in 1934 and later on to California, Adorno escaped the Holocaust and the battlegrounds of World War II. During his exile in the United States of America, he and his co-refugee, friend, and mentor Max Horkheimer, coined the term »Kulturindustrie«. Popular music (like jazz), cinema, journals and illustrated magazines, radio programs, fashion and, most of all, advertising – all of what today might be called mass media or the creative industries – was part of Kulturindustrie.[1] Adorno and Horkheimer, the two representatives of what was not yet called critical theory, invented this term to mark the difference between folk art and mass culture. They wanted to avoid the impression »that it [the Kulturindustrie] is a matter of something like a culture that arises spontaneous-

---

1   Diedrich Diedrichsen, The Adequacy of Signs: Adorno versus Jazz and Pop, in: Nicolas Schafhausen, Vanessa Joan Müller & Michael Hirsch (Eds.), *Adorno. The Possibility of the Impossible*, Berlin 2003, 33–44.

ly from the masses themselves, the contemporary form of popular art. From the latter the culture industry must be distinguished in the extreme.«[2]

Kulturindustrie does not include original products by individuals. It is a powerful instrument of the ruling class – in Berlin, Moscow, Rome or Hollywood alike – to silence people, to sedate critique, to curtail civic rights and to keep all citizens in a passive state of consumption. Independent and self-reliant thought and the philosophical ideals of enlightenment are eroded by Kulturindustrie, which is itself a result of enlightenment. No act that helps to keep up the mechanisms of consumption can be truly creative. That is because there is no originality and no inventive quality in recreating a system that already exists. Fulfilling the will of any given authority cannot bring something new into the world, but only perpetuate the old and traditional.

As long as there is a »constraint of the client or the market« – as long as design is used to produce consumer goods or items of trade only – there will be no creativity.[3] Art must completely rid itself of the character of ware. As this concept of creativity is in some ways indebted to nineteenth century ideas of the original genius and a model of the autonomous subject in the tradition of German idealistic philosophy, Adorno's point of departure may be questionable. Within the framework of the relationship between art and advertising two primary questions arise at this point: the first is why is Adorno so strident? The second is, what would art that exists outside of a consumerist world look like?

No Poems after Auschwitz

Adorno's uncompromising attitude was a direct result of his experience of German National Socialism, the aggressive and racist anti-Semitism culminating in the Holocaust, and the aesthetic politics of propaganda with the help of radio and cinema, newspapers, architecture, mass performances or the doctrine of »Entartete Kunst«. Affected personally as a Jew and intel-

---

2   Theodor W. Adorno, Theodor, Culture Industry Reconsidered. (translated by Anson G. Rabinbach), in: *New German Critique*, 6, Fall 1975, 12.

3   Theodor W. Adorno, Résumé über Kulturindustrie, in: id., *Ohne Leitbild. Parva Aesthetica*, Frankfurt a. Main 1967, 11.

lectually as a sociological researcher he found that the traditional occidental concept of culture annihilated itself within the Holocaust. A tradition that led into inhumanity must be inhuman:

»It (culture) abhors the stench, because it stinks; because, as Brecht put it in a magnificent line, its palace is built of dogshit. Years after that line was written, Auschwitz irrefutably proved the failure of culture. That it could happen in the midst of all the traditions of philosophy, art and the enlightening sciences, says more than just that these traditions, the spirit, was not able to seize and to change man. In those fields themselves, in their emphatic claim of self-sufficiency, dwells the untruth. All culture after Auschwitz, including its urgent critique, is garbage.«[4]

A culture that enabled Auschwitz could not produce or convey any truth and so meant nothing but shit and rubbish. After the Holocaust, a culture that traded on its values stank. But that leads directly into a classical dilemma. Even criticizing the dog shit culture is impossible: how could one defend art, if the concept of autarky itself had become dirty? »Not even silence gets us out of this circle«:

»Whoever pleads for the preservation of a radically culpable and shabby culture makes himself its accomplice, while one who denies culture directly promotes the barbarism that the culture has revealed itself to be.«[5]

Those who intended to continue prewar culture were cohorts of the fascists; those who fought culture would bring barbarism. There was no way to escape this constraint by reason. »Die Hure Vernunft«, the whore of reason, without any moral prejudice, obeyed even the organizers and managers of the Holocaust.[6] But this way of thinking was a dead end. It was not only Umberto Eco who saw the impossibility of being active within a culture that had discredited itself in such a fundamental manner.[7]

---

4   Theodor W. Adorno, *Negative Dialektik*, Frankfurt a. Main 1997, 359.

5   Ibid., 360.

6   Ibid., 376.

7   Umberto Eco, *Apokalyptiker und Integrierte. Zur kritischen Kritik der Massenkultur,* Frankfurt a. Main 1989, especially »Vorwort zur deutschen Ausgabe«, 9, 11; and »Einleitung«, 21–22.

Adorno adjusted his position during the following years writing his »Negative Dialectics«, and he found a legitimate case of being productive within a cultural context. A valid form of creativity is the expression of pain:

»Perennial suffering has as much a right to expression as the martyred has to scream. Thus it may have been wrong to say that poems could not be written after Auschwitz.«[8]

The raison d'etre of art can only be one: »to withstand suffering by signalling/marking it.«[9] Enlightenment failed in making human beings more human. Culture is not apt to improve mankind; culture is not even able to relieve the pain of the tortured. But the traditions of literature, of music and visual arts can at least be used to voice the cruelty and to communicate the inhumanity.

Conversely that would mean that Kulturindustrie wants to silence the scream, the cry, the groan. Kulturindustrie pretends that during WWII nothing worth mentioning happened and that everything is back to normal, back to business as usual. Kulturindustrie puts some new paint on the blood spattered walls of occidental tradition ignoring its complete and essential collapse, interpreting the Holocaust as a momentary malfunction or an error of some misled and now eliminated historical figures. In Adorno's eyes the products of Kulturindustrie are meaningless because of this ignorance of the true (that is the failed) nature of western philosophy.

Art that still wants to be art, that still insists on a meaning as revelation of truth has to become anti-art. In his last years Adorno wrote:

»That art which holds onto its concept and refuses consumption, turns into anti-art; its uneasiness about itself, after the real disasters and in the face of future ones, to which its continued existence stands in moral disparity, informs aesthetic theory, to whose tradition such scruples were alien.«[10]

---

8   Adorno: *Negative Dialektik*, 355.

9   Theodor W. Adorno: Diskussionsbeitrag zum ersten Darmstädter Gespräch am 17.7.1950, in: Hans Gerhard Evers (Ed.), *Das Menschenbild in unserer Zeit*, Darmstadt 1950, 216.

10 Theodor W. Adorno: *Ästhetische Theorie*, Frankfurt a. Main 1970, 503.

Adorno wants aesthetical theory to teach »resistance against art as a consumer good.«[11] This is his main target: to fight a capitalist use of culture as
just another way to make money. Advertising has no chance whatsoever to
be judged as an art form. Anti-art is defined rather vaguely, but most of all,
it must not be sellable. Anti-art is not about masterpieces and enduring materials, anti-art is not about timelessness and eternal beauty, anti-art is not
about virtuosity and skill.[12] Anti-art from Adorno's point of view should be
ephemeral, time based, sketchy, open, polysemantic, torn, unsolved, uncompromising, and uneasy. It is defined by the »anti«: It is negative by definition. To the artist as well as to the designer, theory is helpful only to find
out what is to be avoided. The only sense of definitions and standards is to
delineate what is to be rejected.

In this understanding Adorno himself was a decisive advocate of modern art during the 1950s and 1960s. »I identify with the cause of modern art
in its extreme form,«[13] he confessed in 1950. He was a defender of radical
gestures – although he was more into modern music than into visual arts
like painting. Radical – in the etymological significance of a change down
to the roots bare of any compromises – to him meant to substitute works of
art by the act of making them: »To replace artworks with the process of
their own creation« which leads to the conclusion: »Radically-made art
terminates in the problem of its feasibility.«[14]

The process, not the product, a »manipulation of chance«[15], an aesthetics of do-it-yourself, the »self-made«[16] and »the once hidden moment of the
made, the manufactured«[17] are indicators of the new art, the anti-art. In the

11 Ibid., 500.

12 Jay M. Bernstein, »The Demand for Ugliness«: Picasso's Bodies, in: The Town-
    send Center for the Humanities (Ed.), *Art and Aesthetics After Adorno*, Berke-
    ley/ Los Angeles/ London 2010, 210–248.

13 Adorno: Diskussionsbeitrag zum ersten Darmstädter Gespräch am 17.7.1950, in:
    Evers (Ed.), *Das Menschenbild in unserer Zeit*, 215.

14 Adorno: *Ästhetische Theorie*, 46.

15 Ibid., 322.

16 Ibid., 506.

17 Ibid., 46.

heyday of action painting, Adorno supports the handmade, the not cleaned, but process oriented character of manipulations of accidental shapes.

Not function, nor intention, nor purpose, nor communication should be the goals of artists, but an authentic expression of pain. Even to try to be understood by a growing number of persons and to try chum up with the uneducated (like the Nazis) will carry the connotation of the »popular« and by that, will raise the suspicion of making items of trade. Adorno becomes elitist ex negativo.

CRITICAL ADVERTISING?

In his intention of unintendedness, Adorno might have felt this contradiction himself: you cannot command freedom. It is not possible to fight blind obedience with authoritative proclamations. What Adorno was unable to see in his condemnation of Kulturindustrie was that he was led by prejudices. He refused even to take a closer look at what he judged as popular. Perhaps he feared he would be contaminated or affected like he saw so many people become by Nazi propaganda as well as by Hollywood movies. And it could be that advertising and popular media like cinema, comic strips or pop music indeed mainly transport uncritical stereotypes and, in doing so, attract narrow-minded people, who are happy to be told what to do.

On the other hand, Umberto Eco's answer is appropriate for taking a closer look at comic strips like the Peanuts or Superman or at pulp literature like Ian Fleming's James Bond books. Eco presents the argument that no human exists always and only on one and the same side, but that everybody is able read both – high culture lyrics and low culture comic strips. This means that the strict categories of Adorno do not describe the social reality in a proper way.

Moreover it was precisely this discussion on the initial collapse of enlightenment that triggered developments, for instance, within the mass medium of comics that allowed dealing with the Holocaust, like Art Spiegelman did in his *Maus* books – the first Pulitzer Price winning graphic novel. *Maus* shows all of Adorno's characteristics of radical art like the do-it-yourself attitude, the sketchiness, and the reflection on the problems of its own making. The aesthetic genealogy of underground Comix by artists like Robert Crumb and others is uncompromising, torn, and radical, with no simple conclusions and solutions, made by an inspired individual instead of a profit oriented industry. Spiegelman, for sure, was able to voice the scream of the tortured

In the very same moment, *Maus* is without question an item that was produced to be sold and to be understood, a product of Kulturindustrie. The widespread discussions about the legitimacy of a Holocaust comic strip during the 1990s clearly showed that elitist strategy of critical theory was still alive. But it also showed that its contradictions still are unsolved. There is no way for Adorno's artist to survive economically in this world. Or the artist will have to make his money with another job, which may force him to compromise with the failed culture in other ways.

At the same time it is possible to imitate the aesthetic surface of do-it-yourself style in non-autonomous contexts. Advertising indeed does show some of Adorno's characteristics as well. Advertising is ephemeral and time based, sometimes even auto-reflexive, too. Some strategies make use of subculture techniques, for instance, methods of guerrilla marketing using graffiti and street art to attract the attention of specific target groups. In other cases ad strategies aim not at a direct sale of products but are conceptualized as a mere image campaign. Within these concepts advertising can address people's critical sense and their will to think for themselves, even can strengthen a self-reliant and responsible attitude – we do not buy a product, we buy a quiet consciousness. The catchword of »green washing« marks some of these strategies – although there might be business companies that honestly try to deliver moral integrity. Still most people might not be willing to believe that the message of anyone who works for profit is morally integrous.

BEYOND DICHOTOMIES

Adorno was a justly angry man and Eco was similarly justly concerned about what to do. Eco rejected Adorno's strict judgment but he still kept the categories of high and low culture. I would like to suggest, that in the time of Web 2.0 these juxtapositions of two contrasting values like mainstream vs. sub culture, like system vs. individual, like dependency vs. authenticity, like industry vs. consumer are too simple and too undifferentiated either to explain our reactions to advertising or to develop a set of ethical recommendations. No human can be educated enough not to respond emotionally to certain affections. At the same time no one in the western world is a completely helpless slave of the ›Kulturindustrie‹ or an unconscious victim of advertising. We can watch TV and be critical in the same instance. But still Adorno's critique is valid. So the question is: what can be done to keep up the political urge of freedom without nurturing either an imperative or a resigned tone?

What I want to suggest is to modify the categories and, by that, switch the perspective. Freedom is not an absolute term; total freedom is neither thinkable nor desirable. Humans, producers as well as consumers, are always free and dependant in the same instant. There is no way of thinking about a completely hermetic artwork and there is no way of thinking about any kind of ad message that would communicate to or affect each and every person on this planet. The question of freedom is a question of degrees and by that one of conventions. In order to communicate at all, we are all dependent on iconographies and typologies and on prejudices and preconceptions. Even Adorno himself necessarily had to cultivate his prejudices in order to express his horror, his anger, and his despair.

Critical theory cannot speak from outside the world. But it still is important to formulate criteria of judgment to tell the better from the less good. Neither the theory of the gaze nor of semiotics alone are apt to reason a judgment of quality beyond functionality. If Bildwissenschaften can keep up the quest for integrity without the dichotomy between indifference or confirmation, critical theory will be an important source of visual studies. For me it is not so much the decision whether a given phenomenon is to be judged as free or dependent that is important. Of more importance is the question to what degree moral integrity is of concern. This culture may be a palace built from dog shit, as Bertold Brecht suggested. Still it is a palace.

With the Holocaust, enlightenment brought its own dark twin into the world in a dialectical manner, as Adorno diagnosed. Still, the nature of human relationships are too rich to be rendered simply in right or wrong, in free or not free. Seen in this perspective Adorno's theory itself is a piece of art in his definition: a cry of pain.

REFERENCES

Adorno, Theodor W., Diskussionsbeitrag zum ersten Darmstädter Gespräch am 17.7.1950, in: Hans Gerhard Evers (Ed.): *Das Menschenbild in unserer Zeit*, Darmstadt 1950.

Adorno, Theodor W., Résumé über Kulturindustrie, in: id., *Ohne Leitbild. Parva Aesthetica*, Frankfurt a. Main 1967.

Adorno, Theodor W., *Ästhetische Theorie*, Frankfurt a. Main 1970.

Adorno, Theodor W., Culture Industry Reconsidered. (translated by Anson G. Rabinbach), in: *New German Critique*, 6, Fall 1975, 12–19.

Adorno, Theodor W., *Negative Dialektik*, Frankfurt a. Main 1997.

Bernstein, Jay M., »The Demand for Ugliness«: Picasso's Bodies, in: The Townsend Center for the Humanities (Ed.), *Art and Aesthetics After Adorno*, Berkeley/ Los Angeles/ London 2010, 210–248.

Diedrichsen, Diedrich, The Adequacy of Signs: Adorno versus Jazz and Pop, in: Nicolas Schafhausen, Vanessa Joan Müller & Michael Hirsch (Eds.), *Adorno. The Possibility of the Impossible*, Berlin 2003, 33–44.

Eco, Umberto, *Apokalyptiker und Integrierte. Zur kritischen Kritik der Massenkultur*, Frankfurt a. Main 1989.

›… things that people don't need to have but that – for *some reason* – would be a good idea to give them.‹[1]

Discussions on drawing the line between art and advertising

BERNADETTE COLLENBERG-PLOTNIKOV

1. ART, ADVERTISING, AND ART HISTORY

Were you to ask the much quoted common man – or even the less often quoted common woman – about the relation between art and advertising, you might encounter reactions of perplexity more often than not. What could, let‹s say, the *Mona Lisa* possibly have to do with the recommendation of mundane things such as washing powder, TV meals or the latest trend in fashion? Common sense, a conviction that is generally known to have a strong tendency towards conservatism, finds its scientific counterpart in traditional art history research, which understands itself as the scholarly custodian of ›high‹ art which is beyond daily life and its objective manifestations. So, although advertising is a legitimate field of research for

---

1   »An artist is somebody who produces things that people don't need to have but that he – for some reasons – thinks it would be a good idea to give them.« (Andy Warhol, *The Philosophy of Andy Warhol: [From A to B and Back Again]*, New York/ London 1975, 144.).

other sciences such as sociology or psychology due to its manifold aspects, it is not typically a subject of art history.

However, this is not the only or final word on the topic of art and advertising. Rather, the question of the relationship between art and advertising leads immediately to the central academic challenge facing the field today. A set of art historians – including particularly those who see themselves as the avant-garde of their field – regard it as the need of the hour to accommodate the fact that times have culturally changed. Thus everything hints to a radical reciprocal opening of both the spheres of art and of daily life, articulating itself with particular insistence in the aesthetic form of advertising.

To characterize these processes, the formula of the ›dissolution of artistic limits‹[2] has become widely accepted as it also embodies what is probably one of the most characteristic traits of the art world of our days – a fundamental irritation with the meaning of the term ›art‹. Where in the place of art as a more or less clearly marked area within culture, amongst others, a continuing ›aestheticization of the environment‹[3] or a common aestheticization of existence is placed; where no external criterion can be brought forward that classifies an item positively as art, the demarcation between art and non-art becomes questionable.

So the expression of the ›eloped concept of art‹ coined by the art historian Willibald Sauerländer in the 1980s for his field, namely art history, with regard to the fine arts,[4] can also be applied to all forms of art and their scientific reflections. Hence, the question of the relation of art and advertising proves to be part of a drastic problem that has been plaguing not only

2   Cf. esp. the research center ›SFB 626‹ of the Deutsche Forschungsgemeinschaft *Ästhetische Erfahrung im Zeichen der Entgrenzung der Künste*, established in 2003 at the Freie Universität Berlin (http://www.sfb626.de/index.html) [17th March, 2013].

3   Cf. Rüdiger Bubner, Ästhetisierung der Lebenswelt, in: id., *Ästhetische Erfahrung*, Frankfurt a. Main 1989, 143–156.

4   Willibald Sauerländer, Der Kunsthistoriker angesichts des entlaufenen Kunstbegriffs. Zerfällt das Paradigma einer Disziplin? [1985], in: Werner Busch, Wolfgang Kemp, Monika Steinhauser & Martin Warnke (Eds.), *Geschichte der Kunst – Gegenwart der Kritik*, Cologne 1999, 293–323.

the science of art but also cultural studies for quite a while, and also strongly concerns the relationship between art and design.

In the following, the diverging treatment of the field of advertising by art history will first be characterized and put in a context with the history of ideas. In another step, the key question of the reflection in art of the inequality of that which seems equal will be reconstructed by the use of the example of the relation of art and advertising. Furthermore, its aspects will be questioned theoretically in regard to a sustainable self-conception of the discipline of art history today.

2. ADVERTISING IN THE REFLECTION OF ART

2.1 Art and advertising as diametrical opposites

The thesis that art is something completely opposite from advertising has never been more emphatically and effectively advocated than by the US-American art critic Clement Greenberg[5] and by the German philosopher Theodor W. Adorno[6]. It is not an exaggeration to say that the theoretical concepts of art developed by both significantly unfold the difference. However it is not only about marking a difference. It is rather about defining art as a counter-pole to advertising and vice versa: presenting advertising as a counter-pole to art. This contrasting is actually remarkable. In the earlier reflections on art, the difference of art to every-day aesthetic manifestations such as caricatures, applied arts, or advertising was so implicit that it was hardly worth the time to go into further detail. Authors like Richard Muther, Aby Warburg or Alois Riegl, as representatives of the field of art history, occupied themselves with a diversity of ›borderline arts‹ as early as 1900. These were duly noted, but did not have much of an influence on the academic mainstream of a field that remained focused on exploring a European ›high‹ art untouched by daily activities. The verve with which Green-

---

5   Cf. esp. Clement Greenberg, Avant-Garde and Kitsch, in: *Partisan Review* 6/5 (1939), 34–49.

6   Cf. esp. Max Horkheimer and Theodor W. Adorno, *Dialektik der Aufklärung: Philosophische Fragmente* [1947] (= *Gesammelte Schriften*, ed. Rolf Tiedemann, vol. 3), Frankfurt a. Main 1997, 141–191.

berg and Adorno applied themselves to the contrasting of art and advertising around the middle of the twentieth century (both from a decidedly leftist position), attests to a new understanding of art that not only grew from the opposition to everyday aestheticization, but also in a sense formed an idealistic art tradition and became key issue for a radical redefinition of art: the avant-garde. Avant-garde art was ultimately a form of art, which presented and allowed the viewer to experience social conditions embodied in advertising as negative, estranged, and objectified. So only avant-garde art is true art.

Its sociocritical, utopian potential was not only achieved through the formulation of statements in regard to content here, e.g. the exposition of social ills, however legitimate they might have been in detail. Moreover, a critical approach to social contradictions could, in his view, happen exclusively in the radical, unpopular, even hermetically avant-garde creation that – as a contrast to advertising – strictly refused any kind of positive statement about a good life or indulgence. Art must keep itself clean of any influence of trivial culture. It must not mix with the likings of the masses. Furthermore, any approximation of art to the concerns of everyday life and its taste became treason in the estranged present.

With their opinions, Greenberg and Adorno argued a position for avant-garde as art of radical autonomy that, on the one hand, was quite representative of the self-conception of the artist at the time. On the other hand, contemporary art history research and art criticism also associate with this basic definition of the relation of art and life. And finally, the contemporary art-attentive audience, as far as it is ready to get involved with avant-garde, shares this tenor. As ›autonomous‹ art does its part to show the viewer's standards their limit, a new, soon omnipresent and sustainable form for art presentation continues in the same tendency: The ›White Cube‹[7] – an expression coined by Brian O'Doherty in 1976 – gave the ideal of the gallery room as another world, radically cleaned of all the profane, its most concise

---

7   Cf. Brian O'Doherty, Inside the White Cube. Notes on the Gallery Space, Part I, in: *Artforum* 14/7 (March 1976), 24–30; Part II, in: *Artforum* 14/8 (April 1976), 26–34; Part III, in: *Artforum* 15/3 (November 1976), 38–44.

figure: The viewer was not appealed to as a bodily, sensory being but – in antithesis to the strategies of advertising – merely as a ›naked eye‹.[8]

Greenberg's theses about the history of art being a process of on-going formal cleansing were met with resounding success and influenced the understanding of art in many ways until today. The same can be said for the regression and manipulation theses on culture industry advocated by Adorno, which substantially influenced the understanding of art in not only German regions. This position remained the dominant media theory until the 1980s.

2.2 Approximation of Art and Advertising

However, in the course of the new social and political movements around 1970, Adorno's position was increasingly questioned. Thus, under the influenced raised by Critical Theory, the accusation that culture industry exposes the masses to perfect manipulation could now only be branded as a paternalistic underestimation of the recipient's abilities. Overall, the accentuation of the line between art and life that Greenberg and Adorno elevate and attribute to the avant-garde now seems more than questionable. Moreover, Peter Bürger represented his view, against Adorno, with great success in the 1974 publication *Theory of Avant-Garde*. He said the significant attribute of avant-garde was the »negation of the autonomy of art«. The extensive attack of the avant-garde on modern art intended, as Bürger precisely identified, an »annihilation of art in life praxis«.[9]

With this interpretation of avant-garde, Bürger expresses an understanding of art, which has come forward in Europe as well as the USA since the 1960s. In this, one can not only see the tendency to an explicit politicization of art. Characteristically, it is primarily the striving for a leveling of the notorious ›line between art and life‹: It is not the completed piece of art that appears relevant anymore, but the event and the process in which the solidified forms of artistic production and reception are supposed to be pried open. New forms of art like Happening, Performance, Environment, et

8   Cf. esp. Karlheinz Lüdeking, Jenseits des weißen Würfels, in id., *Grenzen des Sichtbaren*, Munich 2006, 227–260.

9   Peter Bürger, *Theorie der Avantgarde*, Frankfurt a. Main 1974, 63 and 69.

cetera, are supposed to realize this minimization of the ›works‹ character of art.

In England, Eduardo Paolozzi, a member of the *Independent Group* from which the English Pop Art emerged, introduced his ›bunk‹ collages, which were inspired by the aesthetics of advertising as early as 1952, including the renowned sheet *I Was a Rich Man's Plaything*. Of course, they were immediately understood as a signal of opposition against ›high‹ art at the time. Moreover it became evident, especially in the USA, that there was a certain weariness against the radicalness which ›pope Clement‹ (Greenberg) had decreed concerning the desire of the recipient for sensuality and pleasure: Instead of formalism and monochromism, there was a demand in art for the same bustling life found in the modern world of consumerism. The triumph of Pop Art, which found its broadest and most hedonistic occurrence in the USA, marked the reclamation of art from mass media and advertising that had long occurred in the opposite direction. It also signaled the end of the era of Greenberg. Andy Warhol, as pope of this new antithetic understanding of art, embraced mass culture explicitly to systematically erase the remainders of autonomous composition:

»Business Art is a much better thing to be making than Art Art, because Art Art doesn't support the space it takes up, whereas Business Art does. (If Business Art doesn't support its own space it goes out-of-business.)«[10]

However, it had also been shown by Warhol that so-called »Art Art« – the accentedly ›artistic‹ autonomous art – was not safe per se from becoming advertising. Thus, the large-sized ›drip paintings‹ by Pollock were used as a dramatic backdrop for a fashion photo shoot of the US-American *Vogue* during an exhibition at the Betty Parsons Gallery in 1951.[11] In fact, was not the Americanization of avant-garde under Greenberg's influence as a triumph of the »American chauvinistic art critique«[12] itself a gigantic advertising campaign for the American ›way of life‹ during the Cold War? The

---

10 Andy Warhol, *The Philosophy of Andy Warhol*, 144.

11 Cf. Thomas Crow, *Modern Art in the Common Culture*, New Haven/ London 1996, 38–48, esp. 38–39.

12 Werner Spies, *Rosarot vor Miami. Ausflüge zu Kunst und Künstlern unseres Jahrhunderts*, Munich 1989, 67.

identification of independence of concreteness with personal and political independence, which seemed so plausible after the War, now appeared to be reductive.

Mass culture and advertising have since taken a permanent place in art, which can portray them in a very different way – affirmatively as characteristic in US-American Pop Art, critically or ironically. Warhol's incredibly successful commercial self presentation furthermore represented the trend of »selling the artist as a brand«.[13] This means that art does not only use advertising in the way that advertising has used art since the beginning as a source of forms and motives, but art becomes also – like almost everything – a subject of advertising itself and celebrates its own market value.

These transformations are also taken up in sophisticated art historical research. One here not only gradually begins to open up so far neglected eras, especially the nineteenth century and the (then) ›new media‹; one also increasingly engages, amongst other things, in everyday culture including advertising. Thus it becomes clear that the latter provokes quite fundamental questions. It is certainly true that advertising in the narrower sense is a »relatively young cultural phenomenon« which only established itself at the beginning of the twentieth century »as its own differentiated communication between producer and recipient«.[14] However, is advertising to be understood in the broader sense, as an offensive recommendation of certain material or ideological content brought forward by aesthetic means: Has art not always been, to considerable length, advertising itself, especially for individuals or their interests, for regimes or for religions? Ultimately, with regard to other artistic epochs, it becomes clear that the radical, purist understanding of art as defined by Greenberg and Adorno is rather an exception.

Werner Hofmann concerned himself intensively with the diversity of the so-called ›borderline arts‹ such as salon paintings, trivial art, and advertising mainly in the 1970s during his time as the director of the Hamburg Kunsthalle – picking up a research tradition founded by Aby Warburg,

---

13 Scott Lash & Urry, John, *Economies of Signs and Space*, London/ Thousand Oaks, Cal./ New Delhi 1994, 137.

14 Gregor Schwering, Werbung, in: Ralf Schnell (Ed.), *Metzler Lexikon Kultur der Gegenwart. Themen und Theorien, Formen und Institutionen seit 1945*, Stuttgart/ Weimar 2000, 535.

which had been disrupted by National Socialism.[15] In the title of the exhibition, Hofmann puts the question that had been central since the 1960s in a nutshell: *What is art?*[16] Examples that show how old, mythological themes can be manipulated and applied within advertising are supposed to deliver food for thought.

The relation of *High and Low* which is up for debate here, eventually became the idea for the title of programmatically viewed exhibition in 1991, staged by curators Kirk Varnedoe and Adam Gopnik at the *Museum of Modern Art* in New York, which advocated a similar view as Hofmann had suggested in exhibitions and publications about twenty years earlier: Modern, avant-garde art and trivial art have the same historical roots: big city life as it developed since the nineteenth century. Moreover, the iconography of day-to-day life and mass media seems to be the red thread of modern art that keeps rejuvenating and renewing it through encounters with the vital creativity of the everyday. »In the above-mentioned exposition modern art appeared as a veteran in staying alive despite its permanent struggles with ›low culture‹.«[17]

It is true that the position of art criticism that derived its energy from the opposition to the dominant idea of an autonomous ›high‹ art as an exclusive world beyond everyday life, prefigures current tendencies. It has already been rendered historical, however, from the perspective of these tendencies. Its approach to give art its rightful place ›in life‹ according to effect and origin, is now itself an idealistic relict which stays fixated on the ultimately anti-authoritarian idea of ›art‹.

In contrast, the claim is now that the nineteenth century onset and steady extension of the concept of art becomes dubious if *everything* potentially experienced can become subject of aesthetic consideration. However, it is precisely this that has been happening since the 1960s. In the course of the long lasting fight for attention, the aesthetic education and reputation of

15 Cf. esp. the anthology of Werner Hofmann, *Bruchlinien. Aufsätze zur Kunst des 19. Jahrhunderts*, Munich 1979, 149–165, 166–179, 180–200.

16 Werner Hofmann, *Kunst – was ist das?*, catalogue Hamburger Kunsthalle 1977, Cologne 1977.

17 Hans Belting, *Art History after Modernism*. Transl. by Caroline Saltzwedel, Mitch Cohen, and Kenneth Northcott, Chicago 2003 (German: *Das Ende der Kunstgeschichte: Eine Revision nach zehn Jahren*, Munich 1995), 80.

marketing specialists has progressed so much that, since the 1980s, one increasingly encounters the conviction that »advertising itself becomes art«.[18] Thus the art historian and image theorist Hans Belting states:

»Today, visual advertising has been a commodity in its own right, and with a quasi-autonomous aesthetic: it sells itself; the market-success of Calvin Klein proves this sufficiently. [...] By aestheticizing our environment, it is seizing control of some of art's public realms. In this interchange, art retains only the role of exposing and revealing the illusion inherent in the advertising products.«[19]

It is no longer about art being entrapped in manifold ways in advertising and everyday life. His diagnosis is that now the non-artistic is upgraded and presented in a world completely defined by media and in such a way that its aesthetic character imposes itself upon it. Art as a paradigm of the aesthetic experience steps back for this very reason. What is more: It has pulled ahead of art in quantity as well as in its meaning for the human awareness – i.e. quantitatively as well as qualitatively. The historical period that postulated art as an autonomous area therefore seems to be dissolving. And this is surely not about the celebration of the hegemony of an event culture: In the face of authoritarian art judgementalism, »genie cult, uniqueness and performance myths« as well as »tax payer insanity« that the concept of art seems to be catering to today, the ›avoidance of the concept of art‹ appears to be progressive in this day and age.[20]

The aesthetic discussion accounts for this dissolution of artistic limits and voidance of the concept of art by moving different, more inclusive terms to the centre of reflection instead of the concept of art itself. With these, especially the shift to the ›image‹ as a new paradigm of a media-created culture of dissolution, gains importance. When it comes to the theo-

---

18 Mark Siemons, *Schöne neue Gegenwelt: Über Kultur, Moral und andere Marketingstrategien*, Frankfurt a. Main/ New York 1993, 54.

Cf. esp. Mark Napierala & Tilman Reitz, Warenästhetik/Kulturindustrie, in: Karlheinz Barck, Martin Fontius, Burkhart Steinwachs & Friedrich Wolfzettel (Eds.), *Ästhetische Grundbegriffe*, Stuttgart 2000–2005, vol. 6 (2005), 479.

19 Hans Belting, *Art History after Modernism*, 79.

20 Diedrich Diederichsen, Kunst und Nichtkunst, in: id., *Eigenblutdoping. Selbstverwertung, Künstlerromantik, Partizipation*, Cologne 2008, 214 and 216.

retical dispute about the aesthetic aspects of commodities and advertising, the preferred choice of words is the more neutral ›mass culture‹ over the controversial ›culture industry‹. It is about analyzing the producers' competency to manipulate »as competency to design, or even communicate«.[21] The polemical term ›commodity aesthetics‹ is replaced with neologisms like ›product culture‹, ›media aesthetics‹, ›aesthetic communication‹, ›communication design‹, ›business communication‹, ›social communication‹ or ›visual culture‹ that are supposed to express the meaning of the dissolute aesthetic and at the same time tear down the demarcations of the old academic interdisciplinary fields of research.[22]

From an art historical perspective that agrees to this view of things, this means nothing less than its loss of the object of art, meaning art as specific cultural context. The concept of art functions therefore merely as relict of an anachronistic Euro-, Christo- and Logocentrism – in short: as »mortgage of thought« (Denkhypothek).[23] For this reason, the ›end of art history‹ serves Belting and many of his colleagues as the central challenge for the readjustment of the field.

The redesign of the traditional field of study to a common science of the visual that – with the greatest possible contrast to the limitations of ›high‹ and Christian-European art – devotes itself to a new field of research: ›Visual Culture‹ is considered a solution. The terms ›art history‹ or ›science of art‹ then merely refer to the inertia of institutional structures.

3. Unequal Equality – The Discrimination between Art and Advertising as Basis for a Destination of Art History today

The processes that are being discussed as the ›dissolution of artistic limits‹ can be denied only by accepting a radical loss of application in today's world. After all, in considering the relation of art and advertising by taking

---

21 Mark Napierala & Tilman Reitz, Warenästhetik/Kulturindustrie, 478.

22 Cf. ibid.

23 Hans Belting, Mit welchem Bildbegriff wird gestritten?, in: *Frankfurter Allgemeine Zeitung* 117 (21st May, 2001), 9.

into account such dissolution, it is doubtful that the purpose of a certain object – work of art or advertising – can be identified with certainty. This does not only concern newer developments. For example, one may think of Watteau's *Shop Sign of the Art Dealer Gersaint*, a shop sign that Frederick the Great bought in the 1740s for his gallery at a price then commonly considered ›exorbitant‹. Does such a case not show firstly, that art that is supposed to be sold also inevitably becomes a matter of advertising and, secondly, that advertising has – as early as the eighteenth century – become art? Even more: Does this not reveal that advertising can *be* art and art can *be* advertising? Evidently the line between art and advertising is somewhat diffuse as both are similar in many aspects. To name a few, both work with aesthetic means (the decided abandonment of ›artificiality‹ is also a part of this), both approach their recipient (this is to say, both want to transport a message in the medium of the senses), and both are objects of collective emotion and identification.

On the other hand, the acceptance of a categorical difference between art and advertising is by no means a necessary testament to blind traditionalism and an anachronistic defense of the professional interests of art history. It has to be noted that the concept of art in the sense of fine arts – however understood – is still institutionally and linguistically present. Therefore, it seems likely that it is »not semantically empty but possesses specific meaning«.[24] The abandonment of art history as science of the (fine) arts, seemingly the rescue of the disciplinary reference to reality under one aspect, has, from a different perspective, to be criticized as reduction of more differentiated cultural facts. One reaches this conclusion not only via a linguistic-analytical but also through an ideology-critical perspective.[25] After

---

24 Reinold Schmücker, Ästhetik und allgemeine Kunstwissenschaft. Zur Aktualität eines historischen Projekts, in: Alice Bolterauer & Elfriede Wiltschnigg, *Kunstgrenzen: Funktionsräume der Ästhetik in Moderne und Postmoderne*, Vienna 2001, 61.

25 Among the art historians cf. esp. Hal Foster, *Design and Crime: And Other Diatribes*, London/ New York 2002, esp. 3–12 and 83–103; Wolfgang Kemp, Reif für die Matrix. Kunstgeschichte als Bildwissenschaft, in: *Neue Rundschau 114/3* (2003), 39–49; Willibald Sauerländer, Der Kunsthistoriker angesichts des entlaufenen Kunstbegriffs; id., Iconic turn? Eine Bitte um Ikonoklasmus, in: Christa Maar and Hubert Burda (Eds.), *Iconic Turn: Die neue Macht der Bilder*, Co-

all there is no need for the concept of art – as is especially pointed out by the critique of the »strong concept of art« – to carry the »stigma of the elitist«. Although *de facto*, as the critics of the concept of art claim, »the ability to occupy oneself with an item beyond its everyday function be a sign of the ruling class«, this fact, however, »does not criticize the content of the privilege but its unjust distribution«.[26]

Facing the stated diffuse line, there certainly is no scope to return to a »strong concept of art«[27] in the sense of Greenberg or Adorno. Also, regarding the modified conditions of living in present times, it would be missing the mark to keep alive the traditionally widespread fixation with European and Christian art of the German-speaking region in principle. It has become a social consensus to view the dissolution of artistic limits and accordingly the permeability of demarcations of different types as a central factor of the current experience of reality. And the dominance of an experience is already an adequate argument to deliberate it scientifically. However, such deliberation does not necessarily contain the argument that the dispute of demarcations means the irrelevance of demarcations. On the contrary, the tendency to dedifferentiation can also be seen as cause for the redetermination of definition. Ultimately, even a striking resemblance does not necessarily indicate identity – any encounter with a pair of twins underlines this argument. So it turns out to be a platitude that mere similarity (as also noted e.g. by Nelson Goodman), says nothing about the essence of a thing

---

logne 2004, 407–426; id., Kunstgeschichte und Bildwissenschaft, in: Josef Früchtl and Maria Moog-Grünewald (Eds.), *Ästhetik in metaphysikkritischen Zeiten: 100 Jahre »Zeitschrift für Ästhetik und Allgemeine Kunstwissenschaft«* (= *Zeitschrift für Ästhetik und Allgemeine Kunstwissenschaft*, special issue 8) Hamburg 2007, 93–108.

Among the philosophers of the Berlin research center SFB 626 cf. esp. the works of Juliane Rebentisch, e.g.: Autonomie? Autonomie! Ästhetische Erfahrung heute, in: Sonderforschungsbereich 626 (Ed.), *Ästhetische Erfahrung: Gegenstände, Konzepte, Geschichtlichkeit*, Berlin 2006, http://www.sfb626.de/ver oeffentlichungen/online/aesth_erfahrung/aufsaetze/rebentisch.pdf [17th of March 2013].

26 Diedrich Diederichsen, Kunst und Nichtkunst, 214–215.

27 Ibid., 214.

or being. In one way or another, every thing is similar to an arbitrary other.[28]

Nonetheless the obvious similarity of art and advertising is not trivial. It can, as has already happened within the last couple of years with the relations between art and design,[29] art and image[30] – or even art and art forgery[31] – be used as a starting point for a redefinition of art and art history in the face of a permeable demarcation with everyday life.

3.1 Art History and Art Theory

In this context, arguments by the US-American philosopher Arthur C. Danto as a specialist for differences in the similar can be helpful. Danto's philosophical, and more specifically art-philosophical interest in general, inflamed with the so-called »phenomenon of confusable counterparts«,[32] holds that items, which are albeit physically indistinguishable, belong to different ontological categories. For Danto, this phenomenon, in which it becomes impossible to make a distinction simply through classification – as there is no perceivable and hence empirically scientific difference – poses a question of *philosophical* explanation. In these cases, it is not a matter of detecting the ›natural‹ but much more of analyzing the ›categorical‹ differ-

---

28 »That a two given things are similar will hardly be notable news if there are no two things that are not similar.« (Nelson Goodman, Seven Strictures on Similarity, in: Lawrence Foster & Joe William Swanson (Eds.) *Experience and Theory*, Massachusetts 1970, 25.)

29 Cf. Jakob Steinbrenner, Wann ist Design? Design zwischen Funktion und Kunst, in: Julian Nida-Rümelin & Jakob Steinbrenner (Eds.), *Ästhetische Werte und Design*, Ostfildern 2011, 11–30; Catrin Misselhorn, Die symbolische Dimension der ästhetischen Erfahrung von Kunst und Design, in: ibid., 75–96.

30 Cf. esp. Willibald Sauerländer, Der Kunsthistoriker angesichts des entlaufenen Kunstbegriffs; and id., Iconic turn?

31 See esp. Reinold Schmücker, Lob der Fälschung, in: Julian Nida-Rümelin & Jakob Steinbrenner (Eds.), *Original und Fälschung*, Ostfildern 2011, 71–91.

32 Arthur C. Danto, *The Transfiguration of the Commonplace. A Philosophy of Art*, Cambridge, Mass./ London 1981, 138.

ence in ›structure‹.[33] As he explained in reference to the analytic philosopher Peter Strawson in the essay, *The Artworld*, which started his art-philosophical career in 1964, this can be the difference between a material body and a person.[34] The difference does not arise from the perceived or even the perceivable differences, but rather from the different *interpretations* of the perceived. Nonetheless this kind of distinction is not trivial, but rather it is essential for human perceptions of reality. If it is amiss, the ontological status of the object will be misinterpreted. The confusion or identification of both ›counterparts‹ is therefore not only wrong, but »categori[c]ally false«.[35] This means that philosophical problems arise at a time when we face »perceptually indiscernible counterparts«[36] which belong to different ontological categories.

It is contemporary Pop Art which, in Danto's eyes, made this phenomenon virulent for art by elevating the selectively enacted possibility shown by Duchamp in his *ready mades* that even objects of day-to-day life can be, without obvious visible interference – as Danto later puts it – »transfigured«[37] to art, to the central art principle. Self-made legend has it, that it was the exhibition of Andy Warhol's *Brillo Boxes* in a New York gallery in 1964 that inspired Danto to write *The Artworld* and accompanied his reflections on art. These objects were ›transfigured‹ to art: Even though they were reconstructed from plywood, they were indistinguishable from the mundane boxes of cardboard for steel wool sponges by Brillo, which filled countless shelves in American supermarkets everywhere.

For innovative objects like Warhol's *Brillo Boxes* to be approved as art, one has to include convincingly, as linguistic analytic diction has it, an object which is ›a candidate for the status of artwork‹ into an art theoretical and art historical context: »To see something as art requires something the

---

33 Cf. e.g. Arthur C. Danto, Philosophizing Literature, in his *The Philosophical Disenfranchisement of Art*, New York 1986, 163–186, esp. 170–171.

34 Cf. Arthur C. Danto, The Artworld, in: *The Journal of Philosophy* 61/19 (1964), 571–584; reprinted e.g. in: *Aesthetics and the Philosophy of Art. The Analytic Tradition. An Anthology*, ed. Peter Lamarque and Stein Haugom Olsen, Malden [Mass.]/Oxford 2004 (Blackwell philosophy anthologies. 21), 27–34, esp. 30.

35 Arthur C. Danto, *The Transfiguration*, 139; cf. 192.

36 Ibid., 133 e.g.

37 Ibid., 61.

eye cannot descry – an atmosphere of artistic theory, a knowledge of the history of art: an artworld«.[38] The object understood as work of art is therefore radically under-identified and differs from his material substrate by its linkage to art theory and art history. Hence, the acknowledgement as a work of art is not at all an arbitrary act by some artworld authority. Moreover, it is through an institutionalized »discourse of reasons«,[39] that players in the art world find out if the object can be plausibly integrated in a particular art theoretical and art historical context. The interpretation of the work of art, too, is by no means arbitrary and can, in fact, be correct or wrong – depending on the compatibility of the art historically and art theoretically situated meaning and the embodied work of art.[40] Narrowing in on the relation of art and advertising as an exemplary case of such »confusable counterparts«,[41] Danto distinguishes three possible constellations that mark an art theoretical and an art historical sequence at the same time. On the one hand, artists had developed a style, especially characteristic for the time around 1900 with Toulouse-Lautrec, which »had an instant application in producing visual excitement in commercial messages«. Secondly, the advertising industry could make identifiable works of high art its own – as in the above-mentioned fashion photo shoot in front of the Pollock backdrop in the 1950s – that »in order to give a certain inflection to their messages, in turn calculated to create a certain attitude in the viewer's mind toward the product actually advertised«. Crucial for this relation is »that the art used as a visual associate for the product advertised have no direct association with that product, or with commerce in fact at all«. Advertising builds on the cultural dominance of a ›strong‹ concept of art in its target group and paradoxically lives on it. From Danto's perspective, the constellation becomes philosophically interesting when – as in the 1960s with Warhol at the head of the movement – »works of art draw on certain idioms of advertising which themselves need to have had no special artistic intention at all«. The

38 Arthur C. Danto, The Artworld, 32.
39 Arthur C. Danto, The Art World Revisited. Comedies of Similarities, in: id., *Beyond the Brillo Box: The Visual Arts in Post-Historical Perspective*, New York 1992, 40.
40 Cf. Arthur C. Danto, Appreciation and Interpretation, in id., *The Philosophical Disenfranchisement of Art*. 23–46, esp. 43–46.
41 Arthur C. Danto, *The Transfiguration*, 138.

»boundary between high and low« so to speak, is not annihilated from ›below‹ but the other way around from ›above‹. The opposition to the strong concept of art, which was the premise for the second relation, becomes so extreme that this version of the relation of art and advertising »was less an artistic breakthrough« than a cultural revolution« utilizing mere items of daily use, »to transform means into meanings« and therein envision, what objects are to a human being or at least could be.[42]

These considerations signify firstly that art history is *possible,* even when facing diffuse lines, and secondly, that it does not have to lean solely on immanent formal analysis for the identification of its objects, but has to *argue* decisively in an *art historical* and *art theoretical* way. That is already a lot to begin with. However, it is not surprising that the concept of art can be supported by art history as well as art theory. Such an argumentation, if it stops there, is circular and is unable to leave the ›artworld‹ as the elitist exclusivity described by Danto. The latter has been accused of this on various occasions.[43]

However, in recourse to Danto's just cited statement, one can definitely develop arguments that not only make it plausible that art history is possible, but that it is *meaningful* and culturally significant today: In contrast to the mundane objects he utilized, Warhol was able ›to transform means into meanings‹.

3.2 The cultural meaning of Art History

The specific potential of art to transform means into visual meaning, is, according to Danto, the grace of its self-reflecting, ›metaphoric‹ structure: In contrast to non-artistic forms of representation, a work of art presents its content always in a way that never adds up simply in the purpose of trans-

---

42 Arthur C. Danto, High Art, Low Art, and the Spirit of History, in id., *Beyond the Brillo Box*, New York 1992, 151–155 – Cf. esp. Id., Hand-Painted Pop, in his *The Madonna of the Future. Essays in a Pluralistic Art World*, Berkeley/ Los Angeles/ London 2001, 11–19, esp. 12–13.

43 Cf. esp. Richard Shusterman, *Surface and Depth. Dialectics of Criticism and Culture*, Ithaca 2002, esp. 175–190; cf. also id., Art in a Box, in: Mark Rollins (Ed.), *Danto and his Critics* (= Philosophers and their critics. 4), Oxford/ Cambridge, Mass. 1993, 161–174.

porting a message. Moreover, the form of representation itself is part of the content, as much as the content is part of the form of representation:

»Any representation not an artwork can be matched by one that is one, the difference lying in the fact that the artwork uses the way the nonartwork presents its content to make a point about how that content is presented.«[44]

At this point, one might argue against the considerations of Danto that the modality of presentation is always relevant – and this applies to the non-artistic space as well: There is absolutely no content without form, no form without content. This is exactly what the US-American philosopher and cognitive scientist Jerry Fodor considers in dealing with Danto and brings to bear in concrete context with a categorical distinction between art and advertising.[45]

According to Fodor, the decisive difference between art and elocution (he classifies advertising as a case of elocution) is »not in the *effects they aim at*, but in the *means that they employ* to make their effects«. Art and advertising both initially appeal to an audience they would like to address. One can imagine examples, says Fodor, »in which the two aim at much the same effect«. And both likewise suffice the »reflexive condition« of any act of communication. Works of art *and* advertising »are intended to affect audiences in certain ways, and to do so partly in consequence of the audience's recognition of this intention«.[46]

Fodor recognizes the *difference* between art and advertising in the fact that advertising utilizes this ›reflexive condition‹ merely as a means to a

---

44 Arthur C. Danto, *The Transfiguration*, 146.

45 Later, Danto himself has taken into account the fact that every artifact, not only a work of art, is an embodied meaning by characterizing the difference between the ›real‹ Brillo boxes und Warhol's boxes no longer as the difference between ›reality‹ and ›art‹, but between ›commercial art‹ and ›fine art‹. – Cf. Arthur C. Danto, Art and Meaning, in: id., *The Madonna of the Future*, XVII–XXX, esp. XXIII–XXX.

46 Jerry Fodor, Déjà vu All Over Again. How Danto's Aesthetics Recapitulates the Philosophy of Mind, in: Mark Rollins (Ed.), *Danto and his Critics* (= Philosophers and their critics. 14), second ed., Malden, MA 2012, 61–62. (first ed. Oxford/ Cambridge, Mass. 1993, 41–54). 61–62.

cause – the marketing of a product. It ultimately aims for, when it comes to means of representation, the status of sheer transparency. Works of art, on the other hand, says Fodor, specifically put their ›reflexive condition‹ in the front: The way representation is supposed to carry a meaning is not only the means to accomplishing an end but stands, moreover, in the centre of attention:

»I take the moral to be that the intention that the reflexive condition be satisfied is *primary* in the case of the artwork but only *secondary* in the case of the ad. In so far as a thing is not primarily intended to satisfy the reflexive condition, it is not intended to be an artwork. [...] So that's what distinguishes artworks from ads (and, *mutatis mutandis*, from other sorts of rhetorical gestures).«[47]

Fodor concludes that the difference between art and advertising is merely quantitative one in regard to the ›satisfaction of reflexive condition‹. However, there are good reasons – as in any categorical difference – to argue that it is a matter of *qualitative difference.* The difference between art and advertising does not lie in the rhetorical, respectively the argumentative element. It also does not lie in the criteria of the aesthetic or in the grade of refinement the aesthetic is presented in. And it does not lie in the aspect of commercial or convenient as such. In the end, and in most cases, art can and should also be sold, and in the course of the history of art, it has taken on a variety of non-artistic functions. However, there is a specific purpose to advertising and a specific purpose to art.

Advertising is always about a direct or indirect manipulation of the human (buying) pattern. This also generally applies not only to goods like washing powder, which are supposed to be sold, but also to an attitude of life. So advanced advertising nowadays tries to reinforce the ostensible appeal to buy through the labored aestheticization tailored to target groups, in order to create new taste and belief alliances and to award the produced object »cult status«.[48] But here as well, advertising that does not intend strategically to influence and that does not want to sell a product, is not advertis-

---

47 Ibid., 63.

48 Hubert Mohr, Kult. IV. Kultästhetik als Forschungsgegenstand, in: *Ästhetische Grundbegriffe*, vol. 3 (2001), 507.

ing. In contrast, art that does not strategically intend to influence and does not want to sell, is still art.

Art is principally geared to make the ›reflexive condition‹ *as such* a topic – independent of the ever-present potential intention to market one's works, use them as means for propaganda, et cetera. This links art to science, which deals with the ›reflexive condition‹ not with the senses, but rather with conceptual means. However, it differs from advertising. It only loses its status as art, when it renounces its ›reflexive condition‹ as *conditio humana* – the need for self-conception in a sensory medium. One can even identify works of art as those objects of perception that differ from others by suggesting a question for meaning,[49] as they are characterized by an idiosyncratic »need for interpretation«:[50] In contrast to day-to-day experiences as delivered by advertising, aesthetical art experience »*flows into an effort for understanding*«.[51]

According to Danto, however, this difference between art and advertising is none that would be recognizable on a level of the senses – without the sensory being irrelevant in the work of art: In a basic principle following this argument, an object can be advertising, and its physically indistinguishable ›counterpart‹ can be art. Which is which, says Danto, has significantly »something to do with its history, with the way in which it arrived in the world«. To experience that the ›history‹ of an object is artistic, therefore means »that it has qualities to attend to which its untransfigured counterpart lacks, and that our aesthetic responses will be different«.[52] This means that reactions differ depending on what we know about the ›history‹ of the object. Historical and art theoretical knowledge is therefore necessary for the identification of works of art as works of art.

The extension of subjective experience through such knowledge is necessary for the appreciation of the potential for meaning as a way of self-communication in the visual medium, which has received different appearances in the course of art history in different epochs and cultures.

---

49 Reinold Schmücker, Ästhetik und allgemeine Kunstwissenschaft, 60.
50 Jens Kulenkampff, *Kants Logik des ästhetischen Urteils*, Frankfurt a. Main 1978, 160.
51 Reinold Schmücker, Lob der Fälschung, 84.
52 Arthur C. Danto, *The Transfiguration*, 44 and 99.

Advertising can utilize works or means of art without being art, as well as art can use advertising or the strategies of representation of advertising without becoming advertising. Furthermore, art history can list many examples where advertising, once its advertising purpose is merely present as historical knowledge, can become art. (A parallel case of such ›becoming art‹ lies especially in sacral works of art that are placed in a museum with their religious functions present merely as historic knowledge.) A little more delicate is the implied question of whether a work of art utilized for the purpose of advertising (which does not necessarily have to change its art character) becomes advertising itself.

How are we to understand, for example, the case of Watteau's *Shop Sign of the Art Dealer Gersaint*, which obviously fulfilled both functions? In this, various positions are possible and can be constructed with valid arguments: On the one hand, one can advocate the relativistic, respectively institutionalistic thesis that the object painted by Watteau may be art or advertising, depending on the functional and institutional framework it is in. Basically this means that it could be removed from the art museum it is in today and placed in its original place on the facade of a picture gallery to attract customers. In this context, the object would be advertising (for art) rather than art. On the other hand, one can argue – and this would be Danto's ontologistic position – that once an object is acknowledged as art, it can only lose its place in the artworld again at the price of barbarism. For the difference between art and daily objects is, says Danto, ultimately »not institutional, it is ontological. We are dealing with an altogether different order of things«.[53] The road to artistic acknowledgement, therefore, would be a one-way street.

What do these contemplations imply for the self-conception of the field of art history? After all, the question has to be settled why an engagement with art would not only be possible in principle but would also be culturally significant.

The social relevance of art history lies, *firstly*, in the prevention of categorical mix-ups through the reconstruction of an art historical and art theoretical context – the ›histories‹ of how the works came to be – and in the provision of a foundation for the peculiar ›need for interpretation‹ of art. *Secondly,* it lies in keeping the potential of art available by appropriate con-

---

53 Ibid., 99.

servation and presentation of art objects; and *thirdly,* in the exemplary involvement in the process of interpretation that answers ›the need for interpretation‹ of art, to give a voice to its historically and culturally bound
presence of meaning in the sensory. In conclusion, art is – especially in
contrast to advertising – not lastly:

»the only socially guaranteed area in which I am still ready to listen to this, whose
voice is normally too weak and nothing penetrates the filters of my ego-
management. And it is about taking this area, enlarging it and reinforcing its reso-
nance.«[54]

An art history that takes over this social function has to be a field that understands itself decidedly as science of art but also accounts for the fact that
this subject can (now) only be identified and understood in relation to non-
artistic subjects – that is to say, in a context of cultural constellations. It has
to refer to a concept of art that places the function of art in a continuum of
rooms of human experience and activity, but also identifies them by their
specific features. Or to put it differently: If it does not want to shift into the
research of overlapping cultural coherences but rather stay the history of
art, art history must operate as cultural history. The ultimate goal is to research the function of art and culture, namely its meaning as portrayal of
›the wisdom of the people‹.[55]

---

54 Diedrich Diederichsen, Kunst und Nichtkunst, 234.
55 Cf. Georg Wilhelm Friedrich Hegel, *Philosophie der Kunst oder Ästhetik: Nach*
    Hegel. Im Sommer 1826 (lecture notes by Hermann von Kehler) (= jena-sophia.
    I.2 ed. Annemarie Gethmann-Siefert and Bernadette Collenberg-Plotnikov) Mu-
    nich 2004, 2.

REFERENCES

Belting, Hans, *Art History after Modernism*. Transl. by Caroline Saltzwedel, Mitch Cohen, and Kenneth Northcott, Chicago 2003 (German: *Das Ende der Kunstgeschichte: Eine Revision nach zehn Jahren*, Munich 1995).

Belting, Hans, Mit welchem Bildbegriff wird gestritten?, in: *Frankfurter Allgemeine Zeitung* 117 (21st May, 2001), 9.

Bubner, Rüdiger, Ästhetisierung der Lebenswelt, in: id., *Ästhetische Erfahrung*, Frankfurt a. Main 1989, 143–156.

Bürger, Peter, *Theorie der Avantgarde*, Frankfurt a. Main 1974.

Crow, Thomas, *Modern Art in the Common Culture*, New Haven/ London 1996.

Danto, Arthur C., Appreciation and Interpretation, in: id., *The Philosophical Disenfranchisement of Art*. 23–46.

Danto, Arthur C., Art and Meaning, in: id., *The Madonna of the Future*, XVII–XXX, esp. XXIII–XXX.

Danto, Arthur C., High Art, Low Art, and the Spirit of History, in: id., *Beyond the Brillo Box*, New York 1992, 146–160.

Danto, Arthur C., Philosophizing Literature, in: id., *The Philosophical Disenfranchisement of Art*, New York 1986, 163–186.

Danto, Arthur C., The Art World Revisited. Comedies of Similarities, in: id., *Beyond the Brillo Box: The Visual Arts in Post-Historical Perspective*, New York 1992, 32–53.

Danto, Arthur C., The Artworld, in: *The Journal of Philosophy* 61/19 (1964), 571–584; reprinted e.g. in: Peter Lamarque & Stein Haugom Olsen (Eds.), *Aesthetics and the Philosophy of Art. The Analytic Tradition. An Anthology* (= Blackwell philosophy anthologies 21), Malden, Mass./ Oxford 2004, 27–34.

Danto, Arthur C., *The Transfiguration of the Commonplace. A Philosophy of Art*, Cambridge, Mass./ London 1981.

Diederichsen, Diedrich, Kunst und Nichtkunst, in: id., *Eigenblutdoping. Selbstverwertung, Künstlerromantik, Partizipation*, Cologne 2008, 213–240.

Fodor, Jerry, Déjà vu All Over Again. How Danto's Aesthetics Recapitulates the Philosophy of Mind, in: Mark Rollins (Ed.), *Danto and his*

Critics (= Philosophers and their critics. 14), second ed., Malden, MA 2012, 55–68 (first ed. Oxford/ Cambridge, Mass. 1993, 41–54).

Foster, Hal, *Design and Crime. And Other Diatribes*, London/ New York 2002.

Goodman, Nelson, Seven Strictures on Similarity, in: Lawrence Foster & Joe William Swanson (Eds.) *Experience and Theory*, Massachusetts 1970, 19–29.

Greenberg, Clement, Avant-Garde and Kitsch, in: *Partisan Review* 6/5 (1939), 34–49.

Hegel, Georg Wilhelm Friedrich, *Philosophie der Kunst oder Ästhetik: Nach Hegel. Im Sommer 1826 (lecture notes by Hermann von Kehler)* (= jena-sophia. I.2, ed. Annemarie Gethmann-Siefert and Bernadette Collenberg-Plotnikov) Munich 2004.

Hofmann, Werner, *Bruchlinien. Aufsätze zur Kunst des 19. Jahrhunderts*, Munich 1979.

Hofmann, Werner, *Kunst – was ist das?,* catalogue Hamburger Kunsthalle 1977, Cologne 1977.

Horkheimer, Max & Adorno, Theodor W., *Dialektik der Aufklärung. Philosophische Fragmente* [1947] (= *Gesammelte Schriften*, ed. Rolf Tiedemann, vol. 3) Frankfurt a. Main 1997.

Kemp, Wolfgang, Reif für die Matrix. Kunstgeschichte als Bildwissenschaft, in: *Neue Rundschau* 114/3 (2003), 39–49.

Kulenkampff, Jens, *Kants Logik des ästhetischen Urteils*, Frankfurt a. Main 1978.

Lash, Scott & Urry, John, *Economies of Signs and Space*, London/ Thousand Oaks, Cal./ New Delhi 1994.

Lüdeking, Karlheinz, Jenseits des weißen Würfels, in: id., *Grenzen des Sichtbaren*, Munich 2006, 227–260.

Misselhorn, Catrin, Die symbolische Dimension der ästhetischen Erfahrung von Kunst und Design, in: Julian Nida-Rümelin & J. Steinbrenner (Eds.), *Ästhetische Werte und Design*, Ostfildern 2011, 75–96.

Mohr, Hubert, Kult. IV. Kultästhetik als Forschungsgegenstand, in: *Ästhetische Grundbegriffe, vol. 3* (2001), 497–510.

Napierala, Mark & Tilman Reitz, Warenästhetik/Kulturindustrie, in: Karlheinz Barck, Martin Fontius, Burkhart Steinwachs & Friedrich Wolfzettel (Eds.), *Ästhetische Grundbegriffe*, Stuttgart 2000–2005, vol. 6 (2005), 461–481.

O'Doherty, Brian, Inside the White Cube. Notes on the Gallery Space, Part I, in: *Artforum* 14/7 (March 1976), 24–30.

Id., Part II, in: *Artforum* 14/8 (April 1976), 26–34.

Id., Part III, in: *Artforum* 15/3 (November 1976), 38–44.

Sauerländer, Willibald, Der Kunsthistoriker angesichts des entlaufenen Kunstbegriffs. Zerfällt das Paradigma einer Disziplin? [1985], in: Werner Busch, Wolfgang Kemp, Monika Steinhauser & Martin Warnke (Eds.), *Geschichte der Kunst – Gegenwart der Kritik*, Cologne 1999, 293–323.

Sauerländer, Willibald, Iconic turn? Eine Bitte um Ikonoklasmus, in: Christa Maar & Hubert Burda (Eds.), *Iconic Turn: Die neue Macht der Bilder*. Cologne 2004, 407–426.

Sauerländer, Willibald, Kunstgeschichte und Bildwissenschaft, in: *Ästhetik in metaphysikkritischen Zeiten: 100 Jahre »Zeitschrift für Ästhetik und Allgemeine Kunstwissenschaft«* (*Zeitschrift für Ästhetik und Allgemeine Kunstwissenschaft*, special issue 8, ed. Josef Früchtl & Maria Moog-Grünewald), Hamburg 2007, 93–108.

Schmücker, Reinold, Ästhetik und allgemeine Kunstwissenschaft. Zur Aktualität eines historischen Projekts, in: Alice Bolterauer & Elfriede Wiltschnigg (Eds.), *Kunstgrenzen: Funktionsräume der Ästhetik in Moderne und Postmoderne*, Vienna 2001, 53–67.

Schmücker, Reinold, Lob der Fälschung, in: Julian Nida-Rümelin & Jakob Steinbrenner (Eds.), *Original und Fälschung*, Ostfildern 2011, 71–91.

Schwering, Gregor, Werbung, in: Ralf Schnell (Ed.), *Metzler Lexikon Kultur der Gegenwart. Themen und Theorien, Formen und Institutionen seit 1945*, Stuttgart/ Weimar 2000.

Shusterman, Richard, Art in a Box, in: Mark Rollins (Ed.), *Danto and his Critics* (= Philosophers and their critics. 4), Oxford/ Cambridge, Mass. 1993, 161–174.

Shusterman, Richard, *Surface and Depth. Dialectics of Criticism and Culture*, Ithaca 2002.

Siemons, Mark, *Schöne neue Gegenwelt. Über Kultur, Moral und andere Marketingstrategien*, Frankfurt a. Main/ New York 1993.

Spies, Werner, *Rosarot vor Miami. Ausflüge zu Kunst und Künstlern unseres Jahrhunderts*, Munich 1989.

Steinbrenner, Jakob, Wann ist Design? Design zwischen Funktion und Kunst, in: Julian Nida-Rümelin & Jakob Steinbrenner (Eds.), *Ästhetische Werte und Design*, Ostfildern 2011, 11–30.

Warhol, Andy, *The Philosophy of Andy Warhol: From A to B and Back Again*, New York/ London 1975.

Internet sources

Juliane Rebentisch, Autonomie? Autonomie! Ästhetische Erfahrung heute, in: *Ästhetische Erfahrung. Gegenstände, Konzepte, Geschichtlichkeit*, ed. Sonderforschungsbereich 626, Berlin 2006, (http://www.sfb626 .de/veroeffentlichungen/online/aesth_erfahrung/aufsaetze/rebentisch.pd f) [17th March, 2013].

The research center ›SFB 626‹ of the Deutsche Forschungsgemeinschaft *Ästhetische Erfahrung im Zeichen der Entgrenzung der Künste*, established in 2003 at the Freie Universität Berlin (http://www.sfb626.de /index.html) [17th March, 2013].

Authors

Aulinger, Barbara, studied art history and sociology in Graz, postdoctoral degree (Habilitation) in art history and art sociology in 1999. Has taught at the Karl-Franzens-Universität Graz, at the University of Salzburg and the Fachhochschule Joanneum Graz for Industrial Design. Her research interests are art theory, design, 19th century and classical modernism. Various publications in the fields of art sociology and art history, including *Die Geschichte der Östereichischen Banknoten vom Gulden zum Euro* (The History of Austrian Paper Money from the Gulden to the Euro).

Collenberg-Plotnikov, Bernadette, studied art history, Latin languages, and philosophy at the Universities of Bochum, Paris, and Constance. She received her doctorate in 1996 at Freie Universität Berlin, postdoctoral degree (Habilitation) in 2009 at FernUniversität in Hagen. She has held lectureships at Folkwang Universität der Künste (Essen) and at the Department of Design of Fachhochschule Dortmund. She is currently a researcher at the Hegel-Archiv of Ruhr-Universität Bochum and teaches at FernUniversität Hagen.

Flath, Beate, Dr.phil., studied musicology, art history and business at the University of Graz. She was awarded a scholarship from the Faculty of Arts and Humanities and completed her doctoral thesis with an experimental study on the influence of sound-qualities on the perception of a product's image within the context of TV commercials in 2009. She has worked in several research projects in the field of emotional and social sound design and as assistant professor at the Department of Musicology at the University of Graz. Her research focuses on music/sound at the intersection of mass media, aesthetics and economy and on methodological issues of empirical research.

Jauk, Werner, Ao. Univ.-Prof. Priv.-Doz. Dr. phil., Professor at the Department of Musicology at the University of Graz; studies in experimental psychology, composing electronic/digital musics and jazz-guitar in Graz; postdoctoral degree (Habilitation) in musicology on „*The musicalization of everyday-life in digital culture*"; research and artistic work on the intersection of cybernetics, music-cognition, music-sociology/anthropology, (music-)technology and media arts; papers and lectures at international scientific congresses and artistic festivals (Ars Electronica, Cynetart, steirischer herbst, Biennale di Venezia et al).

Kettemann, Bernhard, Emeritus Professor Mag. Dr. phil., was Professor and head of the department of English Linguistics at the Department of English Studies, and Dean of Studies of the Humanities, at the University of Graz. He is founder and editor of the critical journal *Arbeiten aus Anglistik und Amerikanistik*; author and editor of over 20 books in the field of English linguistics and has authored over a hundred scholarly articles. His research interests include cultural constructionism, critical-discourse analysis and corpus linguistics, and social semiotics of the media.

Klein, Eva, Mag. Dr., art historian, has worked since 2003 in various museums and institutions. Since 2009 she has been on the faculty of the *Institut für Kunstgeschichte* (Institute of Art History) and the *Forschungsstelle Kunstgeschichte Steiermark* (Research Centre for Styrian Art History) at the University of Graz and on the faculty of the *Institut für Kunstgeschichte* (Institute of Art History) at the Ludwig-Maximilians-University Munich. She studied art history and communication design. Ph.D. (with honors) in 2011. She is active in research and teaching in the following areas: modern and contemporary art, design theory, visual communication, political and feminist art and has received a number of academic awards.

Matthes, Jörg, PhD, University of Zurich, is professor of communication science at the Department of Communication, University of Vienna, Austria, where he chairs the division of advertising research and media effects. His research focuses on advertising effects, the process of public-opinion formation, news framing, and empirical methods. Since 2011, he has chaired the Methods division of the German Communication Association (DGPuK), and he is Associate Editor of the journal Communication Methods & Measures. From 2005 to 2010, he was also chair of the Methods division of the Swiss Communication Association (SGKM).

Prisching, Manfred, Studies in Law (Dr. jur. 1974) and Economics (Mag. rer. soc. oec. 1977); Assistant Professor at the Departments of the Philosophy of Law, of Economics and of Sociology at the University of Graz; postdoctoral degree (Habilitation) 1985; Associate Professor 1994. Guest professorships and research fellowships: 1987–88 at the Rijksuniversiteit Limburg, Maastricht, Netherlands; 1995–96 at Harvard University, Boston, USA; 2005–06 at the University of Lousiana at New Orleans, University of Arkansas at Little Rock and University of Nevada at Las Vegas; and at several Austrian universities. 1997–2001 Rector of the University of Applied Sciences (FH Joanneum) in Graz; Member of the Austrian Academy of Sciences.

Rolshoven, Johanna, Professor of Cultural Anthropology and head of the department of Folklore and Cultural Anthropology at the University of Graz. 1987 diploma (University of Aix-Marseille), 1990 doctorate (University of Marburg), 2005 postdoctoral degree (Habilitation) at the University of Zurich; since 1990 research and teaching at the universities of Basel, Frankfurt a. M., Fribourg, Hamburg, Joensuu, Marburg, Neuchâtel, Turku, and Zurich; guest professorships in Hamburg, Marburg and Innsbruck. 2004–2008 scientific director of the Centre for Cultural Studies in Architecture at the Architecture Department of ETH Zurich. Focus: everyday culture, mobilities, multilocality, material culture, technology, biography, youth studies, science studies, visual studies, city-space cultural studies.

Schramm, Holger, Dr., born 1973, is Professor and Head of the Media and Business Communication Department at the Human-Computer-Media Institute at Julius-Maximilians-University, Würzburg. He is the author or (co-)editor of more than ten books, e.g., Handbuch Musik und Medien (Handbook of Music and Media) and Handbuch Medienrezeption (Handbook of Media Processes). His numerous articles have been published in edited books, and in national and international journals. His research focuses on music and media, sports communication, entertainment, and advertising effects.

Spence, Charles, is Head of the Crossmodal Research Laboratory, at Oxford University's Department of Experimental Psychology. He is also Head of Sensory Marketing at the JWT Ad Agency, and at Condiment Junkie (a sonic branding agency). Prof. Spence has published more than 500 articles on the topic of multisensory perception. His research calls for a radically new approach to the multisensory design of products, packaging, and the places in which those products are purchased and used. Ultimately, the aim of the industry-funded research carried out at the Crossmodal Research Laboratory is to enhance the multisensory design of products and services through a better cognitive neuroscience understanding of the multisensory nature of human perception.

Stadlober, Margit, Ao.Univ.-Prof. Dr., is a professor at the Institute of Art History at the University of Graz. Since 1998, she has been head of the *Forschungsstelle Kunstgeschichte Steiermark* (Research Centre for Styrian Art History) and editor of the *Styrian Art History Research Reports* which has included numerous special issues; since 2007 member of the *Denkmal Steiermark* advisory board; since 2008 head of the Excellence in Art History Award committee; and since 2011, a member of the Graz Commission of Experts on Historic City Architecture (Altstadt-Sachverständigenkommission). She has published widely on the painting, graphic art and architecture of the Middle Ages, on the 19th-century Danube Style and on Styrian modernity.

Ruth, Nicolas, M.A., born 1986, studied musicology at the Justus-Liebig-University Gießen and Popular Music and Media (musicology, media science and economics) at the University of Paderborn. He has a variety of experience in television and radio, and has been an event manager at the international Emergenza Festival since 2009. In 2012, he became a scientific assistant in the Media and Business Communication Department at the Human-Computer-Media Institute at Julius-Maximilians-University, Würzburg. Ruth's research focuses on popular music on radio, copyright, sound studies and ideological music. He is also an active musician.

Weltzien, Friedrich, is Professor for Creativity and Psychology of Perception at the University of Applied Sciences and Arts Hannover. He holds a PhD in Art History from the University of Cologne and a postdoctoral degree (Habilitation) from the Free University Berlin. His range of interests includes art theory from Romanticism to today, cultural studies, and aesthetics of production.